Leadership for a Better World

SECOND EDITION

Leadership for a Better World

Understanding the Social Change Model of Leadership Development

Susan R. Komives, Wendy Wagner, and Associates

JB JOSSEY-BASS™
A Wiley Brand

Copyright © 2017 by John Wiley & Sons, Inc. All rights reserved.

Published by Jossey-Bass
A Wiley Brand
One Montgomery Street, Suite 1000, San Francisco, CA 94104–4594—www.josseybass.com

No part of this publication may be reproduced, stored in a retrieval system, or transmitted in any form or by any means, electronic, mechanical, photocopying, recording, scanning, or otherwise, except as permitted under Section 107 or 108 of the 1976 United States Copyright Act, without either the prior written permission of the publisher, or authorization through payment of the appropriate per-copy fee to the Copyright Clearance Center, Inc., 222 Rosewood Drive, Danvers, MA 01923, 978-750-8400, fax 978-646-8600, or on the Web at www.copyright.com. Requests to the publisher for permission should be addressed to the Permissions Department, John Wiley & Sons, Inc., 111 River Street, Hoboken, NJ 07030, 201-748-6011, fax 201-748-6008, or online at www.wiley.com/go/permissions.

Limit of Liability/Disclaimer of Warranty: While the publisher and author have used their best efforts in preparing this book, they make no representations or warranties with respect to the accuracy or completeness of the contents of this book and specifically disclaim any implied warranties of merchantability or fitness for a particular purpose. No warranty may be created or extended by sales representatives or written sales materials. The advice and strategies contained herein may not be suitable for your situation. You should consult with a professional where appropriate. Neither the publisher nor author shall be liable for any loss of profit or any other commercial damages, including but not limited to special, incidental, consequential, or other damages. Readers should be aware that Internet Web sites offered as citations and/or sources for further information may have changed or disappeared between the time this was written and when it is read.

Jossey-Bass books and products are available through most bookstores. To contact Jossey-Bass directly call our Customer Care Department within the U.S. at 800-956-7739, outside the U.S. at 317-572-3986, or fax 317-572-4002.

Wiley publishes in a variety of print and electronic formats and by print-on-demand. Some material included with standard print versions of this book may not be included in e-books or in print-on-demand. If this book refers to media such as a CD or DVD that is not included in the version you purchased, you may download this material at http://booksupport.wiley.com. For more information about Wiley products, visit www.wiley.com.

Library of Congress Cataloging-in-Publication Data

Names: Komives, Susan R., 1946- author. | Wagner, Wendy (Wendy Elizabeth)
Title: Leadership for a better world : understanding the social change model
  of leadership development / Susan R. Komives, Wendy Wagner, and Associates.
Description: Second edition. | San Francisco, CA : Jossey-Bass, [2017] |
  Includes bibliographical references and index.
Identifiers: LCCN 2016029343 (print) | LCCN 2016031054 (ebook) | ISBN
  9781119207597 (pbk.) | ISBN 9781119207603 (pdf) | ISBN 9781119207610 (epub)
Subjects: LCSH: Universities and colleges–Administration. | College
  administrators–Professional relationships. | Educational leadership. |
  Social change.
Classification: LCC LB2341 .K66 2017 (print) | LCC LB2341 (ebook) | DDC
  378.1/01–dc23
LC record available at https://lccn.loc.gov/2016029343

Cover Design: Wiley
Cover Image: © Ralf Hiemisch/Getty Images, Inc.

Printed in the United States of America
SECOND EDITION

PB Printing   10   9   8   7   6   5   4   3

Contents

Foreword   ix
     Alexander W. Astin

Preface   xiii

Acknowledgments   xxi

About the National Clearinghouse for Leadership Programs   xxiii

About the Authors and Editors   xxv

PART 1   UNDERSTANDING THE SOCIAL CHANGE MODEL OF LEADERSHIP DEVELOPMENT   1

1. Transitions and Transformations in Leadership   5
   Dennis C. Roberts

2. An Overview of the Social Change Model of Leadership Development   17
   Kristan Cilente Skendall

PART 2 INDIVIDUAL VALUES — 41

3. **Consciousness of Self** — 43
   Sherry Early and Justin Fincher

4. **Congruence** — 66
   Tricia R. Shalka

5. **Commitment** — 87
   Ashlee M. Kerkoff and Daniel Ostick

PART 3 GROUP VALUES — 105

6. **Collaboration** — 109
   Jordan England

7. **Common Purpose** — 127
   Marybeth Drechsler Sharp and Alex Teh

8. **Controversy With Civility** — 149
   Cecilio Alvarez

PART 4 SOCIETY/COMMUNITY VALUES — 171

9. **Citizenship** — 175
   Jennifer Bonnet

PART 5 ON CHANGE — 197

10. **Change** — 201
    Wendy Wagner

11. **Examining Social Change** 233
Wendy Wagner

12. **Applying the Social Change Model** 261
Marguerite Bonous-Hammarth

Epilogue 275
Susan R. Komives and Wendy Wagner

Additional Resources 277

Index 283

Dedicated to
Helen S. Astin
1932–2015
Activist, thinker, leader, scholar, friend
Cocreator of the Social Change Model of Leadership Development

Foreword

If you were to ask academics to list their most important learning goals for students, they would most likely include outcomes such as knowledge acquisition, the development of critical thinking skills, and the like. However, what most academics probably don't realize is that the student quality most frequently mentioned in the official mission statements of their colleges and universities is *leadership*.

The process that created the Social Change Model of Leadership Development (SCM) in many respects "modeled the model." From the beginning it followed one of the basic precepts underlying the Social Change Model: that "leadership" is something carried out by a group rather than by an individual. Individuals can, of course, initiate. In fall 1993 my dear late wife and colleague Helen (Lena) Astin initiated the process when she dropped by my office to inform me that a young friend of ours, Goodwin Liu (another "initiator"), had brought to her attention a new federally funded program that might interest us. Known as the Dwight Eisenhower Leadership program, it provided funds for the creation of student leadership projects on college campuses. Because both Lena and I had previously conducted research on leadership, the project intrigued us. Our understanding of the leadership process suggested that what was really needed was a framework, or model, that could guide students in developing their leadership skills. We wanted the model to help instill in young persons a strong sense of social responsibility and a desire to become instruments of positive social change.

Because neither of us was particularly knowledgeable about matters relating to student leadership development, we naturally turned to the folks who do this for a living: student affairs practitioners. Most American college campuses are home to student affairs professionals who are deeply involved in the process of facilitating student leadership development, so we felt that the ideal model would be one that capitalized on the knowledge and experience of some of these experts. Lena and I started calling our friends in the student affairs field, including several who were or had been presidents of NASPA and ACPA, the field's two leading national professional associations, to identify individuals who were regarded as experts in student leadership development. The first few experts we contacted were also helpful in identifying additional colleagues to be recruited for the group that eventually came to call itself the *working ensemble*. Our ensemble comprised 15 individuals, including 8 leadership experts from the field of student affairs, 4 UCLA doctoral students, the Astins, and Carole Leland, Lena's coauthor of their landmark study of 77 women leaders, *Women of Influence, Women of Vision*. Carole had been working for the Center for Creative Leadership in North Carolina, and Lena was a member of the board of the center. Other members of the original ensemble included one of this book's editors—Susan R. Komives—and two of its chapter authors: Dennis C. Roberts and Marguerite Bonous-Hammarth.

Our ensemble held seven 2-day meetings over a period of more than a year with the aim of forging a preliminary version of a Social Change Model of Leadership Development. The notion of "social change" was embraced by the ensemble in recognition of two principles: (1) that leadership, as opposed to mere "management," necessarily involves change and (2) that "social" change implies service to the others (i.e., "Citizenship"). Ensemble meetings, which were facilitated mainly by Lena, were lively and sometimes contentious, but nearly all participants remained focused on the goal of developing a workable model ("Collaboration," "Commitment," "Common Purpose"). To ensure that the ensemble could capitalize on the collective wisdom of the entire group, Lena actively encouraged each participant to be authentic and to share his or her viewpoints openly ("Congruence").

By its third meeting our working ensemble had come to realize that the model had to be value-based, and to that end we began to create a list of basic values. Members would propose a particular value (e.g., Collaboration) to be added to the list, and we would all debate its pros and cons. One of the key considerations in these discussions was that the individual values be consistent, complementary, comprehensive, and nonredundant. Somewhat tongue-in-cheek, we labeled the preliminary list of values "The Seven Cs."

A preliminary version of the model was presented to a diverse group of outside reviewers whom we invited to attend a 3-day retreat held in fall 1994 at the Airlie House Conference Center in Virginia. Retreat participants included our working ensemble, 9 undergraduate students from diverse institutions, and 19 representatives from national associations, higher education institutions, and governmental agencies. The Airlie House retreat proved to be a crucial (if not initially painful) moment for Lena and me in the development of the model. After the first day and a half of nonstop analysis and criticism, several retreat guests had concluded that our preliminary model was "too nice," that our high-sounding values didn't reflect the rough-and-tumble realities of real-life group change efforts, especially efforts that aimed to effect significant social change. Any such effort, our critics insisted, inevitably involves differences of opinion, debate, and argumentation.

Lena and I didn't get much sleep that second night, and we ended up calling an unscheduled breakfast meeting of our ensemble early the next morning. After considerable discussion, the ensemble agreed that we would add a new C to the model: Controversy With Civility. This value constituted an acknowledgment of two realities about any group change effort: that differences in opinion are inevitable and potentially useful and that such differences must be aired openly but with respect and courtesy.

A second problem had to do with the fact that on the final day we were hoping to present a revised model to the attendees. However, because it seemed to us that a simple list of fundamental values fell short of a fully integrated model, we were searching for some way to present the values in a more holistic fashion. Then, early on the final day, it dawned on us that the Seven Cs naturally arranged themselves into three levels of aggregation: individual, group, and civic (community) values. So in the final presentation that last day we were able to diagram the revised model by arranging the Seven Cs into three groups (symbolized by circles). In particular, this visual rearrangement made it easier to show the reciprocal relationships among the values (symbolized by directional arrows connecting the circles). I think this visual representation of the model has helped to facilitate its real-world application.

Following the Airlie House retreat we were able to get further useful feedback about the model by presenting it at several national meetings and trying it out with several student groups at UCLA. Lena mentored a group of seven undergraduates who approached her because they had heard about the model from several of UCLA's student affairs staff members. After applying the model for nearly 3 months as part of an independent study project, these remarkable students ended up bringing the entire 10th-grade class from a local inner city school to the UCLA campus for a full day of exposure and orientation to the campus life of a research university. This entirely student-conceived and -executed project was implemented without a hitch, and it was a great success. To hear the seven students later recount how they applied the model to the design and execution of such an ambitious community service project was an amazing and inspiring experience for Lena and me.

By early 1996 we had completed the final revision (version III) of the model in the form of a guidebook, *A Social Change Model of Leadership Development Guidebook*. The guidebook has since been distributed to hundreds of college campuses by the University of Maryland's National Clearinghouse for Leadership Programs.

Once the formal work on projects such as the SCM has been completed, more often than not the final report languishes on academic bookshelves or dies a quick death in college libraries. Happily, the SCM project has been able to avoid such a fate, largely because of the efforts of Susan R. Komives and her students and colleagues, who have worked virtually nonstop since the 1990s to further refine the model and promote its use on college campuses across the country. I also like to think that the model's intrinsic appeal and validity had something to do with its widespread popularity, but there is little question in my mind that without Susan's efforts it never would have been so widely accepted and used. This second edition of *Leadership for a Better World* represents still another milestone in the evolution of the Social Change Model, and I for one would like to congratulate and express my deepest admiration and appreciation to Susan, Wendy Wagner, and their colleagues for producing this comprehensive and very readable book.

Alexander W. (Sandy) Astin
Los Angeles, California

Preface

> Leadership is much more an art, a belief, a condition of the heart, than a set of things to do. The visible signs of artful leadership are expressed, ultimately, in its practice.
> —MAX DE PREE

Welcome to a challenging and wonderful journey—a journey about the commitments needed to make this world a better place, a journey exploring how you and the people in the groups you belong to can work together for meaningful change, and, ultimately, a journey into yourself. Dennis Roberts (2007), a member of the team that developed the Social Change Model of Leadership Development (SCM) and author of Chapter 1 in this book, calls this the "journey of deeper leadership" (p. 203).

THE SOCIAL CHANGE MODEL OF LEADERSHIP DEVELOPMENT

Contemporary times require a collaborative approach to leadership that can bring the talent of all members of a group to their shared purposes. The Social Change Model of Leadership Development approaches *"leadership as a purposeful, collaborative, values-based process that results in positive social change"* (emphasis added; Komives, Wagner, & Associates, 2009, p. xii; Higher Education Research Institute [HERI], 1996).

Assumptions About This Approach to Leadership

This approach to leadership is built on several key assumptions:

- Leadership is concerned with effecting change on behalf of others and society.
- Leadership is collaborative.
- Leadership is a process rather than a position.
- Leadership should be value-based.
- All students (not just those who hold formal leadership positions) are potential leaders.
- Service is a powerful vehicle for developing students' leadership skills.

In short, the approach proposed here differs in certain basic ways from traditional approaches that view leaders only as those who happen to hold formal leadership positions and that regard leadership as a value-neutral process involving positional "leaders" and "followers" (HERI, 1996, p. 10).

Goals of the Social Change Model

The SCM focuses on two primary goals:

1. To enhance student learning and development; more specifically, to develop in each student participant greater:
    - **Self-knowledge:** understanding one's talents, values, and interests, especially as these relate to the student's capacity to provide effective leadership
    - **Leadership competence:** the capacity to mobilize oneself and others to serve and work collaboratively
2. To facilitate positive social change at the institution or in the community. That is, undertake actions that will help the institution/community to function more effectively and humanely (HERI, 1996, p. 19)

Introducing the Seven Cs

The SCM includes seven values, referred to throughout the book as the *Seven Cs*, that synergistically become leadership for social change. All seven values work together to accomplish the transcendent C of Change. These values are grouped into three interacting clusters or dimensions: individual, group, and society or community. Individual values include Consciousness of Self, Congruence, and Commitment. Group values include Collaboration, Common Purpose, and Controversy With Civility. The societal or community dimension is presented as Citizenship. A premise of the model is that individuals can develop leadership capacity, groups can develop their leadership process, and communities can develop their capacity to engage groups and individuals in community goals. Although the book is approached to help the individual reader explore personal leadership capacity as an individual, in groups, and within communities, readers are encouraged to explore how groups and communities share leadership and how their process can be more intentional and effective.

The Ensemble

The SCM was developed by a team of leadership educators and scholars who have worked extensively with college students. As described further in the foreword and in Chapter 1, the project was funded by an Eisenhower Grant from the U.S. Office of Education in 1993–1996. The team realized early in the process that, similar to a good jazz ensemble, every member's contributions was essential, energy could flow among members of the group, and the whole was greater than the sum of its parts. This team named themselves *the working ensemble* to reinforce the value of the whole.

    The ensemble was concerned that college students needed to value collective action for social change and to learn to work with others in socially responsible ways. The ensemble was further concerned that old paradigms of leadership emphasized only the role of the positional leader and not the relational, collaborative process of leadership among participants. Grounded in the belief that leadership capacity can be developed by anyone, the ensemble developed this values-based model that focused on how individuals can work effectively with others toward shared social concerns.

    The model developed during a two-year process, including a weekend retreat with leadership educators and students from a diverse range of colleges and universities.

THE SCM BOOK PROJECT

The primary publication of the ensemble was a guidebook (HERI, 1996) designed for the use of leadership educators. This guidebook is available from the National Clearinghouse for Leadership Programs (NCLP; www.nclp.umd.edu). The guidebook was often used as a textbook for students, but it needed to be updated and reframed for undergraduate college students who might be studying leadership and seeking to develop their own effective leadership perspective and practices. Subsequently, professor Susan R. Komives, a member of the original ensemble and scholarship editor for the National Clearinghouse for Leadership Programs, challenged her graduate class of leadership educators in the College Student Personnel Program at the University of Maryland to research what college students needed to learn about leadership and to design and write a book that could be used as a text to teach about the Social Change Model. Leadership educator and former coordinator of the NCLP Wendy Wagner joined Komives to write and edit the first edition of this book, which was widely used in academic leadership courses and in cocurricular leadership programs.

Most of the original authors returned to update their chapters for this second edition joined by three original members of the ensemble, Alexander W. Astin writing the foreword, and Dennis C. Roberts and Marguerite Bonous-Hammarth authoring chapters. Sherry Early, former chair of the NASPA Student Leadership Knowledge Community, also joined the project. Social Change Model Leadership educators in Susan R. Komives's last class before her Maryland retirement developed rubrics for each of the Seven Cs in the SCM that are used in this second edition.

Kristan Cilente Skendall and Daniel Ostick led the development of a facilitator's guide for the SCM. Designed as an instructor's companion to this book, it is also intended to be used by leadership educators using the SCM in cocurricular and other settings. It is available from Jossey-Bass Publishers.

Purpose of the SCM Book

Nearly every college or university acknowledges that its graduates can, will, and, indeed, must be active leaders in their professions, their communities, and their world. Colleges expect their graduates to make this a better world. College students consistently affirm that they want their lives to matter and to make a difference (Komives,

Lucas, & McMahon, 2013). College seniors seek jobs in which they can do well and do good (Levine & Cureton, 1998).

This book is a call to action and a framework for developing your capacity to work with other people as you engage in leadership to address shared purposes. The book encourages raising awareness of social issues that need attention and ways of being with each other that promote effectively addressing those issues.

Alexander Astin (2001), co-facilitator of the ensemble who developed the SCM and author of the foreword to this edition, observes that

> American higher education has traditionally defined a "student leader" either as someone who occupies a formal student office (e.g., student body vice-president or editor of the student paper) or as someone who has achieved visibility on the campus by virtue of athletic or some other form of achievement. This rather narrow approach not only relegates most students to the role of "non-leader," but also creates an implicit "leader-follower" hierarchy, which, in the minds of most students, greatly limits their notions of who can or should "lead." The great power of the non-hierarchical approach to student leadership that characterizes this book is that it expands the number of potential "student leaders" to include virtually all students, while simultaneously transforming the process by means of which leadership is exercised on campus. (p. x)

In this book, the term *leader* is used without regard to a specific role in a group—whether as a positional leader or a participant engaging in the leadership process as a group member. We believe—and research supports—that leadership can be learned and that the capacity to engage in leadership with others can be developed (Dugan & Komives, 2007). This journey into deeper leadership is facilitated by action (practicing leadership and engaging with others) and by reflection (thinking about your experiences and making meaning about your observations). This action and reflection cycle is the heart of experiential learning (Dewey, 1923; Kolb, 1981). This cycle expands the individual's capacity to learn more effective ways of thinking about and engaging in leadership.

An old Hindu proverb says, "There is nothing noble about being superior to some other [person]. The true nobility is in being superior to your previous self." Psychologist Carl Rogers's (1961) concept in *On Becoming a Person* validates the exploration of one's own experiences as the most potent source of knowledge for personal development:

> Experience is, for me, the highest authority. The touchstone of validity is my own experience. No other person's ideas, and none of my own ideas, are as authoritative as my experience. It is to experience that I must return again and again, to discover a closer approximation to truth as it is in the process of becoming in me. Neither the Bible nor the prophets—neither Freud nor research—neither the revelations of God nor man—can take precedence over my own direct experience. (p. 23)

The processes of becoming something—becoming collaborative, becoming congruent, becoming a change agent—moves one from an uninformed consciousness about that awareness to a more informed consciousness able to examine the previous way of being in this process of becoming (Kegan, 1994).

In *On Becoming a Leader*, former university president and noted leadership scholar Warren Bennis (1989) wrote, "To become a leader, then you must become yourself, become the maker of your own life" (p. 40). Each of the chapters of this book asks you to reflect on how you are becoming the specific leadership dimension being presented. Think about the journey toward becoming more conscious of your effectiveness with that leadership value. Indeed, developing each of these leadership values, attitudes, and skills is a journey—the "becoming" process.

Focus of the Book

The ensemble and authors of this book focus on social change and socially responsible actions that readers can take to make the world a better place for everyone. The book is composed of five parts. Part 1 sets the foundation by situating this model in the broader field of leadership studies, particularly those approaches that value collaborative leadership and present the SCM. Parts 2 through 4 present the three key dimensions of the model and the values they contain. Part 5 challenges you to think of yourself as a change agent and explore the change outcomes of leadership, particularly social change.

Part 1 includes Chapters 1 and 2. Chapter 1 describes the development of the model in the context of the broader field of leadership studies. Chapter 2 describes and provides an overview of the Social Change Model of Leadership Development.

Parts 2 through 4 delve into the seven values (the Seven Cs) of the model grouped into three dimensions. Although these values can be examined in any order, we encourage reading them in the order presented. Part 2 presents the values on the individual level, which include the importance of having Consciousness of Self (Chapter 3), Congruence (Chapter 4), and Commitment (Chapter 5) in order to be effective in working with others to make change happen. Part 3 focuses on the group dimension of social change, specifically Collaboration (Chapter 6), Common Purpose (Chapter 7), and Controversy With Civility (Chapter 8). In Part 4, the dimension of society/community explores the value of Citizenship along with how communities work for change.

Part 5 emphasizes that the SCM is all about change. Chapter 10 looks at change as a concept: how individuals and groups can lead for change, and why change may be resisted. Chapter 11 explores the common social problems that people share and some of the processes used to address them. We encourage the reader to think deeply and personally about issues that need shared attention and how people can work collaboratively toward those changes. Chapter 12 examines how to apply the SCM. The epilogue ends the book by encouraging the reader to become a person who will have the courage to make this a better world. Additional resources on the SCM are also included at the end of the book.

Personal Reflection

Encouraging personal reflection is an essential aspect of this book. As Carl Rogers (1961) affirmed, one is always "becoming," and the journey into effective leadership is a process of enhancing, improving, informing, and becoming. Deeper learning in leadership (Roberts, 2007) only happens through experiential learning and personal reflection. Each chapter in the book encourages the reader to reflect on the material through discussion questions and actions and reflections. The discussion questions focus your thinking on how the material relates to your experience and may be used in a class conversation to explore those topics.

REFERENCES

Astin, A. A. (2001). Foreword. In C. L. Outcalt, S. K. Faris, & K. N. McMahon (Eds.), *Developing non-hierarchical leadership on campus: Case studies and best practices in higher education* (p. x). Westport, CT: Greenwood.

Bennis, W. G. (1989). *On becoming a leader.* Reading, MA: Addison-Wesley.

Dewey, J. (1923). *Democracy and education.* New York, NY: Macmillan.

Dugan, J. P., & Komives, S. R. (2007). *Developing leadership capacity in college students: Findings from a national study.* College Park, MD: National Clearinghouse for Leadership Programs.

Higher Education Research Institute (HERI). (1996). *A social change model of leadership development guidebook* (Version III). Los Angeles, CA: University of California, Los Angeles, Higher Education Research Institute.

Kegan, R. (1994). *In over our heads: The mental demands of modern life.* Cambridge, MA: Harvard University Press.

Kolb, D. A. (1981). Learning styles and disciplinary differences. In A. W. Chickering & Associates (Eds.), *The modern American college: Responding to the new realities of diverse students and a changing society* (pp. 232–255). San Francisco, CA: Jossey Bass.

Komives, S. R., Lucas, N., & McMahon, T. R. (2013). *Exploring leadership: For college students who want to make a difference* (3rd ed.). San Francisco, CA: Jossey-Bass.

Komives, S. R., Wagner, W., & Associates. (2009). *Leadership for a better world: Understanding the social change model of leadership development* (1st ed.). San Francisco, CA: Jossey-Bass.

Levine, A., & Cureton, J. S. (1998). *When hope and fear collide: A portrait of today's college student.* San Francisco, CA: Jossey-Bass.

Roberts, D. R. (2007). *Deeper learning in leadership: Helping college students find the potential within.* San Francisco, CA: Jossey-Bass.

Rogers, C. R. (1961). *On becoming a person: A therapist's view of psychotherapy.* Boston, MA: Houghton Mifflin.

Acknowledgments

Great admiration, gratitude, and credit goes to the members of the original ensemble who developed the Social Change Model of Leadership Development (SCM) and the guidebook that was the primary document for presenting this model for 20 years. Special thanks to the original authors of the first edition of *Leadership for a Better World*, whose passion and insight guided readers into more intentional collaborative leadership understandings. The commitment to social change, the drive for collaboration, belief in service as a pedagogy, and wisdom of these scholars and leadership educators live in this new book. This second edition is a tribute to their experience and ideas that have transcended time and context.

Special thanks to coprincipal investigators of the project, the late Helen S. Astin (professor emeritus, University of California, Los Angeles) and Alexander W. Astin (professor emeritus, University of California, Los Angeles), and ensemble members Marguerite Bonous-Hammarth (director of assessment, research, and evaluation, University of California, Irvine), Tony Chambers (associate professor emeritus at the University of Toronto), Len Goldberg (retired vice president for student affairs, University of Richmond), the late Cynthia S. Johnson (professor emeritus, California State University, Long Beach), Susan R. Komives (professor emerita, University of Maryland), Emily Langdon (coordinator of assessment, research, and evaluation, University of California, Merced), Carole Leland (Center for Creative Leadership, San Diego), Nance Lucas (executive director for the Center for the Advancement of Well-Being and associate professor, New Century College, George Mason University), Raechele L. Pope (associate professor, University of Buffalo), Dennis C. Roberts (consultant and former assistant vice president for education faculty and student services, Qatar Foundation, Education City), and Kathy M. Shellogg (consultant). Their affiliations at the time of developing the SCM appear in the 1996 guidebook. Hosted by the National Clearinghouse for Leadership Programs (NCLP), most of this group convened for a reunion of the ensemble in summer 2007 and affirmed the promise and role of this model in student leadership development.

Special thanks to the NCLP, which has promoted best practices in college student leadership development for 30 years. Check out this fine organization at www.nclp.umd.edu. We appreciate the support of longtime NCLP director, Craig Slack.

Wendy and Susan also thank the researchers on the Multi-Institutional Study of Leadership team (especially principal investigator John P. Dugan) for the research on the SCM that is advancing the practice and teaching of leadership for college students. The ongoing research and findings of that study are available at www.nclp.umd.edu and leadershipstudy.net. Special thanks to Bailey Albrecht who worked with her advisor, Paige Haber-Curran, to solicit and edit the many student stories shared in this edition. Bailey managed this process for us as a graduate assistant in the Leadership Institute and a master's student at Texas State University.

Thanks also to the team at Jossey-Bass, particularly former editor Erin Null and current editor Alison Knowles, whose unwavering support and encouragement to continue to bring the SCM to a broader audience made this project possible.

Wendy thanks her parents, Wendell and Cathy Wagner, for their consistent support and lifelong example of community involvement and leadership. Wendy also thanks Susan for mentorship, friendship, and princess tiaras. Susan is always grateful to Ralph, who makes everything possible. Very special thanks also to Ralph for rendering the SCM graphics.

Susan R. Komives
University of Maryland, College Park

Wendy Wagner
The George Washington University, Washington, DC

About the National Clearinghouse for Leadership Programs

The National Clearinghouse for Leadership Programs (NCLP) provides a central clearinghouse of leadership materials, resources, and assistance to leadership educators. NCLP members receive publications, web access to resources, consultation assistance, and networking opportunities with other professionals engaged in leadership education with a focus on college students.

The NCLP supports cutting-edge research on leadership development and the dissemination of knowledge through a member listserv, website, institutes, symposia, virtual seminars, and high-quality publications.

The diversity of leadership programs in higher education and the dynamic nature of the subject challenge student affairs educators and faculty members continually to create and refine programs, training techniques, and contemporary models to fit the changing context of leadership education. The NCLP exists to help meet that challenge.

The NCLP is very proud of the impact of the first edition of *Leadership for a Better World: Understanding the Social Change Model of Leadership Development* and how it complemented other NCLP resources related to the Social Change Model of Leadership Development (SCM). The second edition will extend this work, incorporating evidence from the body of research on the SCM. Among the NCLP resources on the SCM is the socially responsible leadership scale (SRLS), an instrument designed to measure students' SCM leadership capacities. NCLP also sponsors the

Multi-Institutional Study of Leadership, an international research project measuring college students' leadership development using the SRLS.

Visit http://www.nclp.umd.edu for more information on the NCLP and other educational material on the Social Change Model.

Craig Slack
NCLP director

About the Authors and Editors

Cecilio Alvarez is an academic advisor in the College of Liberal Arts and Sciences at the University of Colorado Denver. He is a former coordinator of the National Clearinghouse for Leadership Programs and was engaged with research as a member of the Multi-Institutional Study of Leadership research team. He has served as an associate at the National Leadership Symposium, has taught undergraduate leadership courses, and has presented on leadership at the ACPA: College Student Educators International. He earned a Master of Education in college student personnel at the University of Maryland.

Alexander W. (Sandy) Astin is the Allan M. Cartter Distinguished Professor Emeritus of Higher Education and founding director of the Higher Education Research Institute at UCLA. The author of 23 books and some 300 other publications in the field of higher education, Sandy has been a recipient of awards for outstanding research from 13 national associations, a fellow at Stanford's Center for Advanced Study in the Behavioral Sciences, a recipient of 11 honorary degrees, and is a member of the National Academy of Education. In 1990 and 2010 the *Journal of Higher Education* identified Sandy as the author most frequently cited by others in the field of higher education. Sandy's research has focused on how undergraduate students are affected by their college experience, with particular emphasis on educational opportunity and equity, student persistence, service learning, assessment and evaluation, leadership, institutional transformation, and spiritual development. He and his wife Lena Astin were co-PIs of the Eisenhower grant that resulted in the Social Change

Model of Leadership Development and coauthors of *Leadership Reconsidered*. His most recent book is *Are You Smart Enough? How Colleges' Obsession with Smartness Shortchanges Students* (Stylus, 2016).

Helen S. (Lena) Astin (1932–2015) was professor emeritus in the Graduate School of Education and a senior scholar at Higher Education Research Institute (HERI) at UCLA. This book is dedicated to Lena Astin. She was president of the Division of the Psychology of Women of the American Psychological Association and the American Association of Higher Education. She served as a member of the board of the National Council for Research on Women and as a member of the Committee on Women's Employment and Related Social Issues of the National Research Council. She published numerous articles and 11 books, including *Women of Influence, Women of Vision: A Cross-Generational Study of Leaders and Social Change* (1991). She and her husband Sandy Astin were co-PIs of the Eisenhower grant that resulted in the Social Change Model of Leadership Development and coauthors of *Leadership Reconsidered*. From 1983 to 1987, she served as the associate provost of UCLA's College of Letters and Science. Before coming to UCLA, she was director of research and education for the University Research Corporation in Washington, D.C.

Jennifer Bonnet is a research and instruction librarian at the University of Maine. In her position, she develops course-integrated library instruction, teaches an undergraduate information literacy course, and provides in-depth consultations for students and faculty members at all stages of their research. Previously, she worked with the Leadership, Community Service-Learning, and Student Involvement team in the Office of Campus Programs at the University of Maryland. She has researched, written, and presented on cocurricular leadership programs, community service participation and citizenship among undergraduate students, the library's role in undergraduate learning, and librarian approachability. Jen holds an MSI degree in library and information services from the University of Michigan and a master's in counseling and personnel services from the University of Maryland.

Marguerite Bonous-Hammarth is a director of assessment, research, and evaluation at the University of California, Irvine, Office of the Vice Chancellor for Student Affairs, and a cochair of the NASPA Knowledge Community on Student Affairs Partnering with Academic Affairs. Her work in higher education has spanned academic and administrative roles, including director of undergraduate admissions at the University of California, Irvine; researcher at the Higher Education Research Institute; and instructor and coordinator of a Spencer Foundation graduate research training program at the University of California, Los Angeles. Her publications include *As the World Turns: Implications of Global Shifts in Higher Education for Theory, Research and Practice* (edited with W. R. Allen and R. Teranishi, 2012). She was a member of the ensemble that developed the Social Change Model of Leadership Development. She received a master's in literature from the University of California, San Diego, and a PhD in education from the University of California, Los Angeles.

Sherry Early is an assistant professor at Marshall University's Leadership Studies program. Her dissertation, *An Examination of Mentoring Relationships and Leadership Capacity in Resident Assistants*, used the Multi-Institutional Study of Leadership data. She has spent several years as an administrator in residence life, leadership development, service-learning, and diversity initiatives, and has taught numerous leadership courses. Sherry served as a cochair for NASPA's Knowledge Community for Student Leadership Programs and has presented at the Association for Leadership Educators, Leadership Educator's Institute, and Leadership Education Academy, and has collaborated with the International Leadership Association and ACPA's Commission for Student Involvement. Sherry is a member of the ACPA 2017 planning committee overseeing the candidate experience at placement, and she serves as the NASPA IV–East Representative for the Administrators in Graduate and Professional Student Services Knowledge Community. Sherry received her master's in student affairs administration from Michigan State University and her PhD in higher education administration from Bowling Green State University.

Jordan England is the associate director of international admissions and recruitment at the University of California, Davis, and serves on the committee for Europe, the Middle East, and Africa with the Council of International Schools. She has facilitated courses on leadership at the University of Maryland and the University of Michigan and has coordinated the development of social justice and diversity-oriented leadership retreats for students and staff members at the University of California, Santa Cruz. Jordan has presented locally, regionally, and nationally on topics including leadership development and social identities, collaborative leadership, and the relationship among service, leadership, and civic engagement. She earned a

Master of Education in college student personnel at the University of Maryland and a credential in school counseling at Sonoma State University.

Justin Fincher is the assistant vice president for advancement at The Ohio State University, where he oversees teams that advance the overall constituent experience and philanthropic support for the institution. He previously held roles at Rutgers University and Johns Hopkins University leading teams responsible for assessment and research, marketing and communications, talent management, and constituent engagement. Justin's research is centered on how individuals find their sense of belonging and confidence within diverse environments. He was a member of the Multi-Institutional Study of Leadership research team and earned his master's and PhD at the University of Maryland's college student personnel program.

Ashlee M. Kerkoff is the director of undergraduate career programming in the Office of Career Services in the Smith School of Business at the University of Maryland. In this role, she provides strategic direction for the career preparation, education, and placement of 3,000 business undergraduates. She began her career in the University of Maryland Department of Resident Life developing a residential program aimed to engage students in the academic community and prepare for living and working in a global society. She completed a Master of Education in college student personnel at the University of Maryland and a Bachelor of Science in leadership and management and Spanish at the University of St. Thomas.

Susan R. Komives is professor emerita at the University of Maryland. She is past president of the Council for the Advancement of Standards in Higher Education and ACPA: College Student Educators International. She was vice president of two colleges and is the author or editor of a dozen books including *Student Services, Exploring Leadership, Leadership for a Better World,* and *The Handbook for Student Leadership Development.* She is executive founding editor of the New Directions in Student Leadership series. She was a member of the teams that developed *Learning Reconsidered,* the relational leadership model, the Multi-Institutional Study of Leadership, and the leadership identity development grounded theory. She was a member of the ensemble that developed the Social Change Model of Leadership Development. She is cofounder of the National Clearinghouse for Leadership Programs (NCLP) and a former member of the board of directors of the International

Leadership Association. Susan is a recipient of the ACPA and NASPA outstanding research awards, the Distinguished Leadership & Service Award from the Association of Leadership Educators, and the ACPA Life Time Achievement Award.

Daniel Ostick serves as the assistant director for assessment, communication, and administration in the Adele H. Stamp Student Union–Center for Campus Life at the University of Maryland. Previously, he was the coordinator for leadership curriculum development and academic partnerships. Daniel regularly teaches course work on leadership theory and global leadership and has published articles and chapters on the SCM, diversity and leadership, and LGBT issues and leadership. He has held positions in residence life at the University of Maryland, the University of Texas at Austin, and the University of Illinois at Urbana-Champaign. Daniel earned his PhD in college student personnel from the University of Maryland, received his master's in college student personnel administration from Indiana University, and obtained his undergraduate degree in advertising from the University of Georgia.

Dennis C. Roberts is an independent consultant who works with colleges and universities to enhance their impact in student leadership learning and international understanding. He has served in numerous senior leadership positions in higher education in the United States and abroad. He has authored 4 books and more than 50 book chapters and other articles including the first book advocating for comprehensive leadership development for college and university students in 1981. His book, *Deeper Learning in Leadership* (2007), urged educators to help students find and persist in fulfilling their purpose in life as the central focus of leadership learning. He was a member of the ensemble that developed the Social Change Model of Leadership Development.

Tricia R. Shalka is an assistant professor in the Warner School of Education's higher education program at the University of Rochester. Tricia's primary research interest concerns the intersection of trauma and college student development. She also continues to investigate college student leadership development in her scholarly work, most recently exploring the role of mentorship in leadership development outcomes for international students. Tricia has worked in a variety of areas of higher education administration including institutional assessment, residential life, fraternity and sorority life, and development and alumni relations. She holds a PhD from The Ohio

State University, a master's from the University of Maryland, and a bachelor's from Dartmouth College.

Marybeth Drechsler Sharp is executive director of the Council for the Advancement of Standards in Higher Education (CAS). Previously, she worked with leadership and service-learning in UMD's College Park scholars living-learning program and in residence life at the University of Missouri and the University of Central Missouri. Marybeth served as a research team member for the National Study of Living-Learning Programs and Autoethnographic Research Group. She has researched and presented on topics of student learning outcomes, leadership self-efficacy, dimensions of identity development, student engagement in living-learning environments, and the motives and experiences of faculty members involved with living-learning programs. She completed her doctorate in college student personnel at the University of Maryland, where she also has served as an adjunct instructor and internship supervisor.

Kristan Cilente Skendall is a leadership educator who has worked at Georgetown University, the University of Arizona, and the University of Maryland, College Park. She is currently the associate director of the Gemstone Honors Program, a four-year, interdisciplinary, team research program at the University of Maryland. Kristan has served as a co–lead facilitator with the LeaderShape Institute, has taught numerous leadership courses, has presented at dozens of national and international conferences, and was a member of the Multi-Institutional Study of Leadership research team. She has served on the executive council of ACPA–College Student Educators International, served as chair of the 2015 ACPA annual convention, has been an associate at the National Leadership Symposium, and served as the coordinator for the National Clearinghouse for Leadership Programs. Kristan earned her bachelor's at the College of William & Mary in sociology and history, her master's at the University of Arizona in higher education administration, and her PhD at the University of Maryland in college student personnel.

Alex Teh is the senior manager of the change management practice at Collaborative Solutions, LLC, a finance and HR transformation consultancy specializing on enterprise cloud software. He has spent more than a decade focusing on developing and enabling student and business leaders across the higher education, nonprofit, and private sectors. Alex began his career at the University of Maryland (UMD) as the coordinator of the America Reads program and later UMD's Sport Clubs program, while also teaching leadership and university orientation courses. He has done extensive work in recruitment, training, and human resources with Teach For America. Alex earned a Master of Education in college student personnel at the University of Maryland.

Wendy Wagner is the Honey W. Nashman Fellow for Faculty Development in the Honey W. Nashman Center for Civic Engagement and Public Service and visiting assistant professor of human services and social justice at The George Washington University. Previously, Wendy served as the director of the Center for Leadership and Community Engagement and assistant professor of leadership and community engagement in New Century College at George Mason University. Wendy is a coeditor of *Leadership for a Better World* (2009) and *The Handbook for Student Leadership Development* (2011), as well as *Exploring Leadership: For College Students Who Want to Make a Difference; Facilitator Activity Guide* (2013); and the accompanying *Student Workbook* (2013). She is coeditor of *Leadership Development Through Service-Learning* (2016), an issue in the New Directions for Student Leadership series. She is a 2010 recipient of the American Association of Colleges & Universities K. Patricia Cross Future Leaders Award.

Leadership for a Better World

PART 1

Understanding the Social Change Model of Leadership Development

> We must not, in trying to think about how we can make a big difference, ignore the small daily differences we can make which, over time, add up to the big differences that we often cannot foresee.
> —MARIAN WRIGHT EDELMAN

The Social Change Model of Leadership Development (SCM) is all about positive, social change. Social change often includes acts that aim to improve the human condition or care for the environment. It may also be revealed in the more purposeful ways people work together because they value socially responsible leadership. The SCM embraces both modal and end values (Burns, 1978). *How people engage with each other matters, along with the outcomes and purposes of their change activity.*

Change is a dynamic constant in people's lives. Heraclitus wrote, "Nothing endures but change." Change comes at us all the time. It is the intersection of the way things are with the way they will be. Leadership for social change is the opportunity people have to direct change toward a future we desire.

Futurist Alvin Toffler observed that "change is the way the future invades our lives" (1970, p. 1). Extending Toffler's observation, Komives (2005) asserts "leadership is the way we invade the future" (p. 157). *Leadership means responsibly choosing courses of action toward a desirable future.*

Change is explored fully in Part 5 of this book yet needs to be introduced here to keep the end goal in perspective. Leadership and change are inexorably intertwined. After developing the SCM, several ensemble members went on to develop *Leadership Reconsidered* (Astin & Astin, 2000), which captured this important relationship:

> We believe that leadership is a process that is ultimately concerned with fostering *change*. In contrast to the notion of "management," which suggests preservation or maintenance, "leadership" implies a process where there is movement—from wherever we are now to some future place or condition that is different. Leadership also implies *intentionality*, in the sense that the implied change is not random—"change for change's sake"—but is rather directed toward some future end or condition which is desired and valued. Accordingly, leadership is a purposive process which is inherently *value-based*. (emphasis added; p. 8)

The leadership values of the SCM could guide this purposive process. Chapter 1 sets the context for this approach to collaborative, values-based leadership. Chapter 2 presents an overview of the Social Change Model and a summary of its key values.

REFERENCES

Astin, A. W., & Astin, H. S. (2000). *Leadership reconsidered: Engaging higher education in social change*. Battle Creek, MI: W. K. Kellogg Foundation.

Burns, J. M. (1978). *Leadership*. New York, NY: Harper & Row.

Komives, S. R. (2005). It's all about relationships. In A. B. Harvey-Smith (Ed.), *The seventh learning college principle: A framework for transformational change in learning organizations* (pp. 157–164). Washington, DC: National Association of Student Personnel Administrators.

Toffler, A. (1970). *Future shock*. New York, NY: Bantam.

Transitions and Transformations in Leadership

Dennis C. Roberts

> The adaptive demands of our societies require leadership that takes responsibility without waiting for revelation or request. One may lead perhaps with not more than a question in hand.
> —RONALD HEIFETZ

The Social Change Model of Leadership Development (SCM; Higher Education Research Institute [HERI], 1996), on which *Leadership for a Better World* is based, emerged at a time when numerous researchers and theorists were beginning to think of leadership in different ways. Those who created the model believed that there needed to be a framework for understanding leadership that college and university students could embrace and that would reflect the societal changes that were underway at the time. It is gratifying that so many years later the model remains relevant and is one of the most widely used on college and university campuses throughout the United States and in many other countries around the world (Kezar, Carducci, & Contreras-McGavin, 2006).

The creators of the SCM were uniquely concerned with leadership that started with personal commitment, was transformed through collaboratively sharing the work of leadership with others, and was ultimately intended to serve others and society at large. This focus on individual, organizational, and societal or community transformation was prophetic in anticipating the commitment to social justice and service that we see among many of today's college and university students.

The authors of the Social Change Model wrote:

> a leader is not necessarily a person who holds some formal position of leadership or who is perceived as a leader by others. Rather, we regard a leader as one who is able to effect positive **change** for the betterment of others, the community, and society. All people, in other words, are potential leaders. Moreover, the **process** of leadership cannot be described simply in terms of the behavior of an individual; rather, leadership involves collaborative relationships that lead to collective action grounded in the shared values of people who work together to effect positive change. (HERI, 1996, p. 16) (bold in original)

CHAPTER OVERVIEW

This chapter provides background on how views of leadership have changed over time and how leadership for social change fits in this story. It will also describe how the SCM emerged and how it has now become so important.

As you will see throughout this book, the original team that studied, struggled, and strived together to create the SCM referred to themselves as the *ensemble*. Members of the group were educators who had studied and taught leadership for many years. Several members of the group were also musicians who offered their observation during our meetings that we behaved much like a group of musicians would behave as they practiced and performed. Classical musicians interpret manuscripts written by composers in order to bring ideas, images, and emotions to life through their combined artistry. Jazz musicians improvise individually and collectively but always with the purpose of giving voice to each other. Whether skilled as classical, jazz, or popular artists, musicians know that any group will only be effective in performance if each seeks perfection on their own instrument while also embracing other musicians and their contribution to the ensemble.

In many ways, the study of leadership that you are undertaking through this book is similar to learning to be a skilled musician. You will explore new ideas, engage in critical thinking, compare your ideas and approaches with peers, and ultimately attempt to create an approach that makes sense to you plus relates in meaningful ways to the views and actions of others. First and foremost, leadership is not an individual act or gift—it is done in concert with others and it is likely to be something that evolves over time and through many trials.

LEADERSHIP: AN EVOLVING IDEA AND NEED

The study of leadership has been a fascination for scholars and for those who practice leadership for a very long time (Kellerman, 2001). It has been the subject of literature, theater, and art, and it has been studied through disciplines as diverse as political science and sociology to anthropology, theology, and physics. A critical turning point in the study of leadership took place when scholars began to look at leadership as a process rather than defined only by specific individuals who exercised influence and authority. The shift in scholars' views was complemented by leadership educators who worked primarily in extracurricular programs when they began to advocate that leadership potential should be cultivated among broader numbers and types of students (Komives, Lucas, & McMahon, 1998; Outcault, Faris, & McMahon, 2001; Roberts, 1981).

The numerous definitions and ideas about leadership that are available in many books can sometimes be confusing. The disconnect reflected in some of these books, especially those prior to the middle of the 1970s, is that they tell only the stories of individuals rather than the organizational and shared leadership stories that are consistent with what most scholars of leadership now believe. *Servant Leadership* by Greenleaf (1977) played a central role in bridging industrial-era paradigms of leadership to what we now see as postindustrial views. By advocating that leaders should be servants first rather than expecting to be served or followed, Greenleaf contributed to shifting from a focus on leading to the vision, purposes, and values on which leadership was based. The view that leadership should be based on values and ethics blossomed in Burns's (1978) seminal book, *Leadership*, which is recognized by many as pivotal in the perceptual shift from leadership as vested in an individual to leadership as a process. Understanding leadership as Burns proposed called for transforming relationships among followers and leaders that would result in achieving greater purpose and developing followers into being leaders themselves. He emphasized that the *process* of leadership (modal values or ways of working together) was as important as the *purposes and outcomes* of leadership (end values).

Burns's ideas were echoed by many subsequent authors, who advocated important and evolving notions about leadership. Rost (1991) was the first to use the language of industrial and postindustrial leadership, although the idea was implicit in Greenleaf's and Burns's writing. Rost described a shift from the hierarchy and bureaucracy that was so characteristic of early 20th-century organizations to the flat and inclusive organizations that are now viewed as the most desirable workplaces of the 21st century. Lipman-Blumen (1996) advocated for connective leadership that took advantage of the networking aspects of any human organization. Connective leadership occurs when the attention shifts "from independence to interdependence, from control to connection, from competition to collaboration, from individual to group, and from tightly linked geopolitical alliances to loosely coupled global networks" (p. 226). In addition to many others, Allen and Cherrey (2000) wrote of the importance of collaboration. Their view was that leadership was a systemic phenomenon in an interconnected world that should be redesigned around new ways of relating, influencing change, learning, and leading. Finally, by focusing on the quality of relationships, Komives, Lucas, and McMahon (2013) and Uhl-Bien and Ospina (2012) emphasized that it is through the process of mutual engagement with each other in the relational process of leadership that we can most effectively work for positive change.

Although these descriptions chronicle the shift in the evolution of leadership studies, it is important to acknowledge that for many underrepresented groups, such as women and people of color, the approach to leadership practice had traditionally been relational, inclusive, and focused on values as well as outcomes (Komives & Dugan, 2010). By broadening beyond those who had the social privilege to hold leadership positions, mostly White and male up through the middle of the 20th century, the authors invited more voices into the conversation, including the voices of diverse cultural groups and women. New and innovative perspectives were emerging, and this resulted in the reaffirmation of how many of those who were previously excluded viewed it all along (Komives & Dugan, 2010). One of the greatest benefits of this shift was that it opened the door to a wider spectrum of talent.

The momentum of inclusive leadership is so strong that many now think of followership and leadership as a continuum representing the variety of behaviors we all exhibit in groups as we move through roles as supporters, collaborators, advocates, influencers, and leaders. This more fluid conceptualization of roles is reminiscent of the improvisational jazz ensemble metaphor, in which musicians share turns at playing the lead melody and backup, including allowing room for the occasional solo.

The SCM is an excellent fit for groups whose purpose is to influence positive social change. It is also a great leadership model for groups with other purposes, whose members want to practice socially responsible leadership. The SCM is used successfully to develop leadership for individuals and groups in a variety of contexts: recreational sports teams, for-profit business endeavors, theater groups, and much more. Socially responsible leadership is aimed at creating group processes that are inclusive and collaborative and pursuing the group's goals without causing damage to others or to the environment, nor contributing to the decay of community.

Social change leadership and socially responsible leadership are even more important in the 21st century because of the complexity and competing demands of so many different segments of society. Even though the 21st century is often characterized as a complicated and confusing time, the record of history indicates that generations across the millennia also perceived their times to be complicated, difficult, and in some ways treacherous. There is no reason to believe that the current generation will not be able to address the challenges we face. In fact, it may be the condition of the current times that will call the best out of all in leadership and service. As Heifetz and Linsky (2002) propose, the important issues of the day are the ones many of us avoid. They advise that these issues are best tackled using adaptive leadership that gives the work back to those who are most directly responsible for it.

Leadership is needed in so many places today—the environment, social injustice, economic inequality, and cultural and religious conflict are just a few. The good thing is that, although the dynamics of the 21st century are challenging, there are also conditions that help us find solutions. For instance, we have a better and less-biased view of history than we have ever had before. Knowledge is more readily available than any time in history. Scientific advancements are proceeding at lightning speed, offering possible solutions much more quickly than was available to previous generations (Diamond, 2011).

One of the biggest challenges to finding solutions to contemporary dilemmas is sorting through the evidence and discerning those assertions or insights that will help us versus those that are incomplete or flawed. Particularly at a time when special interest groups often assert self-serving and narrow arguments, those aspiring to lead and who are involved in leadership must be very careful to discern the credibility of those to whom they listen. In our shrinking and connected world, one of the most important issues we face is determining how our personal, local, regional, and national interests relate to the emerging international community.

RETHINKING LEADERSHIP

Building on the refinements of authors and theorists of leadership since the early 1990s, the creators of the Social Change Model of Leadership Development were deeply aware of the transitions under way in thinking about leadership: Greenleaf's view of humble service in leadership; Burns's shift to leadership as a process; Rost's ideas about non-hierarchical organizations; Lipman-Blumen's shifting attention to connections in leadership; Allen and Cherrey's new ways of relating, influence, learning, and leading; and the critical issue of enhancing relationships advocated by Komives, Lucas, and McMahon. In conceptualizing the SCM (HERI, 1996) the ensemble took the additional step of raising the question, "Leadership to what end?" These perspectives led to the premises of the Social Change Model.

The Social Change Model of Leadership Development is based on the following premises:

- Leadership is socially responsible; it affects change on behalf of others.
- Leadership is collaborative.
- Leadership is a process, not a position.
- Leadership is inclusive and accessible to all people.
- Leadership is value-based.
- Community involvement and service is a powerful vehicle for leadership.

Source: Astin (1996), Bonous-Hammarth (2001), HERI (1996).

The opportunity to be involved with the ensemble was orchestrated by Alexander and Helen Astin of the Higher Education Research Institute at the University of California, Los Angeles. The late Helen Astin's research on women and leadership across generations (Astin & Leland, 1991) and Alexander Astin's research on university students' overall experiences (Astin, 1993) and on how approaches to organizational leadership influence campus culture (Astin & Scherrei, 1980) drew them to search for ways to enhance student learning related to leadership. As Alexander Astin noted in the Foreword, the Astins convened a group of diverse educators from around the United States to explore how student learning in leadership could be enhanced. The ensemble participants included some of the scholars in the field and others who were deeply immersed in helping students learning about leadership through their active engagement on campus and the community; this second group came primarily from the ranks of campus student affairs educators. Susan R. Komives and Marguerite Bonous-Hammarath, both involved in this book, were also members of the ensemble.

The ensemble conveners, Alexander and Helen Astin, were revered among the rest of the participants because of their long and productive careers in higher education research. Imagine the surprise, discomfort, and delight when we witnessed the two of them actively disagreeing with each other with passionate and raised voices only to conclude with new shared perspectives and improved ideas. Observing how the Astins could disagree, challenge, yet complement each other was a revelation that would enable all of us to voice our perspectives while working very hard to hear and affirm each other. We became a group that drew the best individual contribution from each other while creating a transcending idea that was better than any individual could ever have conceived—an ensemble.

This book will guide you through the details of the model that the ensemble ultimately developed. Much of the appeal of the model is the use of Seven C values that fall into three important spheres of leadership—the individual, group, and society/community. The ensemble's realization was that the research and theory we studied, the experience of students that we observed, and the reflection on our own work as a group included (1) the individual values of Consciousness of Self, Congruence, and Commitment; (2) the group values of Collaboration, Common Purpose, and Controversy With Civility; and (3) the society/community value of Citizenship. As presented in Figure 1.1 and discussed in more detail in Chapter 2, the values

FIGURE 1.1 The Social Change Model of Leadership Development

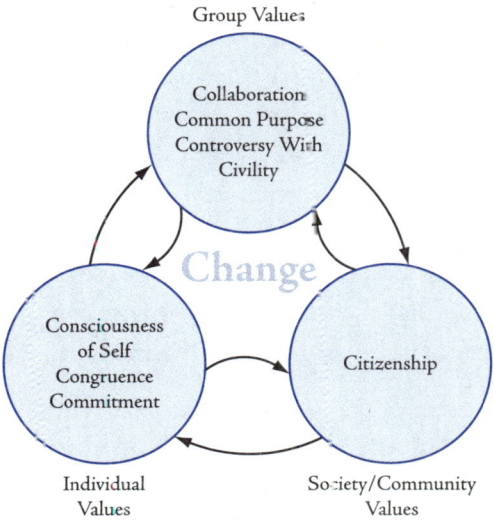

Source: Adapted from *A social model of leadership development* (3rd ed., p. 20) by Higher Education Research Institute [HERI]. Copyright © 1996, National Clearinghouse for Leadership Programs. Reprinted with permission of the National Clearinghouse for Leadership Programs.

not only provided a way to think about how leadership is enacted but also offered a critical lens to determine if the work of a group could be enhanced by greater attention to any one of these values. In this way, the Seven Cs is an analytic and heuristic framework by which we can understand effective leadership in the context of social change and social responsibility.

THE IMPACT OF THE SOCIAL CHANGE MODEL

The SCM has been widely distributed since its first publication in 1996. The model serves as the framework for many campus minors, certificate programs, and staff training, and is the focus of many academic courses.

The dimensions of the model and how this form of socially responsible leadership develops have also been extensively researched through the Multi-Institutional Study of Leadership (MSL). The MSL measures leadership outcomes on the SCM using an instrument called the Socially Responsible Leadership Scale. The MSL was first undertaken in 2006 and is the largest comprehensive measure of college students' leadership learning available today; it provides a method to research high-impact practices, students' leadership self-efficacy, and other issues that have been found central to enhancing students' understanding about and engagement in leadership (Dugan & Correia, 2014). The MSL website (leadershipstudy.net) provides extensive background, resources, published articles, and reports to assist its institutional participants. Select findings from this study are woven throughout this book.

In addition to the documented impact of the SCM in the United States, it has been used in select international locations such as Canada, China, Japan, Lebanon, Mexico, the Netherlands, Turkey, and South Africa. People of many cultures and nations can see themselves in the SCM because of the focus on process and the identification of the elements that make understanding one's own leadership a goal worth pursuing and one that can be done in cooperation and collaboration with others.

INVITATION TO THE ENSEMBLE

We want to invite you into the ensemble by asking that you offer everything you have to the study of leadership for social change. Whether your views of leadership come from what you have seen in popular press and news media, or from your own experience, we are likely to propose some different perspectives in the chapters that follow. This may require some transition as your thinking is shaped in very different ways.

Because leadership is largely socially constructed, researchers and scholars have undergone major transitions in the way they view leadership since the 1970s. The ideas *Leadership for a Better World* will introduce may represent a potential transition for you, challenging you to decide if you will stay with previous understandings of leadership or broaden your view to adopt different perspectives. We ask you to join the ensemble in the chapters that follow—remaining open to new possibilities while keeping your healthy skepticism alive. That's the way we learn best—holding openness and skepticism in our thinking at the same time.

Jake Brewer, formerly of change.org and a senior advisor on technology for the White House, died in 2015 at the age of 34 while participating in a bike ride for a cancer charity. His memorial service filled Washington Cathedral. A sticky note found on his desk read "Cultivate the Karass," a phrase from Kurt Vonnegut's novel, *Cat's Cradle* (1963). A *karass* refers to a group of people who, without being aware of it, are on a shared mission. They "share a cosmic linkage that's not obvious on the surface" (Contrera, 2015, para. 40). The point of cultivating the karass is that many of us working for social change may not realize we are on the same journey. By reading this book, discussing it deeply with your peers, teachers, and mentors, and acting on its principles, you are joining the ensemble in the shared mission of forwarding socially responsible leadership. You also have the potential to cultivate your karass.

CONCLUSION

The idea of leadership continues to evolve. The Social Change Model of Leadership Development is one of the most important contributors to this evolution and offers the potential to transform the way we work together for positive change. Now that you have the background on how our ideas of leadership have changed over time and why the ensemble created the SCM, the authors of the chapters that follow will go into much greater detail as you consider the relevance and application of this model to your own leadership. Enjoy this journey as you seek to understand and cultivate leadership that is dynamic, collaborative, and focused on positive change that benefits others and ourselves.

DISCUSSION QUESTIONS

1. From what sources or experiences have you come to view leadership as you do now?
2. What are the conditions that we face today that call us to critically examine the way we viewed leadership in the past?
3. How do your peers view leadership and how do their views contrast with yours?
4. What metaphor or analogy makes the most sense to you when you think of a high-functioning team?
5. What person or organization have you experienced that you believe personifies the idea of socially responsible leadership? What do they do that you admire?

ACTION AND REFLECTION

1. What did you used to think leadership was when you were young and what do you think it is now? What experiences changed your views or philosophies of leadership? How are your behaviors in groups different than they were as a result of your changed views?
2. Think about a specific context in which you currently engage in leadership with others. How do that group's processes fit the assumptions of the Social Change Model? How do they not?

REFERENCES

Allen, K. E., & Cherrey, C. (2000). *Systemic leadership: Enriching the meaning of our work.* Lanham, MD: University Press of America.

Astin, A. W. (1993). *What matters in college? Four critical years revisited.* San Francisco, CA: Jossey-Bass.

Astin, A. W., & Scherrei, R. A. (1980). *Maximizing leadership effectiveness.* San Francisco, CA: Jossey-Bass.

Astin, H. S. (1996). Leadership for social change. *About Campus, 1*(3), 4–10. doi:10.1002/abc.6190010302

Astin, H. S., & Leland, C. (1991). *Women of influence, women of vision: A cross-generational study of leaders and social change*. San Francisco, CA: Jossey-Bass.

Bounous-Hammarth, M. (2001). Developing social change agents: Leadership development for the 1990s and beyond. In C. L. Outcault, S. K. Faris, & K. N. McMahon (Eds.), *Developing non-hierarchical leadership on campus: Case studies and best practices in higher education* (pp. 34–39). Westport, CT: Greenwood.

Burns, J. M. (1978). *Leadership*. New York, NY: HarperCollins.

Contrera, J. (2015, October 3). She was a conservative pundit. He was a liberal activist. None of that mattered. *Washington Post*. Retrieved from https://www.washingtonpost.com/lifestyle/style/she-was-a-conservative-pundit-he-was-a-liberal-activist-at-home-none-of-that-mattered/2015/10/02/455256b4-66f6-11e5-9223-70cb36460919_story.html

Diamond, J. (2011). *Collapse: How societies choose to fail or succeed*. New York, NY: Penguin Books.

Dugan, J. P., & Correia, B. (2014). *MSL insight report supplement: Leadership program delivery*. College Park, MD: National Clearinghouse for Leadership Programs.

Greenleaf, R. G. (1977). *Servant leadership: A journey in the nature of legitimate power and greatness*. New York, NY: Paulist.

Heifetz, R. A., & Linsky, D. L. (2002). *Leadership on the line: Staying alive through the dangers of leading*. Boston, MA: Harvard Business School Press.

Higher Education Research Institute (HERI). (1996). *A social change model of leadership development* (Version III). Los Angeles, CA: University of California, Los Angeles, Higher Education Research Institute.

Kellerman, B. (2001). Required reading. *Harvard Business Review, 79*(11), 15–24.

Kezar, A. J., Carducci, R., & Contreras-McGavin, M. (2006). Rethinking the "L" word in higher education: The revolution in research on leadership. *ASHE Higher Education Report, 31*(6). San Francisco, CA: Jossey-Bass.

Komives, S. R., Lucas, N., & McMahon, T. R. (1998). *Exploring leadership: For college students who want to make a difference*. San Francisco, CA: Jossey-Bass.

Komives, S. R., Lucas, N., & McMahon, T. (2013). *Exploring leadership: For college students who want to make a difference* (3rd ed.). San Francisco, CA Jossey Bass.

Komives, S. R., & Dugan, J. P. (2010). Contemporary leadership theories. In R. A. Couto (Ed.), *Political and civic leadership: A reference handbook* (Vol. 1, pp. 111–120). Los Angeles, CA: Sage.

Lipman-Blumen, J. (1996). *The connective edge*. San Francisco, CA: Jossey-Bass.

Outcault, C. L, Faris, S. K., & McMahon, K. N. (Eds.). (2001). *Developing non-hierarchical leadership on campus: Case studies and best practices in higher education.* Westport, CT: Greenwood Press.

Roberts, D. C. (Ed.). (1981). *Student leadership programs in higher education.* Washington, DC: American College Personnel Association.

Rost, J. (1991). *Leadership for the twenty-first century.* New York, NY: Praeger.

Uhl-Bien, S., & Ospina, S. (Eds.). (2012). *Advancing relational leadership research: A dialogue among perspectives.* Leadership Horizons Series. Greenwich, CT: Information Age.

Vonnegut, K. (1963). *Cat's cradle.* New York, NY: Random House.

An Overview of the Social Change Model of Leadership Development

Kristan Cilente Skendall

> Even if I knew that tomorrow the world would go to pieces, I would still plant my apple tree.
> —MARTIN LUTHER KING JR.

The Social Change Model of Leadership Development (SCM) was created specifically for college students who seek to lead in a more socially responsible way and who want to learn to work effectively with others to create social change over their lifetimes (Higher Education Research Institute [HERI], 1996). An underlying value and assumption of leadership for social change requires individuals to dig deeper and embrace the plethora of perspectives that exist in our changing world. The Social Change Model advances that the process of engaging in leadership with others should be socially responsible and that leadership should be focused on social change. Social change is happening everywhere and, as a result of the communication and technological revolution, everyone has the ability and responsibility to contribute to a better world (Allen, Bordas, Hickman, Matusak, Sorenson, & Whitmire, 1998; Allen & Cherrey, 2000; Edmunds & Turner, 2005; Rost, 1991; Uhl-Bien, Marion, & McKelvey, 2007).

CHAPTER OVERVIEW

This chapter provides an introduction and overview of the Social Change Model of Leadership Development, specifically the three domains of development and its seven core values. In addition, this chapter will provide an introduction to the use of the Social Change Model as a tool for social change and as a philosophy of socially responsible leadership.

THE SOCIAL CHANGE MODEL OF LEADERSHIP DEVELOPMENT

As described in Chapter 1, the new definitions of leadership that developed during the 1990s generated momentum for leadership educators to recognize that students needed to learn different approaches to leadership (Astin, 1996; Astin & Astin, 2000; Bonous-Hammarth, 2001; Faris & Outcault, 2001; HERI, 1996; McMahon, 2001; Outcault, Faris, & McMahon, 2001). The Social Change Model grew out of the changing tide of leadership perspectives and was widely shared in the United States in 1996. Since then, scholars have observed, "The Social Change Model of Leadership Development . . . [has] played a prominent role in shaping the curricula and formats of undergraduate leadership education initiatives in colleges and universities throughout the country" (Kezar, Carducci, & Contreras-McGavin, 2006, p. 142).

Chapter 1 described how the Social Change Model of Leadership Development was the work of the ensemble (Astin, 1996; Bonous-Hammarth, 2001; HERI, 1996) and grounded in the work of Burns (1978), Rost (1991), and other scholars. Rooted in the postindustrial approach to leadership described by Rost (1991), in which leadership is viewed as a process rather than a position, the model promotes the creation and development of social change agents and the value of socially responsible leadership. As noted in Chapter 1, the SCM rests on the assumption that leadership is socially responsible and is aimed at positive change for and with others. Further, leadership is collaborative, a process, and not a position; it is inclusive and accessible to all people; and it is values-based. Community involvement and service is recognized as a powerful vehicle for leadership development (Astin 1996; Bonous-Hammarth, 2001; HERI, 1996).

> The Social Change Model of Leadership Development approaches leadership as a purposeful, collaborative, values-based process that results in positive social change.

A cornerstone of the model is the concept of a values-based process. The model is rooted in a commitment to core human values, such as self-knowledge, service, and collaboration. Although some approaches to leadership focus on the leader or the position of leadership, the Social Change Model is grounded in the postindustrial paradigm and assumes that leadership describes people's collaborative process, not a position (HERI, 1996; Rost, 1991; Uhl-Bien et al., 2007). The emphasis on relationships in the Social Change Model highlights the importance of the term *process*, which describes the way in which change (and ultimately leadership) occurs (HERI, 1996).

Leadership is not about top-down influence, and it does not happen through the efforts of a single individual with a positional title alone; rather, it is dynamic and collaborative. It is an evolving process that takes place in connection to others. The foundation of this process is relationships. Connections to others through relationships are a core assumption of collaborative leadership and serve as a base for the leadership process. Finally, the intention of positive social change—the hope of helping to make a difference—is the goal of the leadership process.

The model provides a framework for individuals and groups to learn to engage in leadership for social change (see Figure 2.1). The model describes an interaction among seven key values that individuals, groups, and communities should strive for in order to create social change. Each value begins with a C, which is why the Social Change Model is sometimes referred to as the *Seven Cs for Change*. The seven values are grouped into three dimensions: individual, group, and society/community.

The model is also a philosophy of socially responsible leadership, a guide for self-directed leadership development for individuals and groups, and a mechanism for diagnosing and attending to leadership dilemmas. As a philosophy, the Social Change Model provides an approach to socially responsible leadership and enables users to incorporate elements of the model into a personal or group definition of leadership.

The values of the model do not represent a checklist or prescription of how to be a successful leader or how a group can implement an effective process. One does not finish learning about one value and then start learning about the next. Rather,

FIGURE 2.1 The Social Change Model of Leadership Development

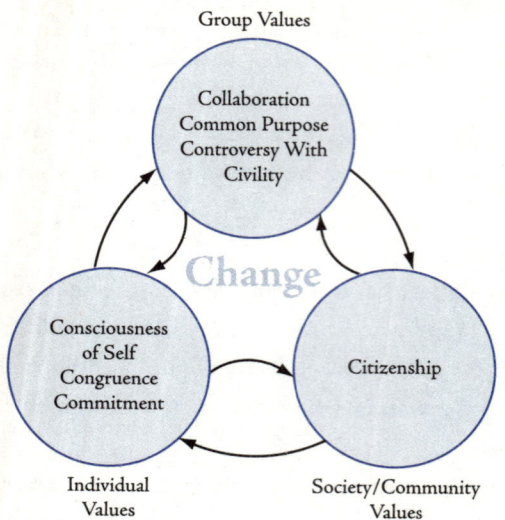

Source: Adapted from *A social change model of leadership development* (3rd ed., p. 20) by Higher Education Research Institute [HERI]. Copyright © 1996, National Clearinghouse for Leadership Programs. Reprinted with permission of the National Clearinghouse for Leadership Programs.

development in each value is ongoing. Applying the values in hands-on experiences of leadership results in understanding each value at a deeper level. The model works in this way because the values are interactive. Growth in one value increases the capacity for growth in the others. Depending on individuals' interest in developing a better understanding of themselves, learning to work effectively in groups, or learning about community issues, they can start learning about and practicing the Seven Cs at any of three dimensions: individual, group, or society/community.

Although the values model may be explored in any order, recent research supports the value of developmental sequencing of each of the dimensions of the model, in which capacity in the individual domain precedes capacity with group values, which precedes society/community (Dugan, Bohle, Woelker, & Cooney, 2014).

Individuals need to develop their capacity to engage in leadership within groups and communities. Similarly, groups need to develop as well. The model offers a framework for groups to improve their ability to function effectively as a collection of people joined to work toward a common goal. The society/community dimension stresses the need for communities to develop perspectives and mechanisms for organizations to work effectively across sectors to address community needs. Development of the individual, group, and community are all emphasized in this model.

Table 2.1 describes each of the Social Change Model values in more detail.

TABLE 2.1 Values of the Social Change Model of Leadership Development (The Seven Cs of Change)

Value	Definition
Consciousness of Self	Consciousness of Self requires an awareness of personal beliefs, values, attitudes, and emotions. Self-awareness, conscious mindfulness, introspection, and continual personal reflection are foundational elements of the leadership process.
Congruence	Congruence requires that one has identified personal values, beliefs, attitudes, and emotions and acts consistently with those values, beliefs, attitudes, and emotions. Congruent individuals are genuine, honest, and live their values.
Commitment	Commitment requires an intrinsic passion, energy, and purposeful investment toward action. Follow-through and willing involvement through Commitment lead to positive social change.
Collaboration	Collaboration multiplies a group's effort through collective contributions, capitalizing on the diversity and strengths of the relationships and interconnections of individuals involved in the change process. Collaboration assumes that a group is working toward a Common Purpose, with mutually beneficial goals, and serves to generate creative solutions as a result of group diversity, requiring participants to engage across difference and share authority, responsibility, and accountability for its success.
Common Purpose	Common Purpose necessitates and contributes to a high level of group trust involving all participants in shared responsibility toward collective aims, values, and vision.
Controversy With Civility	Within a diverse group, it is inevitable that differing viewpoints will exist. In order for a group to work toward positive social change, open, critical, and civil discourse can lead to new, creative solutions and is an integral component of the leadership process. Multiple perspectives need to be understood and integrated, and they bring value to a group.
Citizenship	Citizenship occurs when one becomes responsibly connected to the society/community in which one resides by actively working toward change to benefit others through care, service, social responsibility, and community involvement.
Change	As the hub and ultimate goal of the Social Change Model, change gives meaning and purpose to the other Cs. Change means improving the status quo, creating a better world, while demonstrating a comfort with transition and ambiguity during the process.

INDIVIDUAL VALUES

> No journey carries one far unless, as it extends into the world around us, it goes an equal distance into the world within.
> —LILLIAN SMITH

In order for leadership to occur at the group and societal levels, leaders must do inner work and reflect on leadership at the individual level. The values of this level, shown in Figure 2.2, include developing Consciousness of Self, being Congruent with one's beliefs, and establishing Commitment to follow those beliefs.

Consciousness of Self

Awareness of self and interactions with others are interrelated. The concept of the looking-glass self was introduced in the early 20th century by sociologist Charles Horton Cooley (1902), who posited that how individuals perceive themselves

FIGURE 2.2 The Social Change Model and Individual Values

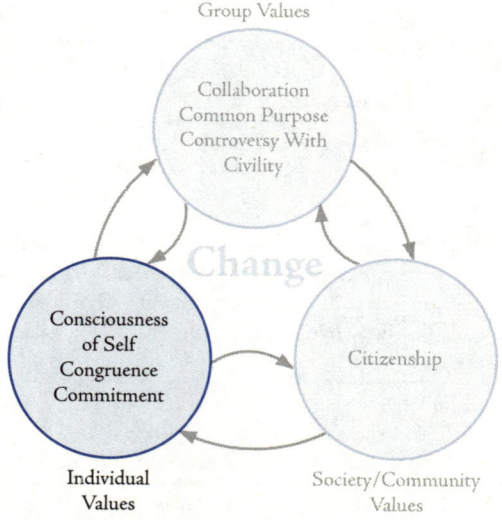

Source: Adapted from *A social change model of leadership development* (3rd ed., p. 20) by Higher Education Research Institute [HERI]. Copyright © 1996, National Clearinghouse for Leadership Programs. Reprinted with permission of the National Clearinghouse for Leadership Programs.

influences how others perceive them. For example, if a person has been told his whole life that he is a talented singer, it is likely that he will have confidence in his singing ability. On the contrary, if the same person has been told he has little musical talent, it is likely that he will avoid opportunities to sing or perform musically. In addition to this concept of how self is defined, individuals also must take time to reflect on who they are in terms of social identities (for example, race or ethnicity, socioeconomic class, gender and gender expression, sexual orientation, religion, or ability); personal identities (for example, sister, parent, friend, or partner); and core values.

In addition to self-awareness, Consciousness of Self involves the ability to observe oneself in the moment. Sometimes referred to as *mindfulness*, it includes being aware of one's current emotional state and making considered responses rather than reacting without thinking. Each of these pieces of the self intersects to define an individual and may evolve or change over time, but self-reflection and mindfulness are critical to the development of leadership. Each individual needs to understand the values, beliefs, motivations, and perspectives that form how he or she approaches working with others (HERI, 1996; Jones & McEwen, 2000).

Consciousness of Self requires continual growth and reevaluation. Because the levels of the Social Change Model are interconnected, as individuals interact with others in groups and engage in the community, their character will likely be influenced. This results in the need to reflect and make meaning of how the sense of self is affected. This continual learning and developmental process is a lifelong endeavor and is essential for the leadership process. Further details and strategies for self-reflection are presented in Chapter 3.

Congruence

Acting consistently with espoused positive values demonstrates the genuineness or authenticity of a person and is a basis of credibility. Everyone can think of people who have not done what they said they would do or have acted in ways inconsistent with what they claim to stand for, for example, friends who profess to be inclusive of diversity but then tell racist jokes are acting inconsistently with their espoused beliefs. Lee and King (2001) describe three ways one holds values: values that are held internally, values that one talks about or states, and values that are "reflected in . . . actions" (p. 62). One of the greatest challenges of leadership is acting consistently even when no one is looking.

People whose actions are Congruent with their espoused positive values instill trust, and trusting relationships support working collaboratively with others. Trustworthy people create brave spaces in groups to engage in Controversy With Civility. Congruence is not only integral to leadership but also it influences how an individual is perceived by others, thereby affecting the other Cs of the model (HERI, 1996). Congruence is presented in greater detail in Chapter 4.

Commitment

Commitment is also grounded in an individual's sense of self. One's passions fuel long-term dedication to a group's efforts and generate resilience from setbacks. Commitment demonstrates each person's responsibility to service and leadership and contributes to the group's Common Purpose.

Commitment is demonstrated by significant involvement, an investment of time, and emotional passion. Commitment is found in the decisions to select a specific major or career field, a life partner, and a focus of community service, and it is found in accepting appointment to a committee that will take time and energy to make a credible contribution. Commitment is the energy that drives action and is a necessary component of change (HERI, 1996). It is crucial in advancing the collective effort. The value of Commitment and its importance to the Social Change Model are explored in further detail in Chapter 5.

GROUP VALUES

> Alone we can do so little, together we can do so much.
> —HELEN KELLER

Whether with a student organization, a group of friends, a group project for class, an office, a research team, or a sports team, groups develop individuals and individuals attend to the development of groups. Groups need to be intentional about their process so that leadership can flourish in the relationships among people in the group. Three specific values, noted in Figure 2.3, interact to support the group being effective in leadership ability: engage in Collaboration with others, come to a Common Purpose, and embrace Controversy With Civility.

FIGURE 2.3 The Social Change Model and Group Values

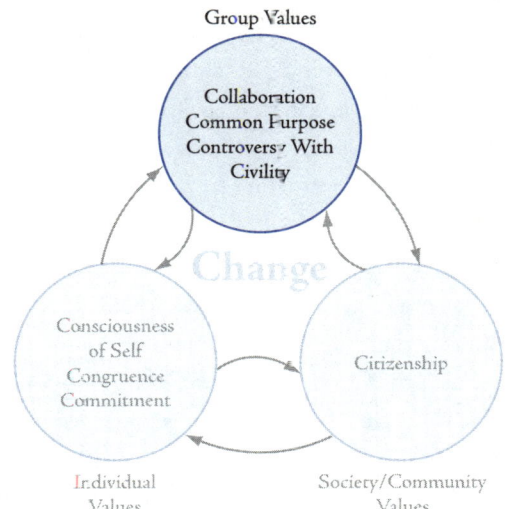

Source: Adapted from *A social change model of leadership development* (3rd ed., p. 20) by Higher Education Research Institute [HERI]. Copyright © 1996, National Clearinghouse for Leadership Programs. Reprinted with permission of the National Clearinghouse for Leadership Programs.

Collaboration

> Collaboration means working together toward common goals by sharing responsibility, authority, and accountability in achieving these goals.... It multiplies group effectiveness because it capitalizes on the multiple talents and perspectives of each group member and the power of that diversity to generate creative solutions and actions. (HERI, 1996, p. 48)

A core value of the Social Change Model, Collaboration is the process through which groups work toward their Common Purpose. Collaboration implies mutually beneficial goals, engaged participants, shared responsibility, and self-aware individuals. Rather than hierarchical leadership approaches in which influence flows top-down from leader to followers, Collaboration means learning to nurture relationships in which influence and good ideas come inclusively from all directions. Collaborative groups benefit from these diverse perspectives (HERI, 1996). Collaboration is explored in greater depth in Chapter 6.

Common Purpose

Group leadership success rests on a Common Purpose. All members or partners in a group need to participate in developing the shared vision of the group, even though each individual may work to accomplish that goal in a different way. Individuals must be engaged in the visioning process and agree on a collective set of aims and group values. Common Purpose is strongest when a group explicitly examines its implicit, or unspoken, values.

When looking at a student organization on campus, it is often easy to identify the common goal of that organization. For example, sororities and fraternities seek to build community among their members centered on a core set of values unique to each chapter on a campus. This Common Purpose unites not only individuals within the campus student organization but also brings together all chapters across the United States, under umbrella organizations such as National Pan-Hellenic Council, the National Panhellenic Conference, and the North American Interfraternity Conference. Many national and global organizations have a mechanism for organizing on campuses and at a larger level, such as the American Society of Mechanical Engineers, the National Association of Black Journalists, Circle K International, or the National Council of La Raza. For more examples of Common Purpose as well as a more in-depth look at this value, see Chapter 7.

Controversy With Civility

Many different ideas and perspectives help group members make sound decisions. It is inevitable in any group that disagreements will arise. Although individuals may have discomfort with conflict, it is necessary for all groups to experience the value of Controversy With Civility, which encourages thoughtful and considered differences of opinion to be heard within a group (HERI, 1996). If a group does not welcome Controversy With Civility, they may not hear the many voices, or perspectives might be lost because individuals do not feel comfortable introducing ideas different from the norm of the group. Avoiding groupthink, the tendency for individuals is to just go along with others even if one holds other views, and engaging in critical dialogue in a respectful manner is crucial for a group's development and ability to achieve Collaboration, work toward a Common Purpose, and achieve positive social change. Controversy With Civility rests on the notion that civil discourse can lead to new, creative solutions and is an essential element of leadership. Read more about Controversy With Civility in Chapter 8.

SOCIETY/COMMUNITY VALUES

> Once social change begins, it cannot be reversed. You cannot uneducate the person who has learned to read. You cannot humiliate the person who feels pride. You cannot oppress the people who are not afraid anymore. We have seen the future, and the future is ours.
> —CÉSAR CHÁVEZ

The Social Change Model calls for leadership directed toward a purpose greater than self for a societal end as illustrated in Figure 2.4. Social change occurs because diverse groups within a community work together to benefit the common good. This level of leadership encompasses all communities of which one is a member, whether that is the campus, the county, the state, the country, or the world; it is necessary that leadership be connected to a larger social purpose. Likewise, communities need

FIGURE 2.4 The Social Change Model and Society/Community Values

Source: Adapted from *A social change model of leadership development* (3rd ed., p. 20) by Higher Education Research Institute [HERI]. Copyright © 1996, National Clearinghouse for Leadership Programs. Reprinted with permission of the National Clearinghouse for Leadership Programs.

to develop effective ways to form coalitions and support social change work across multiple sectors.

Citizenship

Although it may seem overwhelming to work toward positive social change at the societal/community level, the C of Citizenship calls all individuals to see themselves as part of a larger whole. Through this value, individuals and groups or organizations are able to see how their efforts for social change, large or small, play an important role when joined with the many others working toward the same goals in a global effort. This C also calls for communities to examine the strategies and processes in place for groups to come together as a system designed to enhance community goals. Citizenship relies on caring and is characterized by active engagement in service to the community. Community can be defined broadly or specifically, such as a student organization, office, classroom, campus, neighborhood, town, nation, or the world. Service and community involvement are vehicles for implementing this value of the SCM (HERI, 1996).

For the individual, Citizenship requires awareness of local and global issues, active engagement in one's community, and participation in interests beyond oneself. Building relationships with others in the community and working across difference are integral components of Citizenship. There is great privilege in being part of a community, and as a result, a great responsibility to be an active participant in that community as part of the leadership process. Other dimensions of Citizenship are examined in Chapter 9.

CHANGE

> If you ever think you're too small to be effective, you've never been in bed with a mosquito!
> —AMERICAN PROVERB

Change, particularly social change, is the ultimate goal of the Social Change Model (see Chapter 10). As shown in Figure 2.5, it is the hub around which the other elements interact. The model is grounded in the belief that everyone can contribute to making the world a better place for current and future generations. The intention of

FIGURE 2.5 The Social Change Model and Change

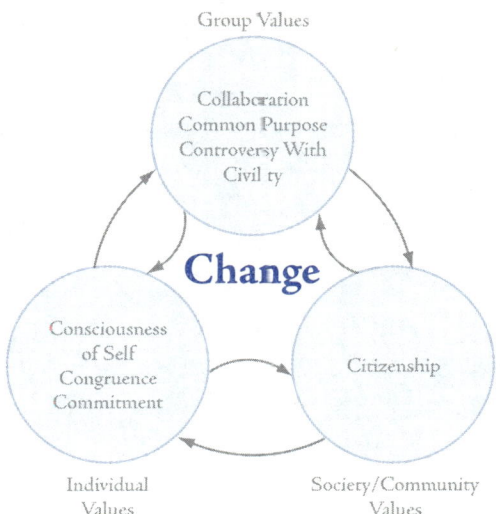

Source: Adapted from *A social change model of leadership development* (3rd ed., p. 20) by Higher Education Research Institute [HERI]. Copyright © 1996, National Clearinghouse for Leadership Programs. Reprinted with permission of the National Clearinghouse for Leadership Programs.

positive social change is at the heart of leadership, regardless of the outcome (HERI, 1996; Rost, 1991).

Change is not easy; it requires learning a new way of being and unlearning past habits, behaviors, and attitudes. It also requires some degree of risk in order to challenge the status quo and go in a new, untested direction. The courage involved in social change is great, and the willingness to take a leap of faith toward a novel idea or a different tactic requires an acceptance of ambiguity, transition, and even discomfort. Although this is a difficult call to action, leadership requires that change (small or large scale) be attempted and, ideally, enacted. Change is explored in greater detail in Chapter 10.

INTERACTIONS IN THE SOCIAL CHANGE MODEL

> For me, a landscape does not exist in its own right, since its appearance changes at every moment; but the surrounding atmosphere brings it to life—the light and the air which vary continually. For me, it is only the surrounding atmosphere which gives subjects their true value.
> —CLAUDE MONET

As Monet indicates, there is a connection between subjects in a piece of art and the environment in which they exist. The reverse is also true; the subjects influence the environment. In the Social Change Model, each level interacts with and influences the other and each value is interconnected to the others. Although each C is a distinct component of the model, positive social change or practicing socially responsible leadership is not possible without the interaction and connection of all of the values. As an individual gains better Consciousness of Self, acts Congruently, and demonstrates Commitment, the individual's ability to contribute to the group's Common Purpose, work with others Collaboratively, and engage in Controversy With Civility increases (as illustrated by arrow *a* in Figure 2.6).

Similarly, engaging with a group's process expects members to Collaborate, work toward a Common Purpose, and civilly engage with others helps individuals clarify their own values and Commitments and learn to act in ways that are Congruent with them (see arrow *b*). This reciprocity exists among all of the values and dimensions of the model. For example, awareness of and involvement in community issues challenges groups (arrow *d*) and individuals (arrow *f*) to continue to clarify and

FIGURE 2.6 Interactions in the Social Change Model

Group Values

Collaboration
Common Purpose
Controversy With Civility

Change

Consciousness of Self
Congruence
Commitment

Citizenship

Individual Values

Society/Community Values

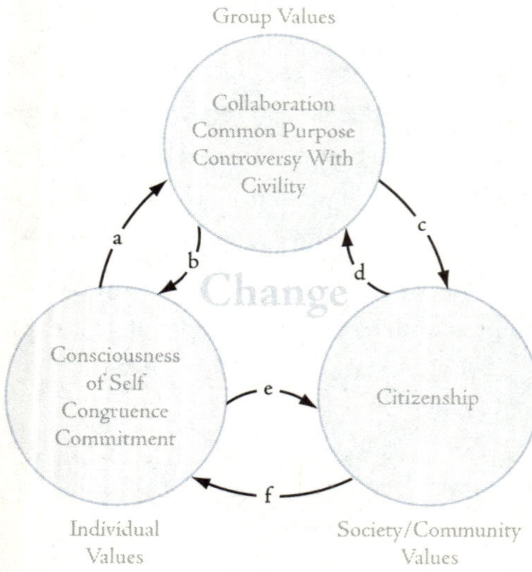

Source: Adapted from *A social change model of leadership development* (3rd ed., p. 20) by Higher Education Research Institute [HERI]. Copyright © 1996, National Clearinghouse for Leadership Programs. Reprinted with permission of the National Clearinghouse for Leadership Programs.

collaboratively act on their values and Common Purposes. Interaction and intersections at each dimension move together to create and facilitate positive social change.

KNOWING, BEING, AND DOING

The interactions within the model are only part of the leadership process. An interaction also exists among one's knowledge, attitudes, and skills involved in leadership and social change. In order to implement the Social Change Model, it is important that one acquires knowledge (knowing), integrates that knowledge into beliefs and attitudes (being), and applies knowledge and beliefs in daily life (doing). This knowing-being-doing framework works especially well for the Social Change Model. Table 2.2 highlights key knowledge, attitudes, and skills rooted in social change and in each value of the model (Komives, Lucas, & McMahon, 2013; National Association of Student Personnel Administrators and American College Personnel [NASPA & ACPA], 2004).

The knowing-being-doing framework can serve multiple purposes. First, this framework helps to further understand the values of the Social Change Model. Next, the framework can be used as a tool to assess oneself and groups on capacities related to knowing, understanding, and applying the core tenets of the Social Change Model. Last, the knowing-being-doing framework provides a full overview of the many ways in which the values of the model can be applied and understood.

IMPLEMENTING THE SOCIAL CHANGE MODEL

> Believe and act as if it were not possible to fail.
> —CHARLES F. KETTERING

As described in Chapter 11, social change is often thought to be large in scope and scale. Popular examples of social change agents are often of heroic people such as Rosa Parks and Martin Luther King Jr. within the Civil Rights Movement or Gandhi's peaceful liberation in India. Grand-scale change can be overwhelming to consider if only viewed through a lens of heroism. Instead, each of these individual change agents worked collaboratively with others as a part of a larger movement. Everyday

TABLE 2.2 Knowing, Being, Doing

Value	Knowing (Knowledge Acquisition)	Being (Attitudes; Knowledge Integration)	Doing (Skills; Knowledge Application)
	Understanding...	Having...	Demonstrating...
Consciousness of Self	Values of self and others How change happens Personal strengths and weaknesses	Self-confidence Openness to feedback Readiness for change Commitment to positive social change	Ability to reflect Meaning-making skills Ability to give and receive feedback Active listening skills
Congruence	Personal values That values are relative to an individual	A commitment to self-evaluation Respect for values different from one's own	Action consistent with personal values An ability to work toward a shared purpose in a group
Commitment	One's personal values and passion The goals or target of a group That change is needed	Self-awareness of personal values Congruence with values and actions Passion Internal motivation Engaged attitude Discipline Energy to move motivation from "should" to "want"	Follow-through on commitments Engagement and involvement Devotion of time and energy Willful action
Collaboration	Intercultural awareness and competence Personal values and perspectives That multiple perspectives are efficient and educational	Belief that working together can generate stronger, more creative win-win solutions Willingness to work toward group trust Willingness to put personal agendas aside to create shared visions	Strong listening, speaking, and reflective dialogue skills Trust and trusting relationships Shared ownership toward a Common Purpose
Common Purpose	How change occurs The role of mission, vision, and core values How groups function Personal core values	A commitment (to the group, the vision, and social responsibility) A visionary approach Inclusive attitude	Ability to identify goals Decision-making skills Creative thinking Ability to work with others and collaborate

An Overview of the Social Change Model of Leadership Development

Value	Knowing (Knowledge Acquisition)	Being (Attitudes; Knowledge Integration)	Doing (Skills; Knowledge Application)
Controversy With Civility	Attitudes, biases, and values Various communication styles Difference in viewpoints is inevitable and contributes to the leadership process	Civility and commitment Inclusive attitude Patience Purpose	Active listening skills Communication skills Engagement in dialogue Ability to mediate and negotiate
Citizenship	Community building Collaboration Social responsibility and larger social issues Personal and community values Rights and responsibilities Social justice/equality	A belief in one's personal ability to make a difference A sense of belonging to one's communities Patience with self and others Optimism and pragmatism Appreciation for diversity Interdependent thinking An ethic of care Tolerance for ambiguity Respect for self and others	An ability to work with others across difference Reflective thought and meaning making Self-motivation and determination Diplomacy Empathy Creativity Critical thinking Interpersonal communication An ability to challenge assumptions Advocacy
Change	That change is a process Resistance to change at the society/community, group, and individual levels Strategies for overcoming resistance Motivations for engaging in change	Positive perceptions of change Comfort with ambiguity and transition Self-confidence Patience Willingness to step outside of one's comfort zone	An ability to influence systems The creation of a sense of urgency An ability to articulate a change vision Willingness to take a risk to make a difference

acts of working together to make a difference is part of the practice of socially responsible leadership and starts a person on a path to deeper commitment to social change.

There are numerous examples of social change by college students at the individual level and group level. Students might find the higher principles in their major that will prepare for a life of meaning: being a teacher to help children, being a lawyer to protect people's rights, being a journalist to reveal the truth, being a musician to lift the spirit, being a biologist to protect the environment, or being an agriculturist to feed the world. Individuals can also make a difference by changing daily behaviors, such as reducing personal electricity use by turning off lights during the day or trading in disposable water bottles for a reusable water bottle. Further, individuals need not limit their engagement in social change to their physical environment. They could engage in dialogue and activism on social media via hashtags, such as #BlackLivesMatter, #YesAllWomen, or #IceBucketChallenge.

To enact social change as envisioned by the Social Change Model of Leadership Development, socially responsible individuals and groups must come together. You can work with others on any side of a complex issue to advance your values about that issue. Social change can clearly embrace conservative or liberal perspectives. Some examples include working with others to do the following:

- Provide scholarships to undocumented students
- Protest university investments that do not uphold social justice values
- Program concerts on campus to improve the sense of community
- Start a composting program in the residence halls or community
- Produce a political play such as *The Vagina Monologues* to raise money for a local women's organization
- Create undergraduate teaching assistant positions in one's department
- Engage in research to advance the common good, such as to develop a Zika virus vaccine, increase the efficiency of solar cells, or explore solutions to cybersecurity threats
- Participate in a community cleanup to rid a neighborhood of trash and protect the environment

As outlined by the SCM, socially responsible leadership and social change happen at the individual, group, and society/community levels. Not only can individuals change personal behaviors to effect change and work with others to make a difference but also groups and communities can come together to forge change. Coalitions are groups of groups who share a common goal and collaborate on their collective efforts to enact large-scale change. Some coalitions are formally organized, such as the U.S. Climate Action Network, a coalition of more than 150 nonprofit advocacy, research, and action organizations (such as Greenpeace, the League of Conservation Voters, and the Sierra Club). Other coalitions are simpler, informal networks among group leaders, for example, a citywide Hunger Coalition linking nonprofits and government agencies that address food security exists in nearly all U.S. cities.

RESEARCH ON THE SOCIAL CHANGE MODEL

> Research is formalized curiosity. It is poking and prying with a purpose.
> —ZORA NEALE HURSTON

As noted in Chapter 1, research on the Social Change Model has been expanding since Tyree (1998) created the Socially Responsible Leadership Scale (SRLS), which became the core of the Multi-Institutional Study of Leadership (MSL). The MSL study participants comprise nearly 400,000 college students from more than 350 different institutions across the United States and in a dozen international countries—including large and small institutions, public and private schools, four-year schools, and community colleges. In addition to the SRLS, the MSL survey collected data on the kinds of college and precollege experience students had, all aimed at identifying the kinds of college involvements that lead to greater socially responsible leadership. For example, students were asked whether they belonged to student organizations and if so which ones, lived on or off campus, had an on- or off-campus job, had attended leadership workshops or courses, and had participated in community service, and dozens of other questions.

Since the inception of the MSL in 2005, data have been collected in 2006, 2009, 2010, 2011, 2012, and 2015 (www.leadershipstudy.net), resulting in numerous studies and publications on various aspects of the model and related concepts, further contributing to the widespread use of the model (Kezar et al., 2006). The outcomes learned from this study about what contributes to leadership learning are briefly highlighted in this chapter and will be included throughout the rest of the book.

Research Informs Understanding the Conceptual Model

One purpose of research is to advance theory building or model validation. As you know from this chapter, the model is presented as three domains in equally interacting circles. Although one can learn the values of the model independently and there are theoretical interactions between each of the domains, research on the Social Change Model has supported the importance of developmental sequencing. Research shows that leadership learning actually is sequential and develops beginning with individual values, which influence group capacities, which influence society/community values. "There were no direct relationships between individual and societal capacities as the relationship was fully mediated by group-level leadership capacities" (Dugan, Kodama, Correia, & Associates, 2013, p. 26). MSL research affirms that leadership capacity develops over time and can be learned. "Overall, college students were confident in their leadership abilities. This confidence increases significantly across college years. All eight of the SCM scales showed significant increases with the largest increase across the value of Consciousness of Self" (Dugan & Komives, 2006, p. 16).

Each domain builds on the previous, but the learning is cyclical in its process. Therefore, learning is continuous and not stagnant, individuals might revisit earlier domains throughout their lifetime.

MSL also examined elements of the Social Change Model in depth. One important finding shows that Collaboration and Common Purpose values have very similar underlying constructs measuring the same outcome. Despite this overlap in measurement of the concepts, Collaboration and Common Purpose remain as separate C values in the Social Change Model because of their importance in group development and process. The inclusion of each C is helpful when using the model to assess oneself or a group.

Interesting MSL Findings

In addition to the developmental sequencing of the model, MSL findings uncover interesting differences within the model when certain characteristics are considered. For example, men scored significantly higher than women on measures of leadership confidence (called *leadership efficacy*), and women scored significantly higher than men on seven of the eight values measured (Dugan & Komives, 2006). This is one of several differences highlighted by research on the Social Change Model; more detail will be included in subsequent chapters.

The MSL particularly studies how a person develops her capacities to engage in this kind of leadership and found that engaging in sociocultural conversations with peers, mentoring relationships, community service, and membership in off-campus organizations "can be considered high-impact practices for building leadership capacity with broad influences across gender, race, and other demographic groups" (Dugan et al., 2013, p. 8). These experiences are important for helping individuals to develop the capacity for socially responsible leadership and ultimately contribute to leadership for social change.

The Model as a Framework for Self-Assessment

The model is an excellent tool for assessing current leadership capacity for individuals and groups, providing a framework for self-reflection and growth in each of the dimensions of the model. Using the SRLS online, individuals and groups can complete an instrument based on the values of the Social Change Model and identify areas of strength and growth (see www.nlcp.umd.edu). Further, the model can be used as a way for individuals, groups, or organizations to address leadership dilemmas that they are facing. The approach to leadership and the values of the Social Change Model provides valuable language that can be used in navigating difficult leadership challenges. For example, if the group is struggling to come to a Common Purpose, members can be asked to think about what motivates their own views and engage on a deeper level to find Common Purpose. Or if several groups in a community demonstrate a common area of shared interest, but they are not collaborating in ways they could be, then the model suggests pathways to foster a more shared sense of mission across the groups. The model would suggest the groups build a stronger sense of Common Purpose by sharing with each other each group's history, mission, and vision, and working together to find their points of alignment.

In addition to using the model as a tool for assessment, it can also be used as a compass for individuals and groups to chart their leadership path. Each subsequent chapter includes rubrics that can be used as a resource for self- and group reflection to measure the way in which that value is being addressed. The rubrics can also be used as a map for a new leadership process as a group comes together to work toward social change.

The world is changing, and with greater abilities to communicate across difference and distance in this networked era of connection and technology, there is a call to action. The Social Change Model provides a framework within which to mobilize oneself and others to address such needed changes.

CONCLUSION

The Social Change Model approaches leadership as a dynamic, collaborative, and values-based process grounded in relationships and intending positive social change. Designed with college students in mind, this model is relevant to student organizations, campus change, and personal development. The model is not a checklist or a prescription for successful leadership; it is a framework for continual exploration of personal values in working with others to attempt change. This approach to leadership requires continual reflection, active learning, involvement, and action. The discussion questions, actions, and reflections at the end of each chapter in this book guide the reader to explore the values of Consciousness of Self, Congruence, Commitment, Collaboration, Common Purpose, Controversy With Civility, Citizenship, and Change (HERI, 1996), and in engaging in social change.

DISCUSSION QUESTIONS

1. This is a model of leadership development. What kinds of experiences do you think would foster leadership development for the individual Cs? What experiences do you think would foster a group's development of the group Cs? Community development?
2. How do multiple perspectives and diversity fit into the Social Change Model?
3. What is the role of ethics in this approach to leadership?
4. How would this approach to leadership work in an organization with clearly defined hierarchical positions of leadership? What benefits would it bring? What would be challenging to implement?
5. Is there anything you would add or remove from the Social Change Model of Leadership?

ACTION AND REFLECTION

1. Take the SRLS online or simply self-assess your own comfort with each value of the Social Change Model given the descriptions in this chapter. (See www.nclp.umd.edu.)

2. Select a group you are a part of and at your next group meeting observe the ways members work together. Can you identify the values of the Social Change Model in action?
3. Reflect on your own person definition of leadership. How is it similar to the Social Change Model of leadership? How is it different?
4. How did you come to leadership? Did you seek out opportunities to lead? Did your desire to make a difference on a particular issue bring you to leadership?
5. How do you want your life to matter? What passions can you identify that are driving any of your actions, such as the major or future career field you are choosing?

REFERENCES

Allen, K. E., Bordas, J., Hickman, G. R., Matusak, L. R., Sorenson, G. J., & Whitmire, K. J. (1998). Leadership in the twenty-first century. In G. R. Hickman (Ed.), *Leading organizations: Perspectives for a new era* (pp. 572–580). Thousand Oaks, CA: Sage.

Allen, K. E., & Cherrey, C. (2000). *Systemic leadership: Enriching the meaning of our work.* Lanham, MD: University Press of America.

Astin, A., & Astin, H. (2000). *Leadership reconsidered: Engaging higher education in social change.* Battle Creek, MI: W. K. Kellogg Foundation.

Astin, H. S. (1996). Leadership for social change. *About Campus, 1*(3), 4–10. doi:10.1002/abc.6190010302

Bonous-Hammarth, M. (2001). Developing social change agents: Leadership development for the 1990s and beyond. In C. L. Outcault, S. K. Faris, & K. N. McMahon (Eds.), *Developing non-hierarchical leadership on campus: Case studies and best practices in higher education* (pp. 34–39). Westport, CT: Greenwood.

Burns, J. M. (1978). *Leadership.* New York, NY: Harper & Row.

Cooley, C. H. (1902). *Human nature and social order.* New York, NY: Scribner's.

Dugan, J. P., Bohle, C. W., Woelker, L. R., & Cooney, M. A. (2014). The role of social perspective-taking in developing students' leadership capacities. *Journal of Student Affairs Research and Practice, 51*, 1–15. doi:10.1515/jsarp-2014–0001

Dugan, J. P., Kodama, C., Correia, B., & Associates. (2013). *Multi-Institutional Study of Leadership insight report: Leadership program delivery.* College Park, MD: National Clearinghouse for Leadership Programs.

Dugan, J. P., & Komives, S. R. (2006). Select descriptive findings from the Multi-Institutional Study of Leadership. *Concepts and Connections, 15*(1), 16–18.

Edmunds, J., & Turner, B. S. (2005). Global generations: Social change in the twentieth century. *The British Journal of Sociology, 56,* 559–577. doi:10.1111/j.1468-4446.2005.00083

Faris, S. K., & Outcault, C. L. (2001). The emergence of inclusive, process-oriented leadership. In C. L. Outcault, S. K. Faris, & K. N. McMahon (Eds.), *Developing non-hierarchical leadership on campus: Case studies and best practices in higher education* (pp. 9–18). Westport, CT: Greenwood.

Higher Education Research Institute (HERI). (1996). *A social change model of leadership development* (Version III). Los Angeles, CA: University of California, Los Angeles, Higher Education Research Institute.

Jones, S. R., & McEwen, M. K. (2000, July/August). A conceptual model of multiple dimensions of identity. *Journal of College Student Development, 41,* 405–414.

Kezar, A. J., Carducci, R., & Contreras-McGavin, M. (2006). Rethinking the "L" word in higher education: The revolution in research on leadership. *ASHE Higher Education Report, 31*(6). San Francisco, CA: Jossey-Bass.

Komives, S. R., Lucas, N., & McMahon, T. R. (2013). *Exploring leadership: For college students who want to make a difference* (3rd ed.). San Francisco, CA: Jossey-Bass.

Lee, R., & King, S. (2001). *Ground your leadership vision in personal vision: Discovering the leader in you; A guidebook to realizing your personal leadership potential.* San Francisco, CA: Jossey-Bass.

McMahon, K. N. (2001). An interview with Helen S. Astin. In C. L. Outcault, S. K. Faris, & K. N. McMahon (Eds.), *Developing non-hierarchical leadership on campus: Case studies and best practices in higher education* (pp. 3–8). Westport, CT: Greenwood.

National Association of Student Personnel Administrators and American College Personnel Association (NASPA & ACPA). (2004). *Learning reconsidered: A campus-wide focus on the student experience.* Washington, DC: Author.

Outcault, C. L., Faris, S. K., & McMahon, K. N. (Eds.). (2001). *Developing non-hierarchical leadership on campus: Case studies and best practices in higher education.* Westport, CT: Greenwood.

Rost, J. C. (1991). *Leadership for the twenty-first century.* Westport, CT: Praeger.

Tyree, T. (1998). Designing an instrument to measure the socially responsible leadership using the Social Change Model of Leadership Development. *Dissertation Abstracts International, 59*(06), 1945. (AAT 9836493)

Uhl-Bien, M., Marion, R., & McKelvey, B. (2007). Complexity leadership theory: Shifting leadership from the industrial age to the knowledge era. *The Leadership Quarterly, 18,* 298–318. doi:10.1016/j.leaqua.2007.04.002

PART 2

Individual Values

> Those of us inspirited by the call to make a difference in the world have no choice but to take the journey of self-discovery.
> —DENNIS C. ROBERTS

Although leadership is a process that takes place among people working together toward positive change, individuals have a responsibility to expand their personal capacity to engage in this collaborative leadership. This journey into self-awareness is essential to be able to relate authentically to others particularly when they are in group settings and to make the personal commitments essential to working toward positive change.

Learning and personal development are a lifelong process. Most people can look back to ways they were when they were younger and realize they have developed more complexity in their thinking, understand themselves in deeper ways, and value interdependence in their relationships. Psychologist Robert Kegan (1994) describes the interaction of cognitive, intrapersonal, and interpersonal development as a stage of consciousness that shifts when one is able to look back on oneself at an earlier time and realize how one is now different in attitudes, beliefs, and skills from then. The thoughtful assessment promoted in this book is intended to enrich a *mindfulness* about self and self in the context of others. This mindfulness describes the process of "becoming" presented in the preface of the book.

In Part 2, the Social Change Model examines leadership development from the individual perspective or level. The ensemble asked, "What personal qualities are we attempting to foster and develop in those who participate in a leadership development program? What personal qualities are most supportive of group functioning and positive social change?" (Higher Education Research Institute [HERI], 1996, p. 19). The three values explored in Part 2 are Consciousness of Self, Congruence, and Commitment.

REFERENCES

Higher Education Research Institute (HERI). (1996). *A social change model of leadership development* (Version III). Los Angeles, CA: University of California, Los Angeles, Higher Education Research Institute.

Kegan, R. (1994). *In over our heads: The mental demands of modern life.* Cambridge, MA: Harvard University Press.

Consciousness of Self

Sherry Early and Justin Fincher

> Until you make the unconscious conscious, it will direct your life and you will call it fate.
> —CARL JUNG

Chris is the chair of the finance committee for his community service fraternity. The group has several grant-funded projects this year, so spending must be tracked project-by-project in order to accurately report to funders how the money was used. At first, things did not go well. Chris learned that although he could set up tracking systems, he was not good at following through with regular record keeping. He kept trying to improve, of course, but after a while he had to accept that keeping track of details in an ongoing way was not something that came naturally to him. Admitting this to the rest of the committee required courage—how can the head of the finance committee be bad with details? But his transparency actually helped turn the group around. Committee members who were great at details were empowered to step forward and now take responsibility for tracking the group's spending. This gives Chris more time to devote to identifying foundations and other potential sources of new funding—something he is great at.

Self-awareness is essential for a collaborative approach to leadership. In order to build authentic relationships within a group or a community, leaders must to be aware of not only their skills, as illustrated in the previous example, but also their values, beliefs, and motivations. Self-awareness "alludes to a deeper process of discovering who one is, that is, learning one's self-concept and self-views, how past events shape current perceptions and behaviors, and how one tends to make meaning of personal experiences" (Walumbwa, Avolio, Gardner, Wernsing, & Peterson, 2008, p. 103).

The ensemble that developed the Social Change Model (Higher Education Research Institute [HERI], 1996) clarified Consciousness of Self as the following:

> Consciousness of Self has two different but closely related aspects. First, it implies an awareness and an acknowledgement of those relatively stable aspects of the self that go to make up what we call "personality": talents, interests, aspirations, values, concerns, self-concept, limitations, and dreams. Second, self-awareness implies "mindfulness," an ability and a propensity to be an accurate observer of your current actions and state of mind. (p. 31)

CHAPTER OVERVIEW

This chapter examines the importance of self-awareness in learning to be effective in collaborative leadership. This practice includes having awareness of your values, skills, personal style, and other important aspects of your identity and ways of being. Practices that foster greater self-awareness include intentional exposure to new experiences, reflection, seeking feedback, and using assessment instruments. The chapter also discusses mindfulness as a form of consciousness of self that occurs while still in the present moment.

DEFINING CONSCIOUSNESS OF SELF

Consciousness of Self includes awareness of your personality traits, values, and strengths, as well as your abilities to be a self-observer who is mindful of your own actions, feelings, and beliefs. This depth of self-awareness includes the understanding of the influence of other people and environmental conditions in shaping your identity.

Having consciousness of self is an ongoing endeavor. People do not achieve a state of self-awareness; rather, they achieve a way of life that continually informs how they see themselves. There is no end point at which one can say, "I've done it. I know myself." Leaders with consciousness of self are observant and reflective and continually developing that awareness.

Some might mistakenly confuse consciousness of self with being self-conscious. People who are self-conscious are afraid to act as they naturally would because they are worried about what everyone else thinks about them. Consciousness of self is quite different. People who are conscious of themselves know where their values come from; they know their strengths and areas for improvement. This results in self-efficacy, or increased internal confidence to act authentically. Although validation from others may be appreciated, it is not required; those who are conscious of themselves have shifted *to* self-approval *from* the approval of others.

CONSCIOUSNESS OF SELF AND LEADERSHIP DEVELOPMENT RESEARCH

Researchers have studied leadership development programs to better understand why some approaches are more successful than others. In addition to many variables that contribute to quality programs, they have also learned that an important contributor to leadership development is the extent to which the learner is "ready." This concept of *developmental readiness* was explored further, and two key components of readiness emerged: the leader's *motivation* to develop and *ability* to learn. *Motivation* to develop leadership comes from having goals that require improved leadership effectiveness and a belief in one's own ability to learn to be a leader, or self-efficacy for leadership. The *ability* to learn leadership comes from self-awareness and the ability to examine one's own thinking (also called *meta-cognitive ability*) (Hannah & Avolio, 2010; Reichard & Thompson, 2016). Although the Social Change Model was created years before this research emerged, it is striking how well connected the Consciousness of Self values align with these findings. This chapter will examine each of these elements.

Another series of research studies has examined how people developmentally come to see themselves as leaders, resulting in the leadership identity development model. Through in-depth interviews with college seniors about their leadership experiences, researchers found that ever-expanding self-awareness was a critical aspect of leadership identity development (Komives, Owen, Longerbeam, Mainella, & Osteen, 2005). Consciousness of self affected this developmental process along five dimensions, which have much in common with the developmental readiness research previously described: (1) deepening self-awareness, (2) building self-confidence,

(3) establishing interpersonal efficacy, (4) applying new skills, and (5) expanding motivation.

The researchers (Komives et al., 2005) found students experienced a deepening self-awareness when they became aware of how they worked with others. In the beginning, students defined themselves by how others saw them. As they had opportunities to work with others and gain experiences, their self-concept began to come from an inner sense of identity. They also became increasingly aware of how their social identities, such as gender, racial, or cultural affiliation, affected how they interacted in groups.

As students became more aware of their skills, personality attributes, and values, they began building confidence in their ability to take on new responsibilities and challenges. This confidence was important to their evolving leadership effectiveness. Self-confident individuals tend to "take on unpopular issues, stand up for their values, and not need peer affirmation" (Komives et al., 2005, p. 600). Self-aware individuals are able to focus on their strengths while understanding their limitations, protecting against overconfidence. Without an accurate perception of one's limitations, leaders can get deep into a task or situation and not realize quickly enough they are not fully prepared for the task and need assistance.

Self-awareness also affected the students' beliefs in their ability to work well with others, or their interpersonal efficacy (Komives et al., 2005). For example, some cultures value building relationships and trust before turning their attention to the task at hand. Students who are aware of having learned this approach from their culture are able to temper their frustration when working in a task-oriented group. "Understanding oneself in relation to others augments the ability to foster social bonds and decreases in-group favoritism enhancing one's overall capacity to engage effectively in group processes" (Dugan, Bohle, Woelker, & Cooney, 2014, p. 3).

People with an awareness of their weaknesses are better equipped to challenge themselves to apply new skills and improve themselves through practice. Students who realize they are not the best listeners can begin to actively seek out opportunities to develop this skill and apply it in different settings. By the same token, students who are aware of their strengths can consider new ways to contribute their talents to benefit their groups and organizations.

Additionally, students who become increasingly aware of their values have an expanding motivation to get involved and address issues most important to them. For example, note the following featured story about Rodrigo Velasquez, whose value for family and solidarity with others provided the deeply felt motivation to become involved on campus in ways that would pave the way for those who came after him, providing support to undocumented students navigating the higher education system. Although Velasquez's leadership involvements certainly benefited many other students on campus, his involvements also helped develop his leadership competence and efficacy, and his clear sense of self.

One of my biggest values is family, which no doubt is based on my personal migration story. My family came to the U.S. and we were undocumented for years. My going to university was a huge step for us. Staying was a challenge. I was not comfortable telling more than a small handful of supportive campus staff members that I was undocumented. It was stressful. What drove me to get involved on campus, as an activist and peer mentor, was partially the need for the scholarships, [which] are the reason I made it to graduation, but mostly so other students like myself wouldn't have to go through what I did.

I consider undocumented people across the country to be my family. No hard-working high school senior who wants to go to college should be blocked by anti-immigrant policies or financial limitations. At a personal level, I want to set an example for my younger brother and cousin.

—Rodrigo Velasquez is a recent graduate of George Mason University, where he served as president of Mason DREAMers and as a peer mentor in the student transition empowerment program. Rodrigo continues to be a tireless advocate for the well-being of immigrants who are undocumented.

ASPECTS OF INDIVIDUAL IDENTITY

There are many factors that make individuals unique and shape their way of engaging in leadership. A few discussed by the ensemble who created the Social Change Model include (1) value, principles, and identity; (2) personal style; (3) talents, skills, and specialized knowledge; and (4) aspirations and dreams.

Values, Principles, and Identity

Values and principles represent the priorities guiding how people live their lives, how they decide what is most important, when to take a stand, and how they know what they are and are not willing to do in order to reach a goal. In 2005, David Foster Wallace once suggested that a fish would not know what it means to be wet. He was describing how difficult it is to have awareness of our values, beliefs, and assumptions when we have not experienced or considered any other ways of being. It may be difficult to even recognize that we have them, but as Jung indicated in the quote at the beginning of the chapter, they direct our lives and shape our identity. One way to come to have conscious awareness of our values and principles is to consider the sources of individual beliefs, such as our culture, faith, family, and generational peers. What values from our contexts have now become part of who we are?

Culture

"The exploration of leadership and culture is a journey both of discovery and practice, related to an understanding of self, an understanding of others, and an understanding of self in relationship and concert with others" (Ostick & Wall, 2011, p. 339). People of a particular culture often share at least a few values in common. For example, the dominant culture in the United States tends to value self-reliance, freedom of choice, and a strong work ethic. There are arguably also some less positive values such as materialism and conspicuous consumption. Ethnic cultures in the United States share some cultural values with their fellow Americans, but they often also possess additional values that are distinct. For example, some of these cultures maintain strong ties to the past. Children are taught to learn from the group's history; particular reverence is given to the wisdom of older family members. In some cultures, people value the needs of the group over the needs of the individual and would look down on someone who lived with independence, seeing that person as selfish, or not having an appropriate regard for or loyalty to others (Bordas, 2012). These are just a few examples of how people's values are influenced by their cultures. Cultural values can shape behaviors and the way one makes meaning of the world.

Faith

For people who grew up with a particular spiritual tradition, messages about how to treat others and how to live a good life are taught from such a young age it might be difficult to be aware of any other way to be. People who are drawn to a particular religious group as adults often choose that tradition because they find the values and principles to be congruent with their own values.

Family

One way to become aware of personal values is to consider what traditions your family maintains and the values communicated in those traditions. What stories about ancestors or grandparents are passed down to children and what values or principles do they reflect? What sayings were common in the family? Examples might be, "Just do your best and forget about the rest," or "There is no room for second place," or "A failure to plan is a plan to fail." Advice and proverbs are often repeated by parents time and again to help children learn to share the same values as the parents and family.

Generational Peers

Peer groups, including baby boomers, generation X, millennials, and generation Z (Seemiller & Grace, 2016), share historical experiences that shape how they interpret events and what they believe to be most important. For example, one value often associated with the millennials (born 1980–1995) is community and connectedness with others. They tend to be joiners rather than going at it alone, and they are often quite committed to the groups and institutions of which they are members. Generation Z (born 1995–2010) have known social media and technology their whole lives and live in a more socially progressive time than previous generations. "Same-sex marriage, for example, has gone from a controversial political issue to a constitutional right recognized by the Supreme Court. For today's 14-year-olds, the nation's first African American president is less a historic breakthrough than a fact of life" (Williams, 2015, para. 11). The terrorist attacks on 9/11 and the Great Recession have influenced generation Z, who have grown up feeling less secure than previous generations. Consequently, generation Z is identified as determined but also risk averse. For example, although millennials use social media to post about their lives, generation Z is more guarded about what they share and tend to use social media to follow others (Seemiller & Grace, 2016).

Personal Style

Personal style refers to different aspects of personality. For example, some people are outgoing and talkative, even thinking out loud; others listen, observe, and share their thoughts after careful consideration. Some people prefer to carefully schedule their time, planning to complete major projects in advance of deadlines. Others prefer spontaneity to a schedule and have learned to adapt to whatever comes along. Personal style includes hundreds of descriptors, such as timid, aggressive, organized, adaptable, optimistic, competitive, easygoing, patient, reserved, or goofy. Being aware of one's own style is useful for understanding interactions with others, particularly with those whose style is different from one's own.

Leadership is certainly influenced by personal style. Some lead through a hands-off approach, letting the group self-organize. Others prefer to control the direction of the group. Some tend to focus on the task or problem the group is working on, others focus on supporting group members and making sure everyone feels included so they can contribute to the group's success. Some are inspirational and are good at motivating people. Others motivate by being a role model, getting their hands dirty right alongside everyone else.

Talents, Skills, and Specialized Knowledge

The ability to persuade others, organize big projects, delegate tasks, keep track of budgets, cheer someone up, or be a good listener are all useful skills that are worth cultivating. Some approach consideration of talents and skills from a negative perspective—listing areas to improve or skills that need to be learned in order to be effective. Although improving on weaknesses is admirable, some research suggests that it is more effective to focus on cultivating one's natural strengths than on improving on one's weaknesses (Rath & Conchie, 2008). Although it takes time, identifying and sharing each team member's unique strengths and talents is beneficial to groups because members can call on one another to share their expertise (Mather & Hulme, 2013). Leadership teams need to be well-rounded to be productive and effective. Studies of personal leadership strengths (Rath & Conchie, 2008) identified these broad domains: executing (making things happen); influencing (reaching a broader audience); relationship building (the glue that binds the team); and strategic thinking (focused on possibilities). Rath and Conchie (2008) posited leadership teams benefit most when there is a representative from each strengths-based domain.

Aspirations and Dreams

Some people have a specific picture of what they want to be doing in 5, 10, or 25 years. Others do not have a time-dated plan, but they could name several things they would like to do someday. Aspirations can take one's strengths into account and include personal and career-related goals; they affect how people choose to invest their time in the present. Evolving a focus of your aspirations can guide the commitments you make and the way you will spend your time.

 A few years ago I was asked a series of powerful questions that made me reflect on my personal history and [wonder] if I was living a fulfilled life. I realized that if I wanted a different society then I needed to assume responsibility and do something. I needed to visualize three things: the power to empower, my passion to pursue, and my happiness These three things will allow me to make a difference in society.

—Yanniz Valadez is coordinator at the Ministry of Social Development of the State and a graduate student from Universidad de Monterrey (UDEM), where she founded IDASE "I Design as a Social Entrepreneur," a social innovation project in which she involved students from UDEM and students from low-income schools to create a change in their communities.

AWARENESS OF HOW OTHERS PERCEIVE US

In addition to having a strong sense of self, it is equally important to know how other people perceive you. How would others describe you, based on their interpretations of the behaviors they witness? Is there alignment between how you perceive yourself and how others do? These are questions that get to the heart of authenticity, integrity, and trust—all important for successful leadership dynamics.

Psychologists Joseph Luft and Harry Ingham developed a now-classic graphic called the *Johari Window* as a tool to improve self-awareness (Luft, 1970). (See Figure 3.1.)

The quadrants of the Johari Window invite reflection in four domains. Quadrant I (open) includes information that is known to oneself and known to others. For example, Hiro is a Yankees fan, loves being a parent, and does not enjoy public speaking. Quadrant II (blind spot) contains information known to others but not to oneself. Hiro's roommate knows that when Hiro is tired from having being up all night, he often snaps at his friends and is irritated by things that usually do not bother him. Hiro is not aware that lack of sleep leads him to behave differently than usual. Quadrant III (hidden) contains information known to oneself but not to others. Hiro's cousin is autistic, which is why he is so devoted to volunteering with children with disabilities. This is information he has not shared with people at college, however, so

FIGURE 3.1 Johari Window

	Known to Self	Unknown to Self
Known by Others	I **Open** or **Public**	II **Blind Spot**
Unknown by Others	III **Hidden** or **Private**	IV **Unknown** or **Undiscovered**

Source: Adapted from Luft, J. (1970). *Group processes: An introduction to group dynamics* (2nd ed.). Palo Alto, CA: National Press Books.

his friends do not know the source of his motivation to be a volunteer. Finally Quadrant IV (unknown) contains information known neither to oneself nor to others. Although Hiro was raised in a family that practiced Catholicism, he has not been to mass while at college. He has not spent any time thinking about why that might be nor about what it means about his faith and beliefs. Neither Hiro nor anyone else knows why he has not been motivated to attend mass.

Having Consciousness of Self would decrease the number of unknown and unaware items and bring thoughtful intentionality to the items that one chooses to reveal to others or keep hidden. The Johari Window offers a clear illustration of how our Consciousness of Self is enhanced by our relationships with others and the ways that understanding how others see us helps us develop a clearer sense of self. The extent to which our behaviors and the way we present ourselves to others are in alignment with our truly held sense of self is an issue for the next chapter, "Congruence."

BECOMING CONSCIOUS OF SELF

As mentioned, Consciousness of Self is not an end point but a lifelong journey. Psychologist Carl Rogers (1961) described a life of development and growth as always being in a process of becoming. The leadership scholarship suggests that the process

Consciousness of Self

of becoming self-aware requires conscious intentional action, including (1) accepting challenging roles and experiences, (2) habitual reflection, (3) openness to feedback, and (4) learning about oneself through assessment (Day, 2013; Komives, Dugan, Owen, Slack, Wagner, & Associates, 2011).

Accepting Challenging Roles and Experiences

Taking on new roles or having new experiences is a powerful way to develop more consciousness of self. Be intentional about what you want to learn about yourself and choose to work in new settings, with new skills, or with new people to facilitate that learning. It is important to find the optimal level of challenge. Staying in the so-called comfort zone results in fewer opportunities for learning experiences, but stretching too far can result in too much anxiety to have an opportunity to make meaning and learn.

I completed four internships during my time at Bethany College. Through each internship I was able to work with those in poverty and [effect] change within the surrounding neighborhoods. I worked with children, older adults, the elderly, and people who were homeless. I now feel that I am a well-rounded professional because each organization had [unique] challenges and rewards, and I learned something new in each internship. Each individual affected my life for the better, and I was grateful to be able to serve the community. Because of these experiences I am highly aware of my beliefs and values that drive me. I have found passion in working with people who live in poverty.

—Monica Westerheide graduated from Bethany College in West Virginia, where among her involvements, she was a resident assistant in the Alpha Xi Delta sorority, a women's college basketball player, and highly involved in campus ministry. Monica is now a residence hall director at Greensboro College and is pursuing her master's degree at the University of North Carolina at Greensboro.

An important concept related to learning from experience is *leadership self-efficacy*, which means confidence in one's ability to engage effectively in leadership (Dugan, Kodama, Correia, & Associates, 2013; Hannah, Avolio, Luthans, & Harms, 2008). Leadership self-efficacy is distinct from actual ability, capacity, or competence; for example, people can be very effective in leadership but not believe they are. Leadership self-efficacy is important for growth and development because these beliefs directly affect willingness to take on new or challenging experiences. It also has an influence on how much effort a leader will expend and how long he or she will persist when problems arise. Multi-Institutional Study of Leadership findings demonstrated that "leadership self-efficacy (LSE) is a key predictor of gains in leadership capacity as well as a factor in whether or not students actually enact leadership behaviors" (Dugan et al., 2013, p. 20).

Given the importance of having challenging experiences for the development of consciousness of self (and other competencies and values related to leadership), it is important to have awareness of when you are avoiding potential opportunities because you doubt your capability. Albert Bandura (1977), an early researcher of social learning theory and the concept of self-efficacy, identified four factors that can contribute to self-efficacy. Table 3.1 identifies those factors and suggests how they would apply to the leadership context.

Habitual Reflection

Reflection refers to thinking back on an experience in an intentional way to facilitate awareness and learning. Reflection activities include writing in a journal; talking with a mentor, group members, or friends; or simply quietly thinking on one's own. Reflection can facilitate the development of Consciousness of Self in several different ways:

- Increase our awareness of how we behave in the presence of others
- Foster exploration of how our values and beliefs influence our behaviors and choices
- Create greater awareness of how our personality, cultural worldview, or skills affect perceptions and actions
- Challenge us to consider whether the same approach that worked in one context will apply in another
- Challenge us to look at the same situation from someone else's point of view
- Identify new skills or approaches that would help us be more effective
- Identify preconceived notions and assumptions we may have had about others

Rather than occasionally remembering to reflect on experiences, developing a habitual practice of reflection can uncover trends in one's own behavior and serve as

TABLE 3.1 Developing Antecedents in Leadership Self-Efficacy

Antecedents in Self-Efficacy for Leadership	Seek Opportunities to . . .
Mastery Experiences Multiple experiences that build skills that can be generalized to other contexts	• Develop new skills • Apply existing skills and competencies to new contexts • Take on new roles and responsibilities • Collaborate with new people and groups, particularly those with perspectives that differ from your own
Vicarious Experience Observations of others successfully performing challenging tasks	• Observe role models and peers engaging in leadership processes and roles • Learn about others' leadership experiences by reading memoirs or watching documentaries • Learn from case studies • Share leadership stories with mentors and advisors
Verbal Persuasion Encouragement that one can successfully face a difficult challenge	• Connect with a mentor, including peers, teachers, supervisors, or other encouraging leaders • Develop formal and informal relationships with other members of organizations you are involved with • Use social networking sites to reinforce leadership dialogue and conversation
Assessment of Physiological and Affective States Mindfully recognizing signs of emotional responses and stress and acting to reduce anxiety	• Reflect on your leadership experiences and future journey • Intentionally take time away from the stress of a multi-tasked, plugged-in, overcommitted schedule to reflect on fears, hopes, goals, and lessons learned • Connect to your spiritual source of strength or examine your sense of what constitutes a life well lived • Wrestle with the big questions and purpose of your leadership journey

Source: Adapted from Wagner, W. (2011). Considerations of student development in leadership. In Susan R. Komives, J. P. Dugan, J. E. Owen, C. Slack, W. Wagner, & Associates (Eds.), *The handbook for student leadership development* (p. 93). San Francisco, CA: Jossey-Bass.

a reminder of the challenging tasks that have already been conquered. Additionally, reflection is a skill that develops with practice. Those who reflect regularly are able to more readily consider perspectives from others' point of view and can make deeper connections more quickly.

When reflective practice is an ongoing habit, it need not take long. Following the completion of a group task, an interaction, or meeting, reflect on the attributes discussed in this chapter. What does the experience suggest about your values, skills, style, or sense of self? Question your initial interpretation and consider how someone different from you in any of these attributes might describe what happened.

Consider what you can learn about yourself from the experience and what you would do differently if it happened again.

It is important to note that reflection is more than simply recollecting what occurred. It should involve complex critical thinking by continually asking oneself, "What assumptions am I making?" This kind of examination often results in the consideration of other valid interpretations of the same event. By starting to consider how others might be making meaning of experiences differently than they do, leaders lay the groundwork for developing the capacity for *social perspective taking* (Selman, 1980), the ability to see and understand issues from the perspectives of people with different worldviews. Social perspective taking is a "higher order cognitive skill reflecting the ability to take another person's point of view as well as accurately infer the thoughts and feelings of others" (Dugan et al., 2013, p. 27). Social perspective taking is critical for working effectively in groups and will be discussed further in Chapter 8.

Openness to Feedback

Another contributor to Consciousness of Self is receiving direct and ongoing feedback. If reflection is seen as an internal process of learning by thinking critically about experiences, then feedback can be seen as inviting external perspectives to that process. Constructive feedback will include positive and negative observations. Sometimes the negative feedback can take a toll on self-confidence and motivation, but it is important to be open to it. To be clear, being open and sincere about receiving feedback from others does not imply one must agree with all aspects of the feedback that is given. Integrating the advice of others with one's own reflections should be done with the awareness that others make assumptions too.

People who are sincerely open to feedback take advantage of opportunities to get it. In fact, they seek out feedback rather than waiting for others to come forward with it. They show they are genuinely interested in what others have to say. Rather than pushing away compliments, they offer a gracious "thank you" and look for further details. For example, if someone makes a very general comment about their "excellent leadership" they might inquire further, "What do you mean? What did I do here that was useful for you?" Likewise, they are open to negative feedback, without getting defensive. Even if they do not agree with the feedback they are hearing, they listen without interrupting, knowing there will be time later to reflect on whether the feedback is accurate or useful.

Learning About Oneself Through Assessment

Many survey-style instruments exist to help expand one's self-awareness, particularly in areas of personal style. Although many of these types of assessments are available on the Internet, it is often preferable to have a qualified professional review the results of the assessment in order to fully understand its meaning. Most colleges and universities offer at least some personal assessments through the counseling center, career center, or leadership development program. The following are a few assessments that are often used in campus leadership development programs:

- Socially Responsible Leadership Scale: https://nclp.umd.edu/srls.aspx
- Myers-Briggs Type Indicator: www.mbticomplete.com
- True Colors: www.truecolors.org
- The Leadership Practices Inventory: www.lpionline.com/
- ANSIR: ansir.com
- StrengthsQuest: www.strengthsquest.com/
- Values Inventory Assessment: https://www.viacharacter.org/survey/
- DISC: http://discpersonalitytesting.com/

MINDFULNESS

Up to now, this chapter has focused on self-awareness, or "acknowledgment of those relatively stable aspects of the self that go to make up what we call 'personality'" (HERI, 1996, p. 31). The other half of Consciousness of Self is having an awareness of our current state of mind, also known as *mindfulness*. According to Ashford and DeRue (2012), "Mindfulness is a 'state of being' where people are actively aware of themselves and their surroundings, open to new information, and willing and able to process their experience from multiple perspectives" (p. 149). People who are mindful can simultaneously act and be observers of themselves acting.

An example of the practical usefulness of becoming more mindful is reflected in an effective way to address procrastination. A student leader tasked with updating her group's website might waste hours on social media and watching television before becoming consciously aware that she is avoiding the work. Once she becomes mindful of the fact that the website work is making her anxious, she can ask herself, "What is it about this project I'm avoiding?" Perhaps she is not comfortable with the technology or her writing skills. Perhaps she is afraid the group will not like the changes she has in mind. The reasons for procrastination are only identifiable by mindful self-observation, but they often stem from fear of failure or feeling incompetent.

Mindfulness is about waking up from a life on automatic pilot and starting to pay attention to what is happening. Many students run from one task to the next without being aware of how they feel. It is possible to be in a bad mood all day but not realize it until you find yourself yelling at a roommate. It is important to learn to recognize when one has unacknowledged stress, just as it is important to be aware of when one is feeling good in order to identify those things that provide personal fulfillment.

Kabat-Zinn (2005) referred to people's constant actions and thoughts as being driven by unconscious impulses rather than being undertaken in awareness. He compared these thoughts and impulses to a river or waterfall, running uncontrollably so that a person gets caught up in it and carried away. Learning to be mindful is similar to consciously deciding to step out of that river and instead sit by its bank and observe it. Imagine the Consciousness of Self that could emerge from taking a few moments a day to be observant of how we spend our time, taking note of how we feel while we are doing it.

The next time you are in a frustrating conversation or are feeling excited and hopeful in a meeting, try being mindful. Observe yourself at that specific moment. See if you can find words to describe your feelings precisely. What is it, specifically, about the experience that is contributing to how you feel about it?

In leadership, being mindful makes it possible to work more effectively with others. It enables group members to recognize when they are being emotionally reactive to others rather than operating from their own principles and values. In leadership contexts, mindfulness makes it possible to "be aware of oneself in the moment, to be able to monitor and self-regulate one's thinking, behaviors, and emotional reactions"

(Wagner, 2011, p. 96). Mindful leaders are affected by others and by situations, but rather than reacting without thinking, they are able to thoughtfully observe and consciously choose how they will respond. The ability to recognize that their response is a choice and not an inevitable result of the circumstances is at the heart of mindfulness and paves the way to effectiveness in groups.

The following hypothetical scenario illustrates what mindfulness can look like in a leadership context. Eboni is the president of the Math Honors Society. One of her goals for the year was to start a volunteer math tutoring program in a nearby high school. Another member named James raises several objections to that idea, many of them valid. As the group continues to discuss the idea, James gets increasingly agitated, interrupting others, and raising his voice. Eboni tries to focus the conversation on the reasons to do the project, describing a conversation she had with one of the high school teachers about focusing particularly on tutoring girls in order to build their confidence and counteract social messages about math being hard for girls. James responds to Eboni bitterly, "If you already have the project all planned out then you shouldn't waste everyone's time pretending to get input."

Although being mindful happens quickly, the following is an example of the kinds of things that Eboni might be thinking:

- *Observation of current emotional state.* "I feel attacked. I cannot believe he just insulted my leadership in front of everyone. I need to calm down before I do anything next; attacking him back will not help."
- *Observation of the situation.* "Although this meeting has been tense, I was fine until that last comment. What shifted? Thinking about it, the argument was about whether to do a service project but the last comment was about me, not the project."
- *Alternative interpretations.* "When I mentioned having met with a high school teacher, I thought that would show I am willing to do a lot of the preparation work. But maybe James and others interpreted my having met with a teacher as trying to control the group too much. The group needs to talk about this. I need to pause the discussion about the volunteer program and have us talk about our roles and input first."

This example illustrates several important outcomes of mindful leadership. First, without attending to her feelings and behaviors in the moment, Eboni might have responded with an equally personal attack on James. Mindfulness makes it possible for the leader to more clearly understand the situation and craft a more productive response to it. Second, mindfulness protects leaders against defining themselves based on other people's projections of them. Eboni can choose to let James's comment damage her perception of herself as a good president, or she can choose to believe that James's comment was distorted by his anger at the current situation. Whether Eboni is enthusiastic or controlling is not a matter of truth but of perspective. The group needs to take a moment to understand each other's motivations better. Third, in this example, mindfulness made it possible for Eboni to stay calm enough to consider James's point of view. Rather than dismissing the attack, rushing to judge him as difficult or unreasonable, Eboni is able to recognize that James is upset and needs to feel heard.

CONNECTION TO THE OTHER Cs

Learning to use the Social Change Model of Leadership Development is an ongoing process of continual improvement, with gains in any particular C resulting in increased capacity to do the other Cs. It is not possible to be successfully Congruent and Committed without having Consciousness of Self. As people become more mindful of their behaviors and more conscious of their values, principles, and preferred ways of being, they cannot help but be more aware of times when their actions are not Congruent with their inner truth. Self-awareness, self-efficacy, and reflection on what is most important are key contributors to Commitment, particularly during those times when a person needs a sense of renewal.

Consciousness of Self also positively affects the group Cs. Groups can foster a more authentic Common Purpose when participants are clear about their personal goals and values for the group. When individuals are knowledgeable of the skills and perspectives they can contribute and are aware of how their personal style affects interactions with others, the group's ability to do Collaboration is greatly enhanced. When individuals in groups are able to practice mindfulness, their ability to monitor their emotional state in the moment makes Controversy With Civility a real possibility. Finally, students' efforts to be of service to their communities through Citizenship are more powerful when the work is an authentic reflection of the individual's personal values and convictions.

CONCLUSION

It is difficult with today's busy lifestyles to take time to stop and think about issues of self-awareness or the lessons that life's experiences are teaching. In Western culture, it is considered a mark of excellence to be busy, always doing, always achieving something. If one is not doing, then he or she is wasting time (Rogers, 2005). Increasingly, simply doing one thing is no longer enough. People find themselves multitasking in order to do even more in the same amount of time. Many students can simultaneously write a paper, eat dinner, and chat with a friend. But this constant busyness does not lend itself to Consciousness of Self.

A lifestyle that fosters an ongoing practice of developing self-awareness needs to include a retreat from all the doing. It would include some point in the day to pause and reflect on bigger questions. Not "What should I do next?" but "Who am I? How would I describe myself? What values am I living by? Why am I here?"

Although some may think this sounds like daydreaming or wasting time, it can lead to greater effectiveness and more clarity about what all the "doing" is for. Kabat-Zinn (2005) said:

> You actually become more alive now. This is what stopping can do. There is nothing passive about it. And when you decide to go, it's a different kind of going because you stopped. The stopping actually makes the going more vivid, richer, more textured. It helps keep all the things we worry about and feel inadequate about in perspective. (p. 12)

Learning to be mindful, having an accurate sense of self and how others perceive us, and approaching leadership from a sense of being in an ongoing state of becoming all contribute to the capacity to engage in leadership processes with others.

❓ DISCUSSION QUESTIONS

1. How would having a conscious awareness of your values and beliefs influence your leadership? What are specific examples of this?
2. How are leadership capacity and leadership self-efficacy connected? How are they distinct?

3. How would the group values of Collaboration, Common Purpose, and Controversy With Civility work differently if everyone in the group were able to practice mindfulness?

 ACTION AND REFLECTION

1. What strengths does your personal style bring to working in groups? In what ways does your style sometimes make group work challenging?
2. What are the personal values that guide how you interact in groups? How do you approach Citizenship in your communities? What values guide your approach to Citizenship and civic engagement?
3. What format of reflection (for example, journaling, quiet time for thought, a discussion partner or group) would be most realistic for you to take up as a regular practice for examining who you are? This week, try a format you have never used before. Does using a different format change the nature of your reflections?
4. Do you seek feedback? How do you react when others give you feedback? Think of someone with whom you have engaged in leadership processes and ask him or her for feedback on your strengths and areas for growth.
5. Use the rubric in Table 3.2 to gauge your development on various dimensions of Consciousness of Self. Reflect on how you could develop this aspect of your leadership capacity.

REFERENCES

Ashford, S. J., & DeRue, D. S. (2012). Developing as a leader: The power of mindful engagement. *Organizational Dynamics, 41*, 146–154.

Bandura, A. (1977). Self-efficacy: Toward a unifying theory of behavioral change. *Psychological Review, 84*(2), 191–215.

Bordas, J. (2012). *Salsa, soul, and spirit: Leadership for a multicultural age* (2nd ed.). San Francisco, CA: Berrett-Koehler.

Day, D. V. (2013). Training and developing leaders: Theory and research. In M. G. Rumsey. (Ed.), *The Oxford handbook of leadership* (pp. 76–93). Oxford, UK: Oxford University Press.

TABLE 3.2 Consciousness of Self Rubric

	Excelling	Achieving	Developing	Needing Improvement
Self-Awareness	Demonstrates a thorough understanding of personal identity, social identity, and core values Able to accurately describe self to others Understands complex multiple identities	Understands core values and many aspects of social and personal identity May struggle a bit with articulating these values or identity to others Still exploring a more in-depth sense of self	Aware of some aspects of personality, identity, and core values but struggling to define and articulate a cohesive sense of self	Unaware of personal values or identity Struggles with identifying social identity Unable to describe self accurately to others
Conscious Mindfulness	Consistently evaluates self and actions Is fully aware of current emotional state and adjusts actions accordingly	Makes an effort to observe oneself in the moment but is inconsistent or struggles Tries to think through the situation before acting	Understands the need to consider one's words and actions but has difficulty actually doing this May occasionally evaluate current emotional state but is unsure what to do about it	Unable to separate emotion and personal feelings from action Lack of awareness of how one's actions affect others
Feedback	Open to positive and negative feedback Seeks such feedback and further clarification Integrates advice into how one goes about future activities Uses discretion	Makes an effort to seek out some positive and negative feedback Works on taking negative feedback as a way to develop	Able to take some positive and negative feedback that is presented Does not seek out feedback Does not use feedback in other situations	Unable to take positive and negative feedback Pushes feedback away Negatively affects self-confidence and motivation
Continual Personal Reflection	Continually takes time during each day to reflect on thoughts, feelings, and experiences Integrates learning and uses it in subsequent experiences Views experiences from other perspectives Reflects on big questions such as "Who am I?"	Often sees the benefit of personal reflection Frequently takes time to reflect on self and experiences	Sees some benefit of personal reflection, such as learning from an experience, and sometimes takes opportunities to reflect on different experiences	Does not see the need or benefits of taking time out of the day to reflect Rarely, if ever, takes opportunities to reflect about daily experiences or pondering big questions

Source: Developed by Colette Fournier and Christina Colasanto.

Dugan, J. P., Bohle, C. W., Woelker, L. R., & Cooney, M. A. (2014). The role of social perspective-taking in developing students' leadership capacities. *Journal of Student Affairs Research and Practice, 51*(1), 1–15.

Dugan, J. P., Kodama, C., Correia, B., & Associates. (2013). *Multi-institutional study of leadership insight report: Leadership program delivery*. College Park, MD: National Clearinghouse for Leadership Programs.

Hannah, S. T., & Avolio, B. J. (2010). Ready or not: How do we accelerate the developmental readiness of leaders? *Journal of Organizational Behavior, 31*, 1181–1187.

Hannah, S. T., Avolio, B., Luthans, F., & Harms, P. D. (2008). Leadership efficacy: Review and future directions. *Management Department Faculty Publications*. Retrieved from http://digitalcommons.unl.edu/managementfacpub/5

Higher Education Research Institute (HERI). (1996). *A social change model of leadership development* (Version III). Los Angeles, CA: University of California, Los Angeles, Higher Education Research Institute.

Kabat-Zinn, J. (2005). *Wherever you go there you are: Mindfulness meditation in everyday life*. New York, NY: Hyperion.

Komives, S. R., Dugan, J. P., Owen, J. E., Slack, C., Wagner, W., & Associates. (2011). *The handbook for student leadership development*. San Francisco, CA: Jossey-Bass.

Komives, S. R., Owen, J. E., Longerbeam, S., Mainella, F. C., & Osteen, L. (2005). Developing a leadership identity: A grounded theory. *Journal of College Student Development, 46*, 593–611.

Luft, J. (1970). *Group processes: An introduction to group dynamics* (2nd ed.). Palo Alto, CA: National Press Books.

Mather, P. C., & Hulme, E. (Eds.). (2013). *Positive psychology and appreciative inquiry in higher education* (New Directions for Student Services, no. 143). San Francisco, CA: Jossey-Bass.

Ostick, D. T., & Wall, V. A. (2011). Considerations for culture and social identity dimensions. In S. R. Komives, J. P. Dugan, J. E. Owen, C. Slack, W. Wagner, & Associates (Eds.), *The handbook for student leadership development* (pp. 339–368). San Francisco, CA: Jossey-Bass.

Rath, T., & Conchie, B. (2008). *Strengths based leadership: Great leaders, teams, and why people follow*. New York, NY: Simon & Schuster.

Reichard, R., & Thompson, S. (Eds.). (2016). *Leader developmental readiness* (New Directions for Student Leadership, no. 149). San Francisco, CA: Jossey-Bass.

Rogers, C. R. (1961). *On becoming a person*. Boston, MA: Houghton Mifflin.

Rogers, J. (2005). Spirituality and leadership: The confluence of inner work and right action. *Concepts & Connections, 13*(2), 1–3.

Seemiller, C., & Grace, M. (2016). *Generation Z goes to college.* San Francisco, CA: Jossey-Bass.

Selman, R. L. (1980). *The growth of interpersonal understanding.* New York, NY: Academic Press.

Wagner, W. (2011). Considerations of student development in leadership. In S. R. Komives, J. P. Dugan, J. E. Owen, C. Slack, W. Wagner, & Associates. *The handbook for student leadership development* (pp. 85–107). San Francisco, CA: Jossey-Bass.

Wallace, D. F. (2005, May 21). *This is water.* Commencement speech delivered at Kenyon College, Gambier, OH.

Walumbwa, F. O., Avolio, B. J., Gardner, W. L., Wernsing, T. S., & Peterson, S. J. (2008). Authentic leadership: Development and validation of a theory-based measure. *Journal of Management, 34*(1), 89–126.

Williams, A. (2015). Move over, millennials, here comes Generation Z. Retrieved from http://www.nytimes.com/2015/09/20/fashion/move-over-millennials-here-comes-generation-z.html

4

Congruence

Tricia R. Shalka

> Happiness is when what you think, what you say, and what you do are in harmony.
> —MAHATMA GANDHI

Nia is faced with a difficult decision that will have a long-term impact on the future of the student group with which she has been actively involved. The choices in front of her do not offer an obvious answer in terms of which decision will be best. To complicate matters further, Nia is hearing conflicting opinions from her friends. Some think she should do one thing, and others suggest she do the other. What does she do? Although it is not an easy decision, Nia knows she can only make it from a place of authenticity. She weighs her options and the opinions of others carefully, thinks critically about her own beliefs and values, and makes a decision that is reflective of her core sense of self. Although some people are disappointed with Nia's final decision, everyone admits to her that they respect the difficult position she was in, and respect even more the fact that she held true to her deepest values and beliefs. They admire her ability to act with Congruence.

What congruent leaders such as Nia do is an authentic reflection of who they are and what they believe. Their inner worlds of values, principles, and priorities match their outer worlds through their decisions and actions, including the way they treat others.

What is the opposite of this? Perhaps you have already witnessed it in your life. Leaders who are not congruent might present a façade. They act in ways that they think others want to see at the expense of representing who they really are. Sometimes this is a conscious choice based on fitting into or being successful in a particular environment, and at other times leaders may lack the self-awareness necessary to align their values and actions. In other situations, Congruence may be less about an individual and more about the social structures within which he or she is embedded. For example, issues of power and privilege complicate what it means to be congruent in certain spaces, particularly when the expectations of an environment are constructed on dominant social norms that are not representative of everyone's experience. Thus, how we address what it means to be congruent is a complex combination of individual and social factors.

DEFINING CONGRUENCE

Congruence is very closely connected to Consciousness of Self, because the work of being a person of Congruence begins with the work of understanding oneself. However, Congruence takes that self-awareness one step further. It asks that we align our interior beliefs and values with our exterior actions and behaviors. This means that our espoused values should match our enacted values. In theory, that may sound relatively simple. In practice, being congruent across the many small and big decisions and interactions we experience in our daily lives can be much easier said than done. This chapter offers a foundation for how to move that good-in-theory concept into the reality of practice.

The ensemble that created the Social Change Model defined Congruence this way:

> Congruence refers to thinking, feeling, and behaving with consistency, genuineness, authenticity, and honesty toward others. Congruent persons are those whose actions are consistent with their most deeply held beliefs and convictions. Clearly, personal Congruence and Consciousness of Self are interdependent.
>
> Developing a clear Consciousness of Self is a critical element in being congruent. Being clear about your values, beliefs, strengths, and limitations is especially important. It is, therefore, imperative to understand your most deeply felt values and beliefs before Congruence can consciously develop. (Higher Education Research Institute [HERI], 1996, p. 36)

CHAPTER OVERVIEW

This chapter begins by describing what it means to be congruent with one's personal values. Some of the challenges that come with being a person of congruence are considered, including the ambiguity that is a part of many situations that involve Congruence. Finally, several suggestions are offered for how to begin fostering a deeper sense of Congruence.

KNOWING THE SELF

Understanding what makes each of us who we are (or Consciousness of Self) is the bedrock of Congruence. Before we are able to embark on the work of Congruence, which is aligning our outer world of actions with our inner world of values and beliefs, we need to have a firm grasp of who we are on the inside. Indeed, self-awareness is foundational to leadership and Congruence. However, being able to articulate clearly one's values and priorities is not enough. Congruence requires acting in ways that reflect those values and priorities. This means that we need to take our knowledge of Consciousness of Self and transform it into action to achieve Congruence.

In many ways, Consciousness of Self and Congruence have a synergistic relationship with each other (see Figure 4.1). We need a strong foundation of self-awareness in order to act with congruence. However, the relationship can work in reverse as well. It is frequently the case that the more we prioritize acting Congruently, the more we learn about ourselves in return. The process of becoming increasingly aware of our actions and how we spend our time can lead to increased self-awareness and a clarification of our priorities.

Congruence is a cornerstone of effective leadership. In their study of more than 200 change agents from diverse backgrounds and interests, Porras, Emery, and Thompson (2007) found that long-term leadership accomplishments had less to do with generally assumed success strategies, such as honing in on the best idea

FIGURE 4.1 The Synergistic Relationship Between Congruence and Consciousness of Self

or organizational structure. Instead, successful leaders were those who could identify what was personally meaningful to them and then pursue it. As Porras and colleagues (2007) explained, "We learned that, for the most part, extraordinary people, teams, and organizations are simply ordinary people doing extraordinary things that mattered to them" (p. 5). In other words, these were leaders who could identify their passions and values and act on them. These leaders were congruent.

The 200 people interviewed spanned a range of personalities and some were even reluctant to think of themselves as leaders. However, what was consistent with all of these identified change agents was their personal commitment to work for the causes and purposes that were congruent with their fundamental core being. That made all the difference. As Porras et al. (2007) noted, enduring success and leadership often occurs "not because you are perfect or lucky but because you have the courage to do what matters to you" (p. 2).

Congruence shows up in the daily decisions we make about how to navigate our lives. For example, the sorority member who challenges her sisters not to attend a party with a racist theme at their neighboring fraternity is being congruent with her values of social justice. Meanwhile, an athlete who believes his involvement in sports has been an invaluable experience might be a volunteer coach for the Special Olympics to provide similar opportunities to others. In both of these examples, these individuals aligned their actions to be congruent with their deeply held values and beliefs.

As a person's awareness of core values grows, the desire to act consistently with those values grows as well. Assessing what matters and why it matters is fundamental to becoming a person of Congruence, but that simultaneously requires a personal commitment to a continuous process of self-evaluation and growth (see Figure 4.1). Sometimes this can be a difficult process, because it demands us to reflect on our core self, the good and the less than stellar. This kind of self-honesty requires effort, but the rewards are great. The ability for individuals to live their lives from places of personal truth can bring comfort and strength.

Upon graduating from Elon University I didn't have a job lined up yet and eagerly continued my job hunt following my graduation day. The weeks after my graduation were filled with job interviews. During the trying job hunt process, I learned more about myself than ever before. From speaking with hiring managers about my strengths, weaknesses, and passions, and sharing other exciting tidbits about my life, I developed into a stronger

advocate for myself. I have always had an understanding of who I am as a person: my beliefs, values, and motivation; however, being tasked to articulate these intangible parts of who I am enabled me to truly solidify them into my psyche. Moving forward into my career, I am excited to maintain a sense of congruence regarding who I am as an individual.

—Danielle M. Biggs is a graduate of Elon University, where she double-majored in arts administration and dance performance and choreography. She held many student leadership positions and she currently serves as a full-time development associate at McCarter Theatre in Princeton, New Jersey.

In a commencement address at the Massachusetts Institute of Technology (MIT), Nobel Peace Prize winner and former secretary general of the United Nations Kofi Annan (1997) reflected on the importance of being guided by one's own internal compass. Annan understood the graduates he was speaking to well, because he himself was once a student at MIT. However, Annan's initial days at MIT brought forth feelings of inadequacy. He talked about feeling overwhelmed in a group of so many talented students and did not know how he would possibly be successful in that environment. Annan went for a walk one morning to consider this dilemma, when he was suddenly struck by a solution. Annan realized the way he would be successful at MIT was to forgo any need to define success on others' terms and instead focus on his own internal voice. And, with that recognition of the need to act from a place of congruence, Annan reported feeling his anxiety instantly start to diminish. As he articulated, "To live is to choose. But to choose well, you must know who you are and what you stand for, where you want to go and why you want to get there" (para. 7).

SELF-AUTHORSHIP

As explained previously, the ensemble that created the Social Change Model of Leadership Development defined Congruence in terms of authenticity and consistency across our thoughts, feelings, and behavior. In other words, Congruence occurs on many levels including how we think, how we feel, and how we act in interaction with our surroundings and with others. Establishing Congruence, then, becomes a process of enabling the inner world of thoughts, feelings, and self-awareness to align with one's behaviors and actions in his or her outer world.

One theory that can help us think about these multiple dimensions in different ways is that of self-authorship. Self-authorship is an aspect of human development that is explained in the work of developmental psychologist Robert Kegan (1994) and further investigated, particularly for college students, through the longitudinal research of higher education scholar Marcia Baxter Magolda (2004, 2009). At the most basic level, self-authorship represents our capacity to take in information from our environments, put that information through the filter of our own values and beliefs, and then use that process to make meaning of our world in ways that are connected to our unique internal voice.

Self-authorship develops as an integration of three separate but very related dimensions of human development, which include the cognitive, intrapersonal, and interpersonal (see Table 4.1). As Baxter Magolda's (2004) work has highlighted, college students often grapple with three dominant questions related to these areas of development: "How do I know?" (cognitive), "Who am I?" (intrapersonal), and "What kinds of relationships do I want to construct with others?" (interpersonal).

How an individual makes sense of these questions could be driven by external or internal forces. For example, two aspiring student leaders could both think, "What kinds of relationships do I want to construct with others?" One student might answer that question by networking with particular people that he or she believes to be in positional leadership roles, because that student may have heard from someone else that your best chance to become a leader in that organization is to know those

TABLE 4.1 Self-Authorship and Congruence

Dimension of Self Authorship	Related Question	What Would Congruence in This Dimension Look Like?
Cognitive	How do I know?	Using your beliefs (as opposed to those of others) to guide your actions
Intrapersonal	Who am I?	Having a deep understanding of who you are and using this information to inform what you do
Interpersonal	What kinds of relationships do I want to construct with others?	Interacting with others in ways that match your values

already in positions of power. Meanwhile, another student might have considered the type of relationships he or she wants in life to reflect authenticity and mutual learning. That student may also network with the same positional leaders, but perhaps it comes from an internal sense of wanting to build meaningful relationships with people who could provide mentorship. Although the outcome might be the same, what is evident in the second example is that the student was able to make a decision from an internal (or increasingly self-authored) point of view as opposed to uncritically relying on what others dictate.

As individuals grapple with the three dominant questions on the journey toward self-authorship, they progress from making meaning of their worlds in ways that are dictated by external forces (as demonstrated in the first example) to making meaning of their lives in ways that are internally driven and deeply connected to individual beliefs and values (as demonstrated in the second example). Self-authorship is the capacity that arrives at the internally driven end of the spectrum. Individuals who are self-authored can take in all the information of their surroundings and make meaning of it in ways that are internally derived.

Here, we can begin to see how Congruence can be connected to self-authorship. Congruence has a degree of difficulty associated with it because we do not exist in vacuums—we are connected to others and environments and this complicates the task of congruence. Congruence is not as simple as just knowing our values and acting on them. Instead, Congruence requires that we identify our values and beliefs, yes, but also that we figure out how to live those values when faced with the ambiguity of being in relation with others.

CONFLICTING VALUES: OUR CONGRUENCE AND OTHERS'

Acting congruently may be tested when engaging with others as we learn to navigate the ambiguity of how our values interact with the values of others. Working with a group can present an important challenge for Congruence: what to do when one's own values and principles are in contradiction with those of others? As business executive Paul Gam (2001) articulated, navigating personal truths alongside the truths of others is an important journey in the life of a leader:

> Does it matter that I am right according to my own truth? The answer is yes in that it is the source of my strength and renewal to stay the course. It is my

> compass and engine. However, the answer is also no, not if I want to be a truly effective leader. When I chose to be a leader, I thought I was electing an elevated stage of influence and privilege. Little did I realize I was actually forgoing an even playing field, and taking on an inferior position. To be a true leader, it is insufficient only to be right. It is not just those who share my truth whom I aim to lead. It is all the others who do not share the same needs or desires. To lead, I must see through their eyes and walk in their shoes. I must recognize their truths as if they were my very own. (p. 91)

Congruence is very much a balancing act. Working congruently with others might be easier if everyone had similar values and beliefs, but that is not reality. We increasingly work and interact with one another across rich diversity and experiences. As the world continues to become more and more globalized, we are frequently challenged to see the multiple perspectives of the situations in which we engage.

A large leadership research project involving more than 200 researchers from around the world highlights this point. The Global Leadership and Organizational Behavior Effectiveness (GLOBE) research project started more than 20 years ago as a way to explore how culture affects leadership (Dorfman, Javidan, Hanges, Dastmalchian, & House, 2012). Many interesting findings have emerged from this project, including the fact that there are multiple leadership traits that are desirable across cultural contexts, such as honesty and trustworthiness. However, this study has also found many examples of traits that are desirable in some cultural contexts and not others, such as an emphasis on rules or encouraging competition within groups. What these results remind us is that values are subjective. One individual or cultural group may place tremendous value on something another individual or cultural group strongly disagrees with or vice versa.

Congruence Gets Complicated

Let's return to the basic concept of Congruence as knowing who we are and then acting in ways that are reflections of that knowledge. Is it always that easy? Certainly not. This is particularly true when we find ourselves in environments that are not congruent with our identities and may even demand us to exist in different ways than what feels authentic. In these situations we need to consider what we are able to control and what we are not able to control. Sometimes this may mean removing ourselves from a particular situation when we can. At other times, that is not an option and then we need to make decisions about how we want to exist within an environment when it seems incongruent with our sense of self.

There are many dimensions of Congruence that are decided and controlled at the level of the individual. However, the larger social structures of power and privilege that surround an individual also play a role in that person's capacity to act congruently. Leadership researchers Dugan, Kodama, and Gebhardt (2012) suggested that much research and education about college student leadership does not give adequate attention to the ways that broader social structures can affect leadership. As a specific example of this, they call attention to the ways leadership approaches can be race blind but reminded readers that "leadership represents a socially constructed phenomenon and as such is directly influenced by other social constructions such as race" (p. 174).

In other words, the social identities that each of us embody (such as race, gender, sexual orientation, nationality, religion, ability, etc.) affect how we interact with the world and one another. Each of these dimensions affect our sense of who we are in the world and, in turn, affect how we will conceptualize Congruence.

Complicating Congruence: Right Versus Right

Congruence is subjective and influenced by who we are and the contexts in which we are embedded. This adds a layer of complexity to how to act with congruence. It can get even more challenging, particularly when we start to think about how to choose between decisions that lack an obvious "right" congruent answer.

Questions of congruence are closely related to similar issues that are explored in thinking about ethical leadership. Former professor, journalist, and founder of the Institute for Global Ethics Rushworth Kidder (2009) observed that most of our difficult ethical decisions are rarely as simple as choosing between a right and a wrong option. Instead, they are challenging because we are faced with a choice between right versus right. In other words, leadership decisions rarely present us with one choice that is clearly congruent with our beliefs and one that is in direct opposition to our sense of what should happen. Rather, as leaders, we often need to make tough decisions when the two choices appear right while simultaneously operating somewhat in opposition to one another.

In his book, *How Good People Make Tough Choices*, Kidder (2009) suggested that these right-versus-right decisions generally fall into four different categories:

TABLE 4.2 Right-Versus-Right Decisions

Category	Related Leadership Decision
Truth versus loyalty	Should I share a truth that could help others, or do I honor the confidence of the person who shared it with me and remain loyal to my promise not to tell anyone?
	Should I share with a group member a truth that will hurt her feelings? Is it more loyal to protect her from this truth or to reveal it?
Individual versus community	If a member's actions are detrimental to the rest of the group, is it right to restrict his or her behavior or should the group adjust to preserve the individual's autonomy?
	Do I support a community decision made with the intent to benefit everyone even if I know at least one individual whose opportunities will be unfairly limited by the decision?
Short term versus long term	Do I act in a way that will be beneficial for the current organization but have questionable outcomes in the future?
	In order for my group to receive much needed additional funding, I must provide evidence of achieving our stated goals. These goals are complex and can't be accomplished in just one year. Do I change our stated goals to make our outcomes achievable?
Justice versus mercy	Do I preserve an objective system by considering only candidates whose applications were submitted by the deadline or do I allow an extra day for a person who is dealing with a personal tragedy?
	Is it right to revoke group membership from a person who fails to achieve the minimum required grade point average, knowing the person's primary motivation to study at all is the ability to belong to the group?

(1) truth versus loyalty, (2) individual versus community, (3) short term versus long term, and (4) justice versus mercy. In each of these categories, we come face-to-face with two "good" or "right" values choices. See Table 4.2 for examples of how these categories might occur in leadership decisions.

Kidder (2005) suggested that understanding these four dominant categories of right-versus-right decisions is important, because it enables us to have the opportunity to better understand the situation we are confronting. This can be particularly useful when we are considering issues of Congruence. If we are struggling with a scenario in which we want to be congruent but feel that we are conflicted about which decision allows us to do that, then considering whether we have a right-versus-right situation can provide important information to help us figure out what we need to do next.

However, as Kidder (2009) explained, just knowing what kind of right-versus-right situation we are in is not generally enough to effectively find a solution to the problem. Instead, we need some tools that can help us analyze the right-versus-right dilemma.

Kidder offered three such thinking frameworks that provide ways to consider what to prioritize when making decisions among tough choices:

1. *Ends-based thinking*. In this framework we prioritize doing whatever will produce the greatest good for the greatest number of people.
2. *Rule-based thinking*. Here, the priority is on establishing behaviors that could become universal law. In other words, rule-based thinking compels us to choose to act in ways that everyone should.
3. *Care-based thinking*. This framework prioritizes putting care and concern for others first and considering what the other person in the scenario would want. This framework encourages us to step into someone else's shoes and see the world through his or her eyes.

To summarize, Kidder offered four categories that right-versus-right decisions often fall into. Then, he suggested that there are three thinking frameworks that we can use to evaluate which right decision we want to make. These frameworks are simply tools, and there is no particular thinking framework that is more right than another. Instead, it is up to each of us to decide which framework (or combination of frameworks) feels the most congruent to us and use it as we think through these difficult decisions.

Consider as an example a student advisory board that determines whether new student groups should be approved for recognition or not. The campus regulations state that student groups must have 20 members to be recognized by the institution. At issue is a new organization for Muslim women that has not been able to reach 20 members. Some members of the advisory board feel they should challenge the campus regulation.

One member states, "I have personally gained so much from being able to connect with other students who share my experiences through the Black Student Union.

I think other students should have that opportunity too." Another member points out that the campus claims to value diversity and helping all students feel welcome and at home, but this regulation would seem to run counter to that claim. "This new organization is particularly needed because there aren't many Muslim women on this campus. That in itself makes it harder for this group to recruit enough members to qualify for recognition." Two members argue in favor of upholding the membership rule. They are concerned that by making exceptions, the group would be inserting subjectivity into a process that is meant to be objective. "An objective process is our only way to protect against some groups being given special favors or preferential treatment."

What types of right-versus-right dilemmas might apply in this scenario? What thinking frameworks are the various members using as they think through what to do?

CONGRUENCE AND AUTHENTIC LEADERSHIP

A concept that is closely related to Congruence is that of authenticity. Authenticity can be thought of as having a firm grasp of who we are, a willingness to objectively acknowledge the desirable and undesirable aspects of who we are, and an ability to act in relation to the external world in ways that reflect those aspects of self-knowledge (Kernis & Goldman, 2006). This sounds very similar to Congruence, doesn't it?

Authenticity undergirds a leadership perspective that has gained considerable attention since the new millennium—authentic leadership (Gardner, Cogliser, Davis, & Dickens, 2011). The idea of authentic leadership originally emerged as a response from leaders and scholars who felt they were witnessing far too many examples of the breakdown of leadership—situations in the late 1990s and early 2000s that challenged ethical concepts of leadership practice.

Since its emergence into the leadership literature, authentic leadership has gained increased attention in research as a leadership model. However, some scholars have suggested that authentic leadership is much broader than just a model of leadership. Instead, some argue that authentic leadership is actually the foundation of many other relational forms of leadership (Avolio & Gardner, 2005).

Authentic leadership has been defined in several ways. However, across many different definitions of authentic leadership there are some key elements that remain fairly consistent. Generally, we can think of authentic leadership as an approach in which the leader has a deep understanding of who he or she is and acts in ways that are congruent with that self-knowledge, and through the trustworthiness that this behavior fosters the leader empowers, motivates, and encourages the strengths of those with whom they work (Gardner et al., 2011).

> In the fall of my sophomore year I decided to join a sorority. As a new member I learned the values and creeds of the organization, but I observed that members within the Greek community were not adhering to those integral aspects of the community. Rather than sacrifice my values and those that I had learned, I decided to run for Panhellenic president and dedicated my efforts to improving the Greek community.
>
> —Meg Royer is a former student at Gettysburg College, where she was involved with the Garthwait Leadership Center, an organization that creates opportunities for alumni and students to develop their leadership skills; she was also president of the Panhellenic Council.

According to leadership scholars Avolio and Gardner (2005), authentic leaders can be characterized by the following:

- They know their strengths and their personalities and are aware of the benefits these bring to the groups of which they are a part.
- Authentic leaders know how they think through issues as well as how they feel about them, and their actions fall in line with their own ethical code.
- In their relationships with others, authentic leaders are transparent about their intentions, values, and priorities.
- They do not attempt to hide their stance on an issue until a popular opinion emerges.
- Although authentic leaders have a firm sense of self, they are equally open to questioning their assumptions and learning from the perspectives of others.
- Authentic leaders are comfortable being challenged by others' perspectives and learning new ways of seeing an issue, but they also have enough strength in their own convictions to avoid hopping onto an idea purely because it is trendy or popular.

Leaders who are inauthentic act in ways they believe others expect them to act rather than being true to who they already are. For example, a student, Felipe, may be aware that he has a more introverted personality, but perhaps he thinks that others do not believe introverts can be good leaders. So, Felipe does not consider the strengths that introversion can bring to leadership, such as the ability to truly listen to others and a tendency to think things through carefully before speaking, rather than thinking out loud. Instead Felipe puts all his energy into trying to get others to think he is an extrovert. The group is not able to benefit from Felipe's true strengths, and because his attempt at extroversion is not real, the group does not benefit from the strengths that natural extroverts bring to groups either.

Leading congruently means believing that who you are is enough—that the personality, values, strengths, and skills that you bring to the table are unique to you and will be useful to the group. Certainly, it is a good thing to continually strive to learn new skills and see situations from different perspectives. However, this is different from being something you are not. Although trying to give others the impression that you are different from who you really are may have short-term appeal in making you feel more comfortable in the moment, it generally results in greater challenges in the long run.

CONGRUENCE AND COURAGE

To be a person of Congruence requires dedication and courage. Congruence demands that leaders commit to a process of frequent evaluation and refinement of their intentions, actions, and motives. Connected to this commitment to continual improvement, Congruence requires a degree of courage. In part, this is because it can be much easier not to be congruent. Being congruent across all aspects of our personal and professional lives demands that we do the right thing even when it is not convenient, popular, or easy. It may mean standing up to friends, risking popularity, or feeling isolated. Additionally, as previously illustrated, doing what is right is not always easy when there are multiple competing right things that could occur. Thus, the congruent leader also has to draw on courage to stay the course when there are no easy answers.

Congruence also requires another form of courage—the courage to believe in one's capabilities and potential. Sometimes, when people tell themselves they are not good enough or worthy enough to be the ones who stand up for what is right, they are acting from a lack of courage to realize their full selves. Marianne Williamson is an author and former head pastor of the Renaissance Unity Interfaith Spiritual Fellowship. Some of her writings address the issue of summoning the courage to believe in our abilities to be change agents. In her book, *A Return to Love: Reflections on the Principles of a Course in Miracles* (1996), Williamson articulated the level of courage it can take to overcome the fear of allowing our outer life to reflect the power of which our inner life is aware:

> Our deepest fear is not that we are inadequate. Our deepest fear is that we are powerful beyond measure. It is our light, not our darkness, that most frightens us. We ask ourselves, Who am I to be brilliant, gorgeous, talented, fabulous? Actually, who are you not to be? You are a child of God. Your playing small doesn't serve the world. There's nothing enlightened about shrinking so that other people won't feel insecure around you. We are all meant to shine, as children do. We were born to make manifest the glory of God that is within us. It's not just in some of us; it's in everyone. And as we let our own light shine, we unconsciously give other people permission to do the same. As we're liberated from our own fear, our presence automatically liberates others. (pp. 190–191)

All people have the potential to shape their surroundings. Sometimes it is easier to look to others to do the right thing—perhaps to the elected leaders or to the outgoing, popular, or well-spoken leaders. However, leadership can come from anywhere in the organization and from any kind of personality. True leadership happens whenever an individual makes the decision to act congruently with the intention of making positive change (Higher Education Research Institute [HERI], 1996). Leadership has less to do with popularity and charm than it does with having a core sense of purpose and the courage to act on it.

Whether in big ways or in small ways, leadership happens when people recognize that the thing that moves them is worth acting on no matter the level of difficulty that may be associated. As Kouzes and Posner (2007) articulated, "leadership begins with something that grabs hold of you and won't let go" (p. 50). Discovering what that something is constitutes the journey of Consciousness of Self. Taking courageous action on that identified something is the journey of Congruence. Sustaining that courageous action is the work of Commitment (see Chapter 5).

CONGRUENCE BUILDING

Many of the ideas discussed in this chapter related to Congruence can seem rather abstract until put into practice. At this point, you may be wondering how to go about building or enhancing your own capacity for Congruence. Following are several ideas to get you started.

1. Learn from others. Identify one to three role models who exhibit congruent leadership. These could be people you know or leaders you can read or learn about from afar. What about these leaders makes them congruent? How do you see evidence of their values and beliefs manifested in how they lead?
2. Practice makes perfect when living out your priorities. Make a list of your top values, beliefs, and priorities. Next, use these core values, beliefs, and priorities to organize a to-do list. Start small. Plan the next day based on prioritizing things that are congruent with your core values and beliefs. If this seems easy, try organizing your weekly to-do list and schedule to prioritize these values and beliefs. Does this change anything about how you think about your to-do list and schedule?
3. Reflection goes a long way. Take some time to sit down and reflect on the past week. In what ways did you act with Congruence this week? In what ways did you not act with Congruence this week? Make a list or journal about the big and small ways you were or were not congruent. What do you notice about this inventory of Congruence? Are there things that surprise you? Are there things you want to do more or less of in the future?

CONNECTION TO THE OTHER Cs

Just as learning to enact the other Cs of the Social Change Model enables a person to be congruent, Congruence increases effectiveness in the other Cs. Having congruence in situations when one's values and principles are questioned improves Consciousness of Self. It also reinforces one's resolve to continue with Commitment.

The group Cs are also positively affected by Congruence. Groups can foster more authentic Collaboration, Common Purpose, and Controversy With Civility when participants are Congruent with their values and challenge others to be Congruent as well. Finally, Congruence with one's own values makes it possible to be more effective as an engaged Citizen. Existing in a society can help individuals be more aware of their own preferences and values and also provide opportunities to seek to understand the perspectives of others whose values may differ from their own.

CONCLUSION

Living one's values is an evolving process. At times, being a person of Congruence means standing alone for what one knows deep down must be done. There may very well be times when acting with Congruence will not be the popular choice and when it will mean taking risks with which others will not agree. Additionally, we exist as individuals embedded within larger structures of social and cultural norms. This means that congruence can be difficult or complicated, particularly in environments that promote expectations and values that are not congruent for all individuals within that environment. But, there are internal and external rewards for those who are able to exhibit Congruence that changes the shape of how we interact with one another in increasingly diverse and interconnected situations. Jewish philosopher Martin Buber described an Hasidic saying, "Everyone should carefully observe which way his heart draws him, and then choose that way with all his strength" (Kramer, 2011, p. 22). Making this choice is embracing Congruence, a fundamental part of being a leader and a change agent in everyday life.

DISCUSSION QUESTIONS

1. How can the personal values of individual group members contribute to or be transformed into shared group values?
2. Describe an example from your own experience that illustrates each right-versus-right dilemma discussed in the chapter.
3. Suppose you begin to realize that your fundamental values are in stark opposition to those with whom you are working. How far should you bend for the good of the group? What is the threshold at which you would walk away from the group or project?
4. Do you think core values can change? Are they fixed or flexible?

ACTION AND REFLECTION

1. Would someone who just met you be able to identify your values by observing your behavior? Do others see you as you see yourself?
2. How do your social identities (e.g., your race, gender, sexual orientation, nationality, religion, ability status, etc.) affect your ability to be congruent or not in various environments? In what situations is it more challenging to be congruent with values?
3. Examine your social media posts over the past few weeks. To what extent does your online presence align with who you really are? Would a person who does not know you have an accurate perception of who you are and what is important to you based on what they see online?
4. Use the rubric in Table 4.3 to gauge your development on various dimensions of Congruence. Reflect on how you could develop this aspect of your leadership capacity.

TABLE 4.3 Congruence Rubric

	Excelling	Achieving	Developing	Needing Improvement
Cognitive Complexity (*Thinking*)	Develops a focused belief system Recognizes personal limitations Analyzes situations and relationship to core values Able to support personal thoughts and viewpoints	Articulates belief system Identifies important problems, questions, and issues in relation to personal values Does not recognize own personal limitations	Begins exploring core values and belief system Limited understanding of what core values mean	Not aware of having a belief system Does not know the source of own opinion Unable to understand own value system
Internal Belief System (*Feeling*)	Feels confident about making educated decisions Strong sense of self Able to tactfully express belief system in the presence of different individuals Authentic Comfortable acknowledging when a mistake is made	Comfortable with internal expression of core values Expresses self but sometimes loses the ability to be consistent with values around certain groups of individuals Still uncomfortable acknowledging a mistake	Starts to develop confidence in one's own belief system Begins to explore roots and reasoning behind core values Still highly uncomfortable expressing self and beliefs	No confidence in oneself and in decision-making skills Does not value one's own thoughts Does not feel that one can contribute to the group Only relies on reassurance from others
Team Membership (*Connecting*)	Balances self and group values Identifies early on when group's values are unethical or different than one's own Seeks group experiences that align with personal vales Able to confront conflict to better align individual and group's values for all members	Works well in a group around a common purpose Communicates a difference in self and group values Still does not encourage positional leaders to align actions with group's mission and values	Begins to develop self and see a difference in values with the group Persists in feeling frustration because of the misalignment of self and group values Has yet to discuss with group or act on difference in values	Unable to see the connection between self and group values Follows along with group activities without understanding how group actions affect others
Acting Congruent (*Behaving*)	Takes a stand on a belief Acts consistently with values Is committed to being genuine and authentic Makes purposeful life decisions Courageous	Behaves in a manner consistent with beliefs Does not effectively voice when situations are inconsistent with core values Still some minor limitations acting Congruent in high-stakes environments	Begins to act in accordance to core values in very comfortable situations Does not always behave in agreement with beliefs	Beliefs contradictory to behaviors Does not act in accordance to one's values or does not have any values to act on Exhibits a façade in many situations

Source: Developed by Ana Maia and Peter DeCrescenzo.

REFERENCES

Annan, K. A. (1997, June 6). Commencement address. Speech presented at the Massachusetts Institute of Technology, Cambridge, MA. Retrieved from http://news.mit.edu/1997/annansp

Avolio, B. J., & Gardner, W. L. (2005). Authentic leadership development: Getting to the root of positive forms of leadership. *The Leadership Quarterly, 16*, 315–338.

Baxter Magolda, M. B. (2004). *Making their own way: Narratives for transforming higher education to promote self-development.* Sterling, VA: Stylus.

Baxter Magolda, M. B. (2009). *Authoring your life: Developing an internal voice to navigate life's challenges.* Sterling, VA: Stylus.

Dorfman, P., Javidan, M., Hanges, P., Dastmalchian, A., & House, R. (2012). GLOBE: A twenty year journey into the intriguing world of culture and leadership. *Journal of World Business, 42*, 504–518.

Dugan, J. P., Kodama, C. M., & Gebhardt, M. C. (2012). Race and leadership development among college students: The additive value of collective racial esteem. *Journal of Diversity in Higher Education, 5*(3), 174–189.

Gam, P. J. (2001). Recognizing others' truths. In W. K. Kellogg Foundation, *Leading from the heart: The passion to make a difference* (pp. 89–93). Battle Creek, MI: W. K. Kellogg Foundation.

Gardner, W. L., Cogliser, C. C., Davis, K. M., & Dickens, M. P. (2011). Authentic leadership: A review of the literature and research agenda. *The Leadership Quarterly, 22*, 1120–1145.

Higher Education Research Institute (HERI). (1996). *A social change model of leadership development* (Version III). Los Angeles: University of California, Los Angeles, Higher Education Research Institute.

Kegan, R. (1994). *In over our heads: The mental demands of modern life.* Cambridge, MA: Harvard University Press.

Kernis, M. H., & Goldman, B. M. (2006). A multicomponent conceptualization of authenticity: Theory and research. In M. P. Zanna (Ed.), *Advances in experimental social psychology* (Vol. 38, pp. 283–357). San Diego, CA: Academic Press.

Kidder, R. M. (2009). *How good people make tough choices: Resolving the dilemmas of ethical living* (Rev. ed.). New York, NY: Harper.

Kouzes, J. M., & Posner, B. Z. (2007). *The leadership challenge* (4th ed.). San Francisco, CA: Jossey-Bass.

Kramer, K. P. (2011). *Martin Buber's spirituality: Hasidic wisdom for everyday life.* Lanham, MD: Rowman & Littlefield.

Porras, J., Emery, S., & Thompson, M. (2007). *Success built to last: Creating a life that matters.* Upper Saddle River, NJ: Wharton School Publishing.

Williamson, M. (1996). *A return to love: Reflections on the principles of a course in miracles.* New York, NY: HarperPerennial.

Commitment

Ashlee M. Kerkoff and Daniel Ostick

> I'm doing what I think I was put on this earth to do. And I'm really grateful to have something that I'm passionate about and that I think is profoundly important.
> —MARIAN WRIGHT EDELMAN

Kara was an incoming first-year student at the university. Having been active in high school, she was excited about attending the involvement fair the first week of class. At the fair, there were tables representing many student organizations and local service agencies. Kara didn't want to miss out on any great opportunities, so she wrote her name on a lot of lists and started getting e-mail notices about welcome meetings for groups. She attended a lot of them, including an acapella group, an intramural soccer team, alternative breaks, the women in engineering group, and another focused on global health. Unfortunately, with classes and a part-time job, Kara found herself stretched too thin. She decided she needed to focus on just a couple groups she felt really passionate about and in which she felt she could really make a difference. In doing so, she met more students with similar interests and values who were excited to work together on a common purpose. Kara was able to dive more deeply into her involvements and make a mark on those organizations. She learned it was OK to say no to some involvements if it meant she could spend more of her time on things that brought her joy and meaning.

Commitment, the final individual C, pulls together the concepts of Consciousness of Self and Congruence and anchors the group effort. In a sense, Commitment serves as the focal point for social change, around which all of the other Cs are integrated. In Kara's case, she had to consider what kinds of involvements meant the most to her and had to prioritize how she spent her limited free time. The ensemble agreed that "some degree of commitment is essential to accomplish change" (Higher Education Research Institute [HERI], 1996, p. 40).

In order for change to occur, one must commit to applying personal values to the collective effort through action. For Kara, moving from making small contributions to many organizations to making significant contributions to fewer groups maximized her influence.

The ensemble defined Commitment as follows.

> Commitment implies intensity and duration. It requires a significant involvement and investment of one's self in the activity and its intended consequences. It is the energy that drives the collective effort and brings it to fruition. (HERI, 1996, p. 40)

CHAPTER OVERVIEW

This chapter explains the concept of Commitment and its role in the Social Change Model of Leadership Development, including the origins of Commitment, the importance of Commitment to leadership effectiveness and personal development, the influence of personal experiences, external factors that affect Commitment, and an exploration of individual commitment within group settings. Issues of sustaining commitments, overcoming burnout, and gaining resiliency are also examined. Questions for further discussion and reflection are offered, along with action steps to further explore personal commitments.

THE MEANING OF COMMITMENT

At the very core of Commitment is the individual's integrity and his or her innate passion or desire. This internal passion inspires Commitment and requires active engagement. Leaders with commitment follow through on promises, are responsible, and persevere despite challenges. Commitment is "the quality that motivates the individual and supplies the energy and passion to sustain the collective effort" (Astin & Astin, 2000, p. 14). Whether in interpersonal relationships, groups, or communities, when difficulties arise, leaders with commitment stay when others might quit.

Commitment means one's investment in the group members and goals runs deeper than casual interest.

> Commitment requires a level of intensity and duration in relation to a person, idea, or activity. It requires a significant involvement and investment of self in the object of commitment and in the intended outcomes. It is the energy that drives the collective effort . . . and is essential to accomplishing change. It is the heart, the profound passion that drives one to action. (Astin, 1996, p. 6)

Sustained commitment is driven by one's deep, internal passions and motivations. The kind of passion that drives one to have commitment is not necessarily something that one should do or something that ought to be done, but rather something that needs to be done because of a personal drive to act. Shoemaker (2015) describes this as the thing you "can't not do." It is a cause, passion, or desire that is so innate that it propels commitment and persistence. Authentic passion and Commitment are not about having to do something because of some external pressure. It does not feel forced or unnatural; rather, the desire to commit to something is compelled by intrinsic motivation, as if it could not be any other way. It is the personal passion that compels one to act to achieve a certain outcome. "It's about leading out of what is already in your soul" (Kouzes & Posner, 2011, p. 26).

Having said that, it is important to know that commitment can be developed and can grow or fade over time. Everyone is capable of commitment and likely expresses the deep commitment explained here in one way or another. Commitment can be seen as a competency that needs to be developed, and in developing this competency, "people not only affect their own level of commitment . . . but also affect the people around them" (Jaffe, Scott, & Tobe, 1994, p. 19). Developing Commitment in oneself and others can therefore be seen as increasing the fuel that powers organizational drive.

QUALITY OVER QUANTITY

Deep Commitment implies full, personal investment in a group's purpose and goals. In order to have deep Commitment, it is important to examine all of one's involvements and the level of Commitment needed and desired for each. Similar to Kara's example from the beginning of this chapter, life offers such a variety of opportunities that it can be difficult to prioritize. Though it may be tempting to be involved with many activities, such breadth of involvement can decrease one's ability to be fully committed, because an individual's energy is spread thin. The Multi-Institutional Study of Leadership research examined which experiences predict leadership development in the values of the Social Change Model. The results confirm the ensemble's feeling that commitment to deep involvement in just a few organizations has greater leadership development outcomes than shallow involvement in many organizations (Dugan & Komives, 2007).

Often, students look for more clubs and organizations to put on their résumés. But it is important to know that potential employers want to see evidence of one's contribution to results and persistence through challenges. A long list of involvements lacks meaning and depth if students are unable to articulate what they have learned from the experiences, how they have contributed, and how their goals are aligned with that of the group. When involvement is shallow, what value is this group providing to the individual? What value is the individual providing to the group?

As a collegiate soccer player, I dedicated a lot of time, motivation, and emotions into playing. I had three concussions in one year and was no longer able to play, which was really difficult for me. However, I powered through my head and neck symptoms and have since made the dean's list every semester. I promised myself my freshman year to be committed to the soccer program, and in my final year I am part of the coaching staff while also advocating for those suffering from career-ending injuries.

—Jenna Marcello was a member of the class of 2016 at Emmanuel College. Marcello interned at Boston Children's Hospital as the digital marketing intern and was also the assistant goalie coach for her former college soccer team.

THE ORIGINS OF COMMITMENT

> When you adopt the standards and the values of someone else . . . you surrender your own integrity. You become, to the extent of your surrender, less of a human being.
> —ELEANOR ROOSEVELT

Commitment that is truly authentic in nature builds Congruence between values and actions. This kind of authentic Commitment must come from within, from motivation that is intrinsic in nature. Although some energy may come from external factors and supports, a sustained effort requires an individual's own motivation and will. For some, this internal drive comes from commitment to a social issue, for others it is from their commitment to the group or the individuals who have put trust in them, for yet others commitment derives from their sense of responsibility and integrity—they follow through because they said they would, pure and simple.

Robin Gerber, author of *Leadership the Eleanor Roosevelt Way: Timeless Strategies From the First Lady of Courage* (2002), learned from studying Roosevelt's life that "finding your leadership passion or mission means being true to your nature. It means finding your 'certain thing'" (Gerber, 2002, p. 88). The origins of Commitment discussed here are related to finding that certain thing and include significant personal experiences, spirituality and faith, and supportive external environments.

Significant Personal Experiences

For many, this passion and Commitment is developed from personal experiences. A person who grew up in poverty may find a passion for helping people with low income find new economic opportunities. A person with a talent for music may find immense joy in promoting the arts in the local community. A person with an inspiring and supportive teacher in high school may find mentoring others to be an incredibly rewarding way to pass those lessons on to others. Looking back and reflecting on struggles, successes, and important life events can provide clarity and focus to personal passion and help direct efforts to areas of personal importance.

Malala Yousafzai grew up in the Swat District of northwest Pakistan in the 2000s. Coming from a family of educators, Yousafzai was already an advocate for learning and education when she was attacked for her views and efforts and shot on her school bus in 2013. Surviving the attack, she became a global ambassador for millions of girls denied education because of sociopolitical barriers. Yousafzai turned her personal experiences into a life cause. The attack wasn't the genesis of her advocacy, but a person with less Commitment would have retreated in fear. Instead she used the incident to draw public attention to the resistance girls face when trying obtaining an education. Yousafzai accepted the Nobel Peace Prize in 2014.

Juana Bordas emigrated from Nicaragua to the United States with her seven brothers and sisters. Her extended family includes Mexicans, Colombians, and

Cubans, and her experiences in the Peace Corps in Puerto Rico and Chile have instilled a deep love for leadership principles rooted in a multicultural American experience. Her life's work is a commitment to cultivating leadership in others by spreading an appreciation of multicultural values. Bordas's (2013) strategies to help leaders actualize their destiny, or *destino*, are described in the following:

- Begin with your family history and traditions (the roots of your destino)
- Tap into your heart's desire or passion (the fire and energy to follow your destino)
- Identify your special skills and talents (your destino knapsack)
- Open the door when opportunity knocks (it's your destino calling you)
- Honor your legacy and personal vision (the destino magnet that pulls you forward) (p. 84)

The life stories of Yousafzai and Bordas demonstrate that there are lessons in one's history. The best way to discover your passions is to examine your life. What have you already demonstrated Commitment to without consciously thinking about it? Find your passion points and talents, and cultivate them.

Spirituality and Faith

For many, spirituality or faith is a significant factor in the development of Commitment. Faith can represent a "canopy of significance, that embraces, orders, and relativizes all of our knowing and being" (Parks, 2011, p. 34). Whether connected to an organized faith tradition or not, people's spiritual beliefs give their lives a sense of direction and reason for being that serves as the drive behind their capacity for Commitment. When your decisions, large and small, are rooted in a greater purpose, it compels you to ask important questions about how you spend your time, what you can depend on, whom you can trust, what matters, and how you live. Astin, Astin, and Lindholm (2011) conducted a multiyear study of thousands of college students in order to explore the development of spirituality. Their findings revealed that many students are becoming more caring, more tolerant, and more actively engaged in a spiritual quest. The researchers identified several specific activities that contributed to this growth, including study abroad and service-learning, along with "inner work" such as self-reflection and actively engaging in questions of meaning and purpose.

Supportive External Environments

Though Commitment originates from within, it is important to recognize the external factors that can help support an individual's commitment to leadership for social change. "No one can force a person to commit to something, but organizations and colleagues can create and support an environment that resonates with each individual's heart and passions" (Astin, 1996, p. 6). By having a supportive environment and being surrounded by others who share similar passions, individuals are encouraged in their own personal commitment and motivation. Additionally, affirmation and validation from a supportive environment can matter greatly in sustaining an individual's commitment (Daloz, Keen, Keen, & Parks, 1996).

Supportive environments can provide strong vehicles for advancing Commitment and the collective effort; however, other external factors also affect an individual's commitment level. Factors, such as financial incentives, recognition for work well done, or status, also need to be identified as personal motivators for some individuals. Facing adversity or being challenged in one's passion can also deepen commitment. Debating with someone who shares a dissenting viewpoint or falling short on a goal, as examples, can be motivators that drive one to further develop that passion and recommit to a cause. Though challenges may be barriers or lead to questioning one's commitments, they can also give motivation to reignite the fire, reexamine one's passions, and reenergize. Identifying the range of external motivators that drive personal passion will help direct and sustain commitment.

FINDING YOUR PASSION

> Your vocation in life is where your greatest joy meets the world's greatest need.
> —FREDERICK BUECHNER

Finding personal passion is an ongoing process of clarifying values and Commitment by identifying the work that gives you meaning. This can be a very powerful experience that helps give direction and energy to an individual's commitments. "When you start living your leadership passion you will be swept forward . . . with the energy that comes from acting on authentic feelings and beliefs. You will carry a touchstone that gives you patience, persistence, conviction, and strength" (Gerber, 2002,

p. 102). This process of discovering one's passion for socially responsible leadership can deepen commitment. As an individual develops a greater consciousness of self, he or she examines those deeply held convictions. Kouzes and Posner (2011) say identifying yourself as a leader

> begins with knowing your own key convictions; it begins with your value system. Clarifying your own values and aspirations is a highly personal matter, and no one else can do it for you. To exhibit harmonious leadership—leadership in which your words and deeds are consonant—you must be in tune internally. (p. 24)

Identifying that internal passion is a first step in being fully committed, and that passion can be intensified by reflection and action.

COMMITMENT, CREDIBILITY, AND LEADERSHIP EFFECTIVENESS

A large national research study on the effective practices of corporate leaders examined, among other issues, what constituents most look for in leaders (Kouzes & Posner, 2012). Put another way, what is it about certain leaders that makes group members *want* to work with them? The findings led the researchers to conclude that the foundation of effective leadership is credibility. When people perceived their immediate manager to have high credibility, they were significantly more likely to feel proud about their organization, feel a high degree of team spirit, feel a strong sense of ownership and commitment to the organization, and be motivated by shared values and intrinsic factors (Kouzes & Posner, 2012).

At its core, credibility involves being competent, honest, and inspiring. Knowing your values, passions, and level of Commitment contributes to your ability to develop and sustain credibility in a group. Leading by an example that demonstrates the intensity and duration of Commitment is the heart of what it means to be credible. Indeed, "loyalty, commitment, energy, and productivity depend on it" (Kouzes & Posner, p. 38). Commitment is a core tenet of credibility, and credibility must be present to effectively lead toward a Common Purpose. Leadership that is built on a foundation of credibility can ultimately lead to a higher functioning group with shared values at its core.

COMMITMENT IN THE GROUP ENVIRONMENT

> [One]'s mind, once stretched by a new idea, never regains its original dimension.
> —OLIVER WENDELL HOLMES

Group effort comes from the collection of individual commitments. The combined energy of individuals is what provides a driving force for the productive functioning of a group. Banding together with others to form a collective commitment to a cause can strengthen efforts.

Students at the University of Vermont employed strategic, well-coordinated activism through a silent yet dramatic protest of the board of trustees to successfully get gender identity and expression included into the university's nondiscrimination statement.

In an ideal world, all groups would operate in such productive ways. However, as previously mentioned, people have different levels of Commitment and may demonstrate that in a variety of ways. Consider a student organization that mentors youth in the community. Though the members may share a common purpose, each individual has the power to affect the functioning of the group. If one member is not fully devoted to the group's intended outcomes, the other members of the group can feel that in group performance—maybe through reaching fewer children, missing opportunities because of ignored e-mails, and so on. Group members must be devoted not only to maintaining that internal motivation but also to following through on tasks necessary to the group's operation. For example, a group member who misses group meetings hinders the productivity of the group in that the individual is unable to contribute his or her energy and perspective to the effort. This can also be seen when a group member does not follow through on assigned tasks. Faltering commitment from one group member then puts added strain or work on other group members and can slow productivity and the energy necessary to accomplish group goals.

When an individual's commitment falters, other group members have an obligation to address it. They should have a hard conversation, and talk about what the group needs from the member and how his or her lack of commitment to the group goal is reducing the effectiveness and morale of the group. The SCM value of Controversy With Civility requires confrontation with compassion in addressing Commitment issues within a group. Leaders with a strong commitment to group purpose have the confidence to address problems head-on rather than avoid them.

An individual's level of Commitment not only has an impact on group outcomes but the group can reinforce an individual's commitment. Positive experiences within a group can reinforce individual commitment and spur motivation. If a person in a group feels needed or that he or she can make a positive contribution, he or she is more likely to be committed to the efforts of the group. Success or positive change rewards Commitment and can deepen it further.

Likewise, an unsupportive or unhealthy group environment can impede an individual's commitment and service to the group. Although there may have been initial internal motivation that led an individual to serve, unsupportive environments may force an individual to question his or her service to that group. These types of situations pose a challenge to individuals who are deeply committed, because they may lead to choosing between remaining loyal to the group or taking care of their own needs.

There are many moments during my time as a student organization leader that I've wanted to completely give up; I felt like I was the only person committed to the organization or felt ignored and belittled by my team. However, I take solace in . . . my love for my organization's purpose and my love for contributing to the community. I remind myself constantly that the value of my work is greater than any occasional discomfort, which motivates me to continue on my path without wavering.

—Vanessa Barksdale is an undergraduate student at the University of Maryland Baltimore County, where she participates in student government and works with an initiative on the development of racial consciousness within her campus.

SUSTAINING COMMITMENT

> Perseverance is not a long race; it is many short races one after another.
> —WALTER ELLIOTT

Commitment takes effort. But thinking of Commitment as only full of challenges and uphill struggles belies that true Commitment comes from a place of positivity and possibility. A relatively recent movement in the field of psychology is to balance the field's research on psychological problems and disorders with new research studying people who thrive despite the usual ups and downs of life (Seligman, 2011). Although commitment can be a challenge to sustain, particularly through disappointments, temporary failures, and relationship tensions, the findings of studies on resilience and flourishing can help bolster one's capacity to stay the course. This research explores how and why people *flourish*: how one can learn to thrive, develop resilience, create meaning and purpose, sustain positive emotions, develop positive relationships, build self-esteem, and bolster engagement.

Addressing Burnout With Self-Awareness

One of the personal barriers to strong Commitment is burnout, which can be considered a type of depression, conveying a sense of hopelessness, as if there is no point in persisting with your activities. Burnout is considered to have three dimensions, including emotional exhaustion because of prolonged work-life stress; depersonalization, personal distancing from others, and ignoring important tasks; and lack of personal accomplishment (Maslach, Schaufeli, & Leiter, 2001).

Burnout can be battled partially through a reframing of its origins, recognizing that true authentic commitment supports sustainability. "It's not that we sustain a commitment; it's more that [we] are sustained by the commitment" (Daloz et al., 1996, p. 196). In other words, we are fueled by the things we have true commitment for, not drained by them. Taking time to reexamine intrinsic motivators can provide a renewed sense of energy as the values and beliefs behind commitment present themselves once again.

My commitment comes from knowing that the organizations that I am a part of are serving a purpose and greater good for my university. I have struggled when I haven't seen the purpose behind what I was doing or was so burnt out that I lost sight of why I was doing it in the first place. I am personally fulfilled when I know that what I am doing is helping others and is meaningful. This is my motivating energy and helps me when I need to work through the night or run between meetings that are back-to-back.

—Kerry Mallett is a former student at Lehigh University, where she was president of the student senate, an editor of the school newspaper, and an executive council member of her sorority, Alpha Gamma Delta.

Building Capacity for Resilience

Balanced self-renewal is crucial to sustaining commitment to values and organizations. A common misconception is that resilience is about being free from negative thoughts or about tamping them down and forcing yourself to be optimistic. Resiliency is actually about developing coping techniques to navigate through tough times.

Resilient leaders see challenges or failure as opportunities to learn. Individual characteristics, such as self-efficacy, confidence, a strong intrinsic motivation, a positive attitude, coping strategies, and supportive relationships with others, are important in developing resiliency. Leaders with resilience do not just survive adversity, they use the experience for growth. In other words, they do not just bounce back, they bounce forward (Allison, 2011/2012).

The research on resilience by Seligman (2011) suggests that an important skill is learning to reframe one's situation and make meaning of it in another way. This new meaning is not a false lens, like rose colored glasses. Seligman emphasizes that the new frame is still a realistic and truthful interpretation of the situation, it is just a look taken from a different angle. Specifically, the new frame should intentionally shift the interpretation of one's situation to recognize it as either (1) temporary or (2) situational. For example, when a person fails to reach a goal, one frame is "I'm a failure." A resilient frame would be either temporary, "I failed this time," or situational, "I failed at this one." Notice that a resilient reframe creates room for learning and another improved attempt—the bounce forward described by Allison (2011/2012).

Resilient leaders can help develop Commitment in others by teaching them to reframe for resilience as well. For instance, when group members say, "University administrators don't care about us," they can be reminded either that "The person we spoke to today didn't care, so we will try talking to someone else" (reframing as situational) or "We didn't convince them this time, so we will think more about what would persuade them and try again" (reframing as temporary).

Allison (2011/2102) shared some signals that your organizational resilience is at risk, which can also serve as personal lessons about how to stay resilient in order to sustain Commitment:

- Keep learning. You are never done learning and should not believe you know everything you need to know.

- Pay attention to key indicators. How do you know if things are going well? What would be the signs? Keep an eye on these so you are ready to respond.
- Focus on what is important. Too many initiatives can drain you, so focus on doing a few things really well instead of a thousand things mediocrely.
- Celebrate success. Celebrating successes reminds others what works and encourages others to do their best.
- Engage in personal renewal. Staying physically and emotionally well will have a direct impact on your ability to bounce back.
- Cultivate networks before challenges occur. Have backup and support in place so they are ready to offer that needed help.

Flow, Thriving, and Commitment

Flow is a concept that describes those moments of intense concentration and hyperfocus that occur when people are applying the very best of their talent. Some describe flow simply as being *in the zone*, doing what they were meant to do, to the extent that they lose all track of time (Csikszentmihalyi, 1991). Achieving flow requires a level of challenge so that one's skills are pushed to their height. Research indicates that experiencing flow is correlated with well-being, life satisfaction, and flourishing (Seligman, 2011).

What makes the idea of flow particularly interesting is to take note that having a life of great satisfaction and well-being is therefore not about being one of the "lucky" ones for whom life is easy and things always go your way. Rather, it is about having opportunities to rise to the occasion and take on challenges that stretch your skills and direct all your energy in the service of something that matters to you. The concept of flow serves as a reminder that having Commitment is not drudgery or a hardship; it is an opportunity to experience the satisfaction that results when we maintain focus on "the thing we can't not do."

CONNECTION TO THE OTHER Cs

Although the other Cs build the capacity to have Commitment, having Commitment also enhances how people experience the other Cs. Being committed to something, deeply and over time, helps people understand their values and personal style more deeply. Similarly, as unforeseen challenges come along, having Commitment puts one's ability to be Congruent to the test. Consciousness of Self emphasizes the importance of self-awareness. In order to be Committed to something, an individual must first understand what it is that is motivating him or her. Further, because Commitment can only be fully realized with action, people must not only have an awareness of their values and beliefs but also they must act in ways that demonstrate those values as part of who they are. And although Commitment ultimately contributes to the collective effort, there is an element of Commitment to the self that is crucial. (For a deeper discussion on the importance of gaining self-awareness, see Chapter 3, "Consciousness of Self.")

The group Cs also clearly benefit from individual Commitment. When individuals are committed to each other through success and challenges, their Collaborations, Common Purposes, and ability to handle Controversy With Civility are challenged again and again. The group can reach a point where it has been through so much together, and members know how to work together so well, that the group Cs can be understood at a more complex level. The group values can go beyond having meaning in terms of one-time cases, such as having a collaborative meeting or working through one tough controversy. Long-term Commitment means knowing what it feels like to be collaborative year-round, and to have Common Purposes that get passed down from graduating seniors to first-year students. There is no way to understand the other Cs at that level without having Commitment.

Finally, it is by demonstrating Commitment that a person can build the trusting relationships in the community that are needed to have active, effective Citizenship. Citizenship requires individuals to be deeply committed to the common good. Commitment is sometimes the one element that makes the difference between a good idea that goes nowhere and one that actually happens and makes a real difference for one's campus, local community, state, country, or world.

CONCLUSION

Commitment implies action—using personal passion and internal motivations to initiate some kind of change. Commitment strongly affects change because it drives action, which means that any individual can be a part of change. "Change starts with one person seeing a possibility and taking action on it. We must each look within ourselves for the wisdom, vision, the ability, and the motivation to change" (Jaffe et al., 1994, p. 252). When individuals find their leadership passion and are authentic in their Commitments, they can find Common Purpose with others and create effective change. Though it may seem as though one individual cannot make a large impact, expressing individual Commitment is the first step to moving others to create change. As Margaret Mead once said, "Never doubt that a small group of thoughtful, committed citizens can change the world; indeed, it's the only thing that ever has" (as cited in Applewhite, Evans, 2003 & Frothingham, 1992, p. 69).

 ## DISCUSSION QUESTIONS

1. How is the individual value of Commitment related to the other individual values of Consciousness of Self and Congruence? How do these three values affect and intersect with each other?
2. Where does Commitment come from? How can sources of personal Commitment be identified to enhance individual and group performance and socially responsible leadership?
3. What are some common barriers to Commitment? How might these be resolved or overcome?

 ## ACTION AND REFLECTION

1. Write down all the student group meetings you had in the past month. Now, order them from most important to you to least important to you. Where do you spend more time: with the groups at the top or bottom of the list? Consider ways in which you can spend more time on the things most important to you.
2. Name a cause or issue that is important to you. Write down the ways you are committed to this cause (or the ways you could be committed). Think of a person on your campus who is also committed to this cause and have coffee with him or her to talk about it. Finding support and common connection is a powerful way to kick-start Commitment.
3. Take a moment to consider your own personal commitments. In general, what motivates you (for example, helping others, recognition, money, making an impact, and so on)?

4. Think of times when you have felt most focused, energized, or satisfied. List the experiences that brought you this feeling. Are there themes that run across these examples (that is, all involve children, all involve working in groups, all resulted in large-scale change, all allowed you to display your creativity)?
5. What do you do to combat burnout and build resilience? What actions have you taken to reflect on your purpose?
6. Use the rubric in Table 5.1 to gauge your development on various dimensions of Commitment. Reflect on how you could develop this aspect of your leadership capacity.

TABLE 5.1 Commitment Rubric

Commitment	Excelling	Achieving	Developing	Needing Improvement
Passion	Acts with conviction for individual and group beliefs Critically reflects on how individual and group beliefs influence change and action Demonstrates engagement through self-reflection combined with action	Usually acts in congruence with one's beliefs Has a solid understanding of how one's beliefs influence one's actions Demonstrates engagement through self-reflection and sometimes links this with action	Feels an internal desire to act on issues of importance but has not found an outlet to do so Demonstrates engagement in easier projects and tasks	Does not feel motivated to act on one's values Is unable to articulate one's values Does not feel connected to any issues outside of oneself
Credibility	Takes pride and responsibility in one's work Willing to take ownership for individual and group work and mistakes Completes all projects at or above expected level Represents self and group in a positive manner Leads by example	Willing to take ownership for one's work and mistakes Completes projects at expected level Displays few flaws in work If mistakes occur, seldom makes excuses Represents oneself in a positive manner	Completes most projects fully but forgets others Blames others for mistakes May not complete projects in a timely manner and at the expected level Seldom fulfills individual and group responsibilities	Work completed below expected levels Does not take ownership for own mistakes Does not represent oneself or the group in a positive manner when given responsibilities Cannot be relied on in group settings
Investment	Thoroughly analyzes all engagements Takes time to understand why one is involved in a project Stays dedicated during distress Devotes time to actions that benefit oneself and others	Analyzes most, if not all, engagements Has a good understanding of why one is involved in certain projects Usually devotes time to actions that benefit oneself	Has many conflicting engagements and responsibilities that have not been well thought out Works to better understand where one's interests lie	Has not dedicated time to any issues bigger than oneself Has not considered where one's interests lie
Persistence	Completes all projects in a timely manner Motivates oneself and group to stay dedicated to goals Overcomes obstacles Checks in to make sure that the process is working	Completes most, if not all, projects Prioritizes one's goals and group goals well most of the time Chooses challenging but not complex projects to complete	Completes some projects Is distracted easily Becomes frustrated with obstacles Becomes forgetful	Completes few to no projects Gives up in the face of adversity Displays levels of apathy
Sustainability	Emphasizes quality versus quantity Sustains deep and meaningful engagements Acts on authentic feelings and beliefs Asks for help when needed and does not take on more than one can handle Rarely becomes overwhelmed	Sustains important engagements Acts on authentic beliefs Usually seeks help when needed Attempts to find daily equilibrium but periodically becomes overwhelmed	Takes on more than one can handle Seldom recognizes one's feelings or beliefs Becomes overwhelmed by multiple projects or tasks Easily becomes burnt out	Takes on too much or too little Has found little direction for what one deems important in one's life Displays frequent burnout or disinterest with one's work

Source: Developed by Jamie Adasi and Evan Witt.

REFERENCES

Allison, E. (2011/2012). The resilient leader. *Educational Leadership, 69*(4), 79–82.

Applewhite, A., Evans, T., & Frothingham, A. (2003). *And I quote: The definitive collection of quotes, sayings, and jokes for the contemporary speechmaker.* New York, NY: Thomas Dunne Books.

Astin, A. W., & Astin, H. S. (2000). *Leadership reconsidered: Engaging higher education in social change.* Battle Creek, MI: W. K. Kellogg Foundation.

Astin, A. W., Astin, H. S., & Lindholm, J. A. (2011). *Cultivating the spirit: How college can enhance students' inner lives.* San Francisco, CA: Jossey-Bass.

Astin, H. S. (1996). Leadership for social change. *About Campus, 1*(3), 4–10. doi:10.1002/abc.6190010302

Bordas, J. (2013). *The power of Latino leadership: Culture, inclusion, and contribution.* Oakland: CA: Berrett-Koehler.

Csikszentmihalyi, M. (1991). *Flow: The psychology of optimal experience.* New York, NY: Harper Perennial.

Daloz, L. A., Keen, C. H., Keen, J. P., & Parks, S. D. (1996). *Common fire: Lives of commitment in a complex world.* Boston, MA: Beacon Press.

Dugan, J. P., & Komives, S. R. (2007). *Developing leadership capacity in college students: Findings from a national study.* A Report from the Multi-Institutional Study of Leadership. College Park, MD: National Clearinghouse for Leadership Programs.

Gerber, R. (2002). *Leadership the Eleanor Roosevelt way: Timeless strategies from the first lady of courage.* New York City, NY: Penguin.

Higher Education Research Institute (HERI). (1996). *A social change model of leadership development* (Version III). Los Angeles, CA: University of California, Los Angeles, Higher Education Research Institute.

Jaffe, D. T., Scott, C. D., & Tobe, G. R. (1994). *Rekindling commitment: How to revitalize yourself, your work, and your organization.* San Francisco, CA: Jossey-Bass.

Kouzes, J. M., & Posner, B. Z. (2011). Leadership begins with an inner journey. *Leader to Leader, 60,* 22–27.

Kouzes, J., & Posner, B. (2012). *The leadership challenge: How to make extraordinary things happen in organizations* (5th ed.). San Francisco, CA: Jossey-Bass.

Maslach, C., Schaufeli, W. B., & Leiter, M. P. (2001). Job burnout. *Annual Reviews Psychology, 52,* 397–422.

Parks, S. D. (2011). *Big questions, worthy dreams: Mentoring emerging adults in their search for meaning, purpose, and faith.* San Francisco, CA: Jossey-Bass.

Seligman, M. (2011). *Flourish: A visionary new understanding of happiness and well-being.* New York, NY: Free Press.

Shoemaker, P. (2015). *Can't not do: The compelling social drive that changes our world.* Hoboken, NJ: John Wiley.

PART 3

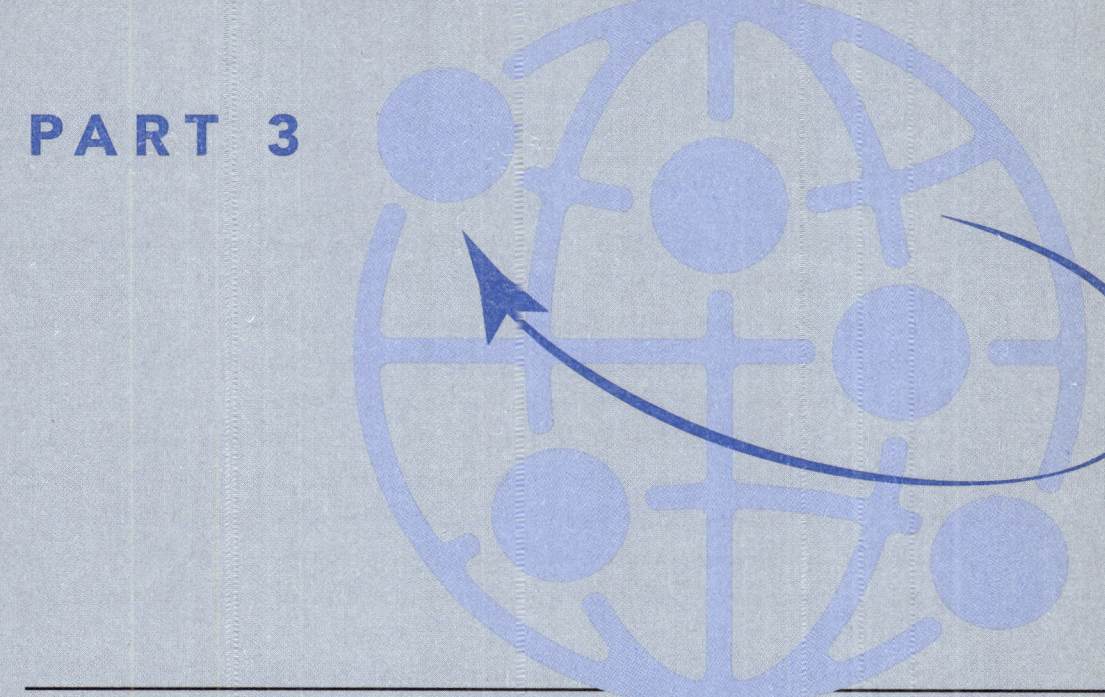

Group Values

> Relationships are the connective tissue of organizations. . . . Over time . . . relationships built on integrity are the glue that holds organizations together.
> —KATHY ALLEN AND CYNTHIA CHERREY

The Social Change Model of Leadership Development recognizes that leadership is inherently a relational process. "Leadership involves collaborative relationships that lead to collective action grounded in the shared values of people who work together to effect positive change" (Higher Education Research Institute [HERI], 1996, p. 16). "[This] requires that individuals learn how to develop relationships among themselves that allow for collaborative action on issues in common" (Morse, 1994, p. 48). People come together in groups to accomplish shared purposes. Whether a study group, an academic class, a staff at work, a student organization, or a local Habitat for Humanity chapter, groups are dynamic and evolve as the members within them develop a breadth and depth working together. Indeed, leadership is all about relationships.

Part 3 explores how leadership happens among individuals in groups as they seek to work toward change. Groups engage in a process of shared leadership among members. Tuckman (1965; Tuckman & Jenson, 1977) studied the evolving nature of groups and observed that they go through predictable stages that are presented in this section. Understanding groups and the leadership dynamics in groups are key to accomplishing shared purposes. Just as individuals grow and develop, so do groups and organizations.

In Part 3, the SCM examines leadership development from the group dimension. The ensemble asked, "How can the collaborative leadership development process be designed not only to facilitate the development of the desired individual qualities [from the last section] but also to effect positive change?" (HERI, 1996, p. 19). The three values explored in this dimension are Collaboration, Common Purpose, and Controversy With Civility.

REFERENCES

Higher Education Research Institute (HERI). (1996). *A social change model of leadership development* (Version III). Los Angeles, CA: University of California, Los Angeles, Higher Education Research Institute.

Morse, S. W. (1994). Educating leaders for the responsibilities of a civil society. *Journal of Leadership Studies, 1*(3), 37–49.

Tuckman, B. W. (1965). Developmental sequence in small groups. *Psychological Bulletin 63*, 384–399.

Tuckman, B. W., & Jensen, M. C. (1977). Stages of small group development revisited. *Group and Organizational Studies, 2,* 419–427.

Collaboration

Jordan England

> Gettin' good players is easy. Gettin' 'em to play together is the hard part.
> —CASEY STENGEL

The #BlackLivesMatter movement began with a simple Facebook message from Alicia Garza—"Black people. I love you. I love us. Our lives matter."—which was reposted by her close friend, Patrisse Cullors, with the hashtag #blacklivesmatter. The original post was in response to the jury verdict acquitting George Zimmerman in the shooting death of 17-year-old Trayvon Martin, but Black Lives Matter has since become a chapter-based national organization and a movement, working for broad scale social change. The movement has done something powerful: it has brought together Black people with diverse and intersecting identities, centering the experiences and concerns of those who bring multiple marginalized identities: "Black queer and trans folks, disabled folks, black-undocumented folks, folks with records, women and all Black lives along the gender spectrum," allowing a new kind of movement with a new kind of leadership to emerge (Black Lives Matter, 2016). Black Lives Matter founders Tometi, Garza, and Cullors-Brignac (2015) assert.

> There are important implications for the possibilities that this new layer of leadership can offer the movement as a whole. We create much more room for collaboration, for expansion, for building power when we nurture movements that are full of leaders, and allow for all of our identities to inform our work and how we organize. (para. 7)

On college campuses across the United States, students participating in the Black Lives Matter movement are bringing their own diverse identities, perspectives, and experiences to these conversations, building understanding and trust, and collaboratively shaping the future of the movement. By centering itself in the diversity of Black lives and experiences, and building a movement that is attentive to the diverse and interesting concerns of Black communities, the Black Lives Matter movement is a poignant example of the power and necessity of Collaboration in the leadership process.

ABOUT COLLABORATION

Collaboration is a core value in the Social Change Model of Leadership Development—in fact, it is part of the definition. Leadership is grounded in relationships between people; in these relationships one develops the ability to work collaboratively with others, which is essential to the leadership process. The ensemble's definition of Collaboration underscores the importance of relationships; the need for shared responsibility, authority, and accountability; and the benefit of having multiple perspectives and talents in a group process.

The ensemble defined Collaboration as follows:

> Working together toward common goals by sharing responsibility, authority, and accountability in achieving these goals. . . . It multiplies group effectiveness because it capitalizes on the multiple talents and perspectives of each group member and the power of that diversity to generate creative solutions and actions. Collaboration underscores the relational aspect in the model. It is about human relationships, how people work together, and how they value and relate to each other. Collaboration mobilizes and enhances the power of the group through the members' commitment to the common purpose. (Higher Education Research Institute [HERI], 1996, p. 48)
>
> Our approach to leadership development views collaboration as more than merely coming together around a predetermined vision or approach. Rather, we see collaboration as being most centrally about how people value and relate to each other across differences in values, ideas, affiliations, visions, and identities (for example, race, gender, culture, religion, sexual orientation, class, and

so on). Collaboration is not only an efficient and effective way to get the "task" accomplished, but it also a powerful way to learn about ourselves and others in the process. (HERI, 1996, p. 49)

CHAPTER OVERVIEW

This chapter explores the concept of Collaboration as it relates to the leadership process. First, the chapter explores the concept of Collaboration—what collaboration is, and what it is not. Next, the chapter delves into concepts critical to making collaboration work, including building trust, having broad-based involvement of all group members, developing purpose and goals, and paying attention to process. Finally, the chapter looks to how Collaboration relates to the other Cs in the SCM.

EXPLORING COLLABORATION

We have all had the experience of working in a team, whether on a group project at school, as part of a student organization, or with a team sport. Collaboration, however, is more than simple teamwork. Collaboration involves these factors:

- Human relationships and how people relate to each other
- A process of developing common visions, goals, and purpose
- Shared responsibility, authority, and accountability in developing solutions and accomplishing goals
- Creating synergy by capitalizing on the multiple perspectives and talents of group members

Instead of looking to a positional leader for answers and direction, collaboration enables us to develop a reciprocal, relational leadership process. In this process, we learn from one another, develop a vision of the change we desire, and work toward that vision.

 Working with others who share the same values, beliefs, and goals is an extremely energizing experience. There is a certain chemistry that is created when passionate people work together. This chemistry allows work to get done. When my teammates and I are planning an event, we often bounce ideas around. Each team member improves upon the previous idea to create a strategy and event that is not only effective, but unique, powerful, and efficient. When that final goal is reached, there is nothing more encouraging than celebrating alongside those who worked so hard to bring it all together. [We create] a meaningful bond and opportunity to improve, learn, and grow and to help others do the same.

—Erin Hudnall was a senior at West Virginia Wesleyan College, where she was a member of a peer-led community service and social justice organization called WE LEAD. She supervised the Children and Youth and Appalachian Experience issue-based action teams within this organization.

Although some may dismiss the concept of Collaboration as overly sentimental, the ability to effectively collaborate is critical for success in today's world and modern workforce (Parker, 2008; Van Velsor & Wright, 2015). Effective collaboration mobilizes and synergizes the efforts of individuals with diverse experiences and perspectives to develop new and innovative solutions to difficult problems—problems for which there may have been no obvious solution using current approaches or existing knowledge.

Fully understanding what Collaboration is and is not requires an exploration of the relationships among the constructs of collaboration: competition, cooperation, and compromise. The following sections discuss each of these concepts and the relationships between them.

Competition

Competition is embedded in many American structures. The adversarial legal system, sports teams, and the competitive free market economy all illustrate the way competition permeates our shared lives (Komives, Lucas, & McMahon, 2013). Some people believe that competition is the most effective way of working toward goals and motivating individuals to achieve their greatest potential; however, the research on achievement has repeatedly refuted the myth that competition leads to greater productivity than cooperation (Kohn, 1992). A classic meta-analysis of more than 100 different studies measuring performance data in competitive, cooperative, or individualistic structures showed that working together typically yields greater achievement (Johnson, Maruyama, Johnson, Nelson, & Skon, 1981). Even in classroom settings, research shows that competition heightens anxiety and promotes a focus on winning rather than on learning. Cooperative learning, however, promotes higher academic achievement, stronger social skills, and higher self-esteem (Kohn, 1992). The SCM promotes the value that individuals working together in the same group toward a shared goal will accomplish more if they collaborate with each other instead of compete with one another for recognition, rewards, or for other motives; likewise, groups working together in the same community will benefit from collaboration instead of isolated action.

The essence of the concept of competition is what Kohn (1992) calls "mutually exclusive goal attainment," meaning one person can only succeed only if the other does not. Competition usually does not motivate people to do the best that they can; it only motivates them to do better than the others. It actually limits how high one's goals are set. It encourages a focus on beating others, rather than focusing on doing well. In that form of thinking, winning is extrinsically motivated, and though it may produce short-term gain, a continued focus on beating others tends to erode one's intrinsic, or internal, motivation to strive toward excellence on a task (Kohn, 1992). This zero-sum thinking illustrates a win-lose philosophy that the more you have then the less I have. Collaboration enables people to imagine a different paradigm, one in which great things can be accomplished in win-win situations.

Mary Parker Follett, a key historical figure in organizational communication and management theory, outlined three approaches to people working together to make decisions (1995): (1) *domination*—when one side "wins" at the expense of another, (2) *compromise*—when both sides give up part of their original interests to come to an agreement, and (3) *integration*—when a new solution is developed that preserves the interests of both parties. The way to achieve Follett's integration is to learn to approach differences of opinion in a new way. Traditionally, each individual states his or her position and defends its merits. For example, one person wants to go out for coffee at Starbucks, the other wants to go to College Perk, a locally owned coffeehouse. The two argue about why each is better, trying to convince the other he or she is right. With an integrative, or win-win, approach, each person would try to understand the criteria behind the other's choice. One person prefers to support locally owned businesses; the other wants to be able to sit outdoors on a patio. Once the criteria are established, it is not about opposing sides anymore. There is no longer a winner and a loser. Instead there are two people on the same side, solving the puzzle together: find a locally owned coffee shop with outdoor seating.

Integration requires each party to determine the criteria that would constitute a win for them, then to set aside "my way" and "your way" of doing things and try to create a whole new option that meets the win criteria of both parties. In the process of forming win-win agreements, Covey (2004) suggests keeping the option of "no deal" on the table. That is, if both parties are not able to come to an agreement that is mutually beneficial, then they agree to walk away peacefully rather than agreeing on a solution that favors the interests of one party over the other. Knowing that neither person will commit to interest in a win if it means a loss for the other person develops trust in working relationships. Win-win solutions are satisfying and beneficial to all parties involved and generate higher levels of commitment from group members.

Working toward integrative solutions builds synergy. Synergy—the concept that the whole is greater than the sum of individual parts—comes from the Greek work *sunergos*, meaning "working together." For organizations, this means the unified efforts of the group working together achieves more than the combined result of same individuals working independently. Reaching the point of synergy is the goal of a collaborative process.

To build synergy, organizations must have a high degree of trust, an essential ingredient in the collaborative process, and truly value the diverse perspectives group members hold. Diversity is key. When members see things differently, they think, "Good! Talking through different perspectives will help us make sure we've really thought this issue through." Members do not need to be "right" or to "win" arguments; instead, they need to feel their perspective was heard and was taken into consideration in the process of developing the outcome.

Cooperation

Cooperation is different from collaboration in a small but important way. A collaborative relationship is developed to achieve mutual goals, whereas a cooperative relationship is meant to help each party achieve its individual goals (HERI, 1996, p. 48). Similarly, Chrislip and Larson (1994) asserted that the "purpose of collaboration is to create a shared vision and joint strategies to address concerns that go beyond the purview of any particular party" (p. 5). As such, win-win solutions can be a part of either cooperative or collaborative processes.

Consider an example of two different community service–based student organizations that are trying to increase undergraduate participation in their respective projects. The two groups may decide to cooperate to help each group achieve their goals by doing a joint mailing to new students about their respective organizations. A collaboration between the two groups would require them to take a step back from their individual goals of increasing participation in their specific projects to develop a common goal: increasing undergraduate participation in community service. Once that purpose has been decided on, the organizations can join together to develop new strategies and interventions focused on the common goal.

Compromise

Even while considering the possibility of integrative solutions, people often believe that working together requires some level of compromise from each party. Crum (1987) says, "Often in life we are so intent on doing the 'fair' thing that we never look at what we are really going for. We never see the possibility that there is enough for each to have everything that he or she needs" (p. 177). Thus, groups often seek solutions that require each person to compromise a little rather than believing and striving for the possibility of a truly win-win solution. The ensemble asserts that

> collaboration is not about "compromise" in the traditional sense of the word. Compromise has traditionally meant that you have to "give something up" for the greater good. We prefer to see true collaboration as requiring each participant to hear and consider the ideas, values, and perspectives of others with the ultimate aim of expanding or redefining individual beliefs and viewpoints. (HERI, 1996, p. 49)

MAKING COLLABORATION WORK

With a better understanding of what Collaboration is, the specific elements that lead to successful Collaborations can be explored. This section will cover four topics: building trust, broad-based involvement and group diversity, group purpose and goals, and the importance of process. Additional topics relevant to the collaborative process, including communication, facilitation of group processes, and Controversy With Civility, will be explored in subsequent chapters.

Building Trust

The ensemble identified trust as the essential ingredient for building and sustaining a collaborative effort (HERI, 1996). To cultivate the level of synergy, creativity, and innovation that is possible in the collaborative process, each group member must feel safe enough to put his or her own ideas forward, listen to others' ideas, and offer and receive thoughtful feedback from other group members. Trust is the path to open communication (Parker, 2008). In the absence of trust, fear of judgment, failure, or "being wrong" may keep people from taking the risks necessary to fully engage with the collaborative process.

Trust does not happen immediately or automatically; it must be cultivated. When groups come together for the first time, people bring their own agendas, values, perceptions, motivations, and histories. Building trust and openness takes time and commitment.

In her book, *Daring Greatly: How the Courage to Be Vulnerable Transforms the Way We Live, Love, Parent, and Lead,* Brené Brown (2012), a researcher focusing on vulnerability, courage, worthiness, and shame, asserts that trust is a "slow-building layered process that happens over time" (p. 47). This process "requires work, vulnerability, attention and full engagement" (p. 53). Brown reminds us that although trust is essential to well-functioning organizations, the *process* of building trust can be scary, involving "uncertainty, risk, and emotional exposure" (p. 34). Discomfort is a usual, even necessary, part of the process.

Chrislip and Larson (1994) offer four suggestions to aid in the process of building and sustaining trust within a group: informal exploring, sharing ownership, celebrating success, and creating powerful, compelling experiences.

Informal Exploring

Informal exploring asks members of the group to put aside preset agendas at the beginning of a group process in order to engage in a process of exploration. This exploration involves getting to know each other's backgrounds, interests, concerns related to the project at hand, and priorities. Informal exploring is an important and necessary step in the collaboration process because it enables the "opportunity to discover common interests, similar ways of defining the problem, and shared aspirations for solutions, as well as the opportunity to get to know individuals as people, [and] is important enough that it must be deliberately built into the process for working together" (Chrislip & Larson, 1994, p. 92). In the exploration process, it is important to make sure that every voice is heard and that some voices do not become more dominant or take up more space than others.

Sharing Ownership

Sharing ownership involves each member of the group taking ownership for the leadership process. Struggles over control and ownership frequently undermine the trust of a group early in the collaboration process. Whether there is a pre-set positional leader or not, sharing ownership asks individual group members to take an active role and be fully engaged in the process. This requires individuals who hold formal leadership positions and those who tend to take on leadership in leaderless groups to use their power and influence with the group to empower the participants to direct the process. Chrislip and Larson (1994) assert that "the more participants take ownership of the process, the more sustainable the collaborative effort will be" (p. 93).

Celebrating Success

Celebrating success is a means of group renewal. Leadership is ultimately about change, which can often be a slow and tedious process. Celebrating small success along the way is necessary to sustain the group's energy in the collaboration effort.

Creating Powerful, Compelling Experiences

Creating powerful, compelling experiences can be a useful way to quickly build trust and establish respect among group members at the beginning of a group process. Examples of powerful, compelling experiences include (but are certainly not limited to) challenge courses, ropes courses, and outdoor challenge trips, as well as interesting classroom projects. Chrislip and Larson (1994) assert "a shared experience of this kind can transform a collection of individuals into a group and unify them around a set of values and a common purpose" (p. 96).

Although group processes and experiences can aid in in the trust-building process, ultimately each individual team member must take responsibility to cultivate openness and trust. Parker (2008) suggests that individual team members can cultivate trust by doing the following:

- Being dependable and trustworthy—someone on whom the team can rely to deliver on commitments, tell the truth, and admit mistakes

- Pitching in and helping other team members who need assistance
- Reading and responding to nonverbal cues that suggest a lack of openness
- Candidly sharing views and encouraging others to do the same (pp. 48–49)

Although trust can take time to build, Kouzes and Posner (2012) suggest that each group member has the power to aid in the trust-building process by being the first to risk opening up, showing vulnerability, and trusting that your teammates will be worthy of the trust you have placed in them. Although this is a scary proposition, "the payoff is huge. Trust is contagious. When you trust others, they are much more likely to trust you" (Kouzes & Posner, 2012, p. 222).

Broad-Based Involvement and Group Diversity

Successful collaboration requires broad-based involvement from members of the group and, if appropriate, relevant stakeholders outside of the group (Chrislip & Larson, 1994; HERI, 1996; Straus, 2002). In today's increasingly diverse society, it is important to consider the role and impact of diversity in the collaborative process. Diversity is the norm in today's workforce, and the ability to collaborate in multicultural environments has been cited by industry leaders as one of the most important competencies for young people entering the workforce in the next 10 years (Van Velsor & Wright, 2015).

> Diversity is an essential part of the collaborative process; it "multiplies group effectiveness because it capitalizes on the multiple talents and perspectives of each group member and the power of that diversity to generate creative solutions" (HERI, 1996, p. 48).

Diverse groups can be more productive, make higher quality and more creative decisions, are better at adapting to changing conditions, and are less prone to groupthink than are groups with homogenous membership (Johnson & Johnson, 2009). As Follett (2003) observed, "Unity, not uniformity, must be our aim. We attain unity only through variety. Differences must be integrated, not annihilated, nor absorbed" (p. 279).

Understanding the role of diversity in the collaborative process requires some exploration of what diversity is. Diversity encompasses complex and intersecting dimensions of identity, including race, ethnicity, national origin, citizenship status, gender, sexual orientation, socioeconomics, age, ability, and religion. Each individual has multiple dimensions of identity that intersect with one another and must be understood in relation to one another and to the environment of the individual (Abes & Jones, 2013; Jones & McEwen, 2000). In addition to one's identities, each individual also brings values, personalities, opinions, attitudes, communication styles, working and learning styles, and strengths and weaknesses to the group process (Johnson & Johnson, 1994).

Diversity is the strength and the challenge of Collaboration. Diversity enables us to capitalize on the multiple perspectives and strengths of the various group members, empowering us to tackle problems with creativity and innovation (Johnson & Johnson, 1994). Although differences within groups are necessary and can lead to stronger outcomes, they can also provide challenges in a group process. Individuals with different values, perspectives, and working and learning styles may come to a group with different ideas of what is important and different notions of how groups should function, and value different styles of communication. These factors can lead to increased conflict and misunderstandings among group members and can create barriers to group effectiveness (Parker, 2008). These dimensions are discussed further in Chapters 7 and 8.

Broad-based involvement is not just about membership; it is about making space for all voices to be heard. Diversity alone does not guarantee a group process that is truly inclusive of diverse ideas and perspectives. "Whether diversity leads to positive or negative outcomes in a group largely depends on the group members' abilities and their willingness to understand and appreciate the diversity that exists in the group" (Johnson & Johnson, 2009, p. 442). Inclusion of diverse voices is only effective if every voice has influence over the process. Throughout U.S. history and social structures, people with certain identities have become accustomed to having more influence than others. Just as an individual's background, perspectives, socialization, and assumptions influence the way he or she communicates his or her messages, these factors will also influence one's ability to hear and understand the messages that others convey, and may result in some voices being privileged and their perspectives having more influence in the process than others.

To make the most of a diverse organization, it is important that every member's point of view is sought out and treated as a valid perspective. It is ongoing work within a group to create a culture in which everyone knows his or her ideas and contributions are equally valued, and each individual makes the effort to ensure that every other voice is heard. If people feel their perspective has been ignored or their values slighted, or if one witnesses another group member's voice being silenced, it is important to be able to bring the issue to the surface and for others in the group to truly listen and engage. These can be uncomfortable conversations, the kind many people prefer to avoid. This discomfort is normal and important in the learning process. The goal is not to avoid difficult conversations but to normalize the discomfort (Brown, 2012). Critical thinking, growth, learning, and change can all be very uncomfortable. Leaning into the discomfort can enable critically important, and sometimes transformative, conversations to take place recognizing it as an essential opportunity for group development.

Group Purpose and Goals

An effective Collaboration requires consensus and clarity among the group of what the group is working toward (Chrislip & Larson, 1994; Parker, 2008). Kouzes and Posner (2012) assert that "the most important ingredient in every collective achievement is a common goal" (p. 230). In a classic study of teams in 30 different companies, Katzenbach and Smith (1993) found that the most effective teams "invest a tremendous amount of time and effort exploring, shaping, and agreeing on a purpose that belongs to them both collectively and individually" (p. 50). Whether the group's purpose is articulated in a mission or vision statement or just a list of goals and objectives, knowing why the group is coming together is an essential first step in the Collaborative process. The importance and process of developing Common Purpose will be explored fully in Chapter 7.

The Sustainable Student Action (SSA) club is an organization at Seattle University that works to increase and improve sustainable practices while empowering students to be advocates for environmental justice, such as driving the university to divest from fossil fuels. Their efforts include educational and advocacy-based events, meetings with administration, rallies to increase visibility, and partnering with community-based organizations. They've worked tirelessly for the last four years to keep this an important dialogue on campus, raising awareness and working through obstacles.

—Bernard (Bernie) Liang is the director of the Center for Student Involvement at Seattle University. In this role, he oversees student advocacy, involvement, tradition, and engagement.

The Importance of Process

Process is critically important in a collaborative effort. How a group proceeds—meaning the process it uses—will affect the outcomes of the project. Although groups should develop agreed-on norms and ground rules early in the process (Chrislip & Larson, 1994), Parker (2008) suggests keeping group meetings as informal, comfortable, and relaxed as possible. On a well-functioning team, people enjoy being around one another, so conversation flows openly. Time spent getting to know one another and building relationships between group members will lead to stronger team efforts.

Communication is, of course, extremely important in the collaborative process. In fact, Straus (2002) asserted that "the single most important factor distinguishing effective teams from ineffective ones is the ability of team members to listen to each other. It is a skill that serves as an underpinning for all the other determinants of effectiveness" (p. 32). Communication in the group process will be explored in depth in Chapter 7.

Also related to engagement and trust, group processes must be (and be perceived as) credible and open. In a process in which information is shared openly and efforts are made to seek out the perspectives of each team member, participants are more willing to fully engage because they believe they have a meaningful voice and role. To aid in the process, it helps to designate a facilitator who will lead the group process but is not in a position of authority over the group (Straus, 2002). The facilitator does not direct the group or dominate discussions but rather works to ensure that all voices are heard and that group norms are followed. Also, keeping a visual representation of the collaboration process, such as a process map or a flowchart, can help group members understand what has already been accomplished and where the group is headed (Straus, 2002).

Finally, important decisions should be made by consensus (Parker, 2008; Straus, 2002). Consensus calls on Follett's concept of integration previously discussed in this chapter. It is important that the group not arrive prematurely at a decision before a range of alternative outcomes have been explored and discussed (Halverson, 2003). Through active sharing, listening, and dialogue, group members can attempt to develop a solution that integrates the various values and priorities of the group. For a consensus to be reached, each group member must agree that he or she is willing to work toward the decision that has been reached. Hearing the depth of others' views helps an individual group member move toward those views and let go of his or her initial position that he or she now sees is not as useful as the ideas of others.

CONNECTION TO THE OTHER Cs

Collaboration is a core value in the SCM and positively influences people's capacity to do the other Cs. It is intricately tied to the other two group values, Common Purpose and Controversy With Civility, and many of the themes integral to the Collaborative process will be further explored in the next two chapters. It is through learning to Collaborate in the process of group development that purposes that are truly shared in common can come to light. It is the Commitment to having a Collaborative process that gives groups the resolve to embrace Controversy With Civility.

The ensemble noted that "when individuals work together to build collaborative relationships, everyone involved is affected or changed by the process" (HERI, 1996, p. 49). Thus, throughout the Collaborative process, individuals' Consciousness of Self, Commitment, and Congruence are likely to deepen and develop. Finally, the ability to work Collaboratively within the diverse communities one is a member of positively influences a person's ability to do Citizenship.

Just as experiences with Collaboration build capacity to do the other Cs, experiences with the other Cs positively affect a person's ability to Collaborate. This is described in more detail in other chapters.

CONCLUSION

The Social Change Model of Leadership Development is a model of collaborative leadership. Individuals must develop their individual capacities of working authentically and effectively with others toward shared purposes. Students looking to develop their skills in Collaboration should consider getting involved in community service, student clubs and organizations, internship programs, peer mentoring or mentoring by student affairs professionals, or short-term leadership programs; all of these programs have been shown to positively influence students' capacity to effectively Collaborate (Dugan & Komives, 2007, 2010). After experiencing an SCM course including a project engaging in the local community, one San Diego State University student observed, "I've learned that leadership is really more about 'us' than it is about 'me,'" illustrating that students understand that leadership is more about a dynamic interpersonal relationships than it is about a position or the individual (Robertson & Lubic, 2001, p. 98). Approaching others in a group to seek true understanding of their perspectives, and reciprocally expecting that they will seek to understand one's own perspectives, is key to working collaboratively. Further, understanding that groups need to develop their capacity to engage with each other in effective, intentional relational processes guides the group to work on its leadership dynamics.

 DISCUSSION QUESTIONS

1. Why is Collaboration so important to the leadership process?
2. What are your personal opinions about competition, cooperation, and compromise? Were the ideas presented in this chapter in line with your opinions, or did they differ somewhat?
3. How can you tell if a group is functioning Collaboratively versus cooperatively? What are the distinguishing factors between the two? Is it possible to move a group from a cooperative effort to a Collaborative effort? What would that process look like?
4. How can diversity among group members contribute to Collaboration? How can diversity make Collaboration challenging? What can leaders do to maximize the benefits of group diversity?

 ACTION AND REFLECTION

1. Reflect on your experiences interacting in multicultural groups. How do your identities, values, and perspectives influence the way you interact with others from different backgrounds? Have you ever felt your voice or perspective was marginalized? Have you ever gotten the sense that someone else in the group didn't feel comfortable sharing?
2. Try to think of an instance when a different perspective helped shed light on a challenging situation. What were the conditions that made that contribution possible? What was the environment like? What are some things that you can

personally do in a group setting that would enable each group member to bring his or her full self (talents, perspectives, and identities) to the conversation?
3. Think of a group that you are a part of. What are some things that you can personally do to help establish and maintain trust within the group?
4. Use the rubric in Table 6.1 to gauge your own development with Collaboration. Reflect on how you can further develop this aspect of your leadership capacity.

REFERENCES

Abes, E., & Jones, S. R. (2013). *Identity development of college students.* San Francisco, CA: Jossey-Bass.

Black Lives Matter. (2016, January 16). About the Black Lives Matter Network. Retrieved from http://blacklivesmatter.com/about/

Brown, B. (2012). *Daring greatly: How the courage to be vulnerable transforms the way we live, love, parent, and lead.* New York, NY: Avery.

Chrislip, D. D., & Larson, C. E. (1994). *Collaborative leadership.* San Francisco, CA: Jossey-Bass.

Covey, S. R. (2004). *The seven habits of highly effective people: Powerful lessons in personal change.* New York, NY: Free Press.

Crum, T. F. (1987). *The magic of conflict: Turning a life of work into a work of art.* New York, NY: Touchstone.

Dugan, J. P., & Komives, S. R. (2007). *Developing leadership capacity in college students: Findings from a national study.* A report from the Multi-Institutional Study of Leadership. College Park, MD: National Clearinghouse for Leadership Programs.

Dugan, J. P., & Komives, S. R. (2010). Influences on college students' capacity for socially responsible leadership. *Journal of College Student Development, 5,* 525–549.

Follett, M. P. (1995). Constructive conflict. In P. Graham (Ed.). *Mary Parker Follett—prophet of management: A celebration of writings from the 1920s* (pp. 67–95). Boston, MA: Harvard Business School Press.

Follett, M. P. (2003). The new state. In J. C. Tonn (Ed.), *Mary P. Follett: Creating democracy, transforming management* (pp. 265–303). New Haven, CT: Yale University Press.

Halverson, C. B. (2003). Group processes and meetings. In C. B. Halverson & S. I. Tirmizi (Eds.), *Effective multicultural teams: Theory and practice* (pp. 111–134). Dordrecht, Netherlands: Springer Science & Business Media B. V.

TABLE 6.1 Collaboration Rubric

	Excelling	Achieving	Developing	Needing Improvement
Cultivating Meaningful Relationships	Relates extremely well to others Has an outstanding awareness of self and how others perceive him or her Works best in a group environment Has a strong awareness that the group can accomplish more than the individual Fully trusts and relies on group members to succeed	Connects interpersonally with others Understands self and how he or she appears to others Works well in a group and has begun to see that the group can accomplish more than the individual Trusts other group members to accomplish the team's mission	Beginning to understand how he or she relates to others Demonstrates an awareness of the benefits of working together in a group setting Beginning to trust and rely on teammates to accomplish goals	Unaware of how he or she is perceived by others Needs improvement when working in a group setting Lacks an understanding that the group is more productive than the individual Feels that the individual can accomplish more than the group Indifferent or resistant to trusting other group members
Encouraging Group Involvement	Always asks for and depends on the input of group members Demonstrates a comprehensive understanding of group members' strengths and empowers group members to best use these strengths Effectively processes group ideas with the help and feedback of teammates	Asks for teammates' ideas and opinions Aware of group member strengths and actively draws on them to help better the team dynamic Empowers teammates to take responsibility regularly	Experiments with asking the group for feedback and contributions Beginning to understand how to best empower group members Aware of group strengths but has not yet capitalized on them	Lacks awareness of group member strengths Rarely asks for feedback or input from team members Fails to empower group members to take on group responsibility
Facilitating a Positive Group Environment	Actively works to create a positive experience for members by including various individuals' thoughts and opinions Always goes out of the way to talk to individuals, and group members are always cared for Maintains a positive attitude despite the current circumstances	Works to create a positive group experience for all members Always shows up with a positive attitude Actively tries to include all members of the group	Active attempts are made to include group members, but some members are missed or not included in conversations Positive attitudes are displayed, but often when there are group troubles, negative or destructive attitudes are apparent	No attempt is made to include group members Often attends group meetings with negative attitudes and is disruptive to the group dynamics Overall group attitude when member is around is hostile
Establishing Trust and Accountability	Can be trusted by group members to complete tasks and uphold commitments without fail Always completes projects or notifies members immediately when problems exist to solicit assistance when needed	Completes all tasks as assigned to uphold group commitments Understands group needs May not always solicit help when needed but will consistently get the task or project completed regardless	Can be trusted to complete basic tasks and contribute to the group as needed Often does not ask for assistance when the task or project becomes unmanageable Needs assistance to complete more-complex tasks or long-term projects	Unable to complete tasks as needed Group unable to trust that projects will be completed with quality Does not ask for help when needed and fails to communicate abilities and needs to other group members

Source: Developed by Patrick Grayshaw and Chelsea Truesdell.

Higher Education Research Institute (HERI). (1996). *A social change model of leadership development* (Version III). Los Angeles: University of California, Los Angeles, Higher Education Research Institute.

Johnson, D. W., & Johnson, F. P. (1994). *Joining together: Group theory and group skills* (5th ed.). Boston, MA: Allyn & Bacon.

Johnson, D. W., & Johnson, F. P. (2009). *Joining together: Group theory and skills* (10th ed.). Boston, MA: Allyn & Bacon.

Johnson, D. W., Maruyama, G., Johnson, R., Nelson, D., & Skon, L. (1981). Effects of cooperative, competitive and individualistic goal structures on achievement: A meta-analysis. *Psychological Bulletin, 89*, 47–62.

Jones, S. R., & McEwen, M. K. (2000). A conceptual model of multiple dimensions of identity. *Journal of College Student Development, 41*, 405–414.

Katzenbach, J. R., & Smith, D. K. (1993). *The wisdom of teams: Creating the high performance organization*. Boston, MA: Harvard Business School Press.

Kohn, A. (1992). *No contest: The case against competition* (2nd ed.). Boston, MA: Houghton Mifflin.

Komives, S. R., Lucas, N., & McMahon, T. R. (2013). *Exploring leadership: For college students who what to make a difference* (3rd ed.). San Francisco, CA: Jossey-Bass.

Kouzes, J. M., & Posner, B. Z. (2012). *The leadership challenge: How to make extraordinary things happen in organizations* (5th ed.). San Francisco, CA: Jossey-Bass.

Parker, G. M. (2008). *Team players and teamwork: New strategies for developing successful collaboration* (2nd ed.). San Francisco, CA: Jossey Bass.

Robertson, D. C., & Lubic, B. J. (2001). Spheres of confluence: Non-hierarchical leadership in action. In C. L. Outcalt, S. K. Faris, & K. N. McMahon (Eds.), *Developing non-hierarchical leadership on campus: Case studies and best practices in higher education* (pp. 90–98). Westport, CT: Greenwood.

Straus, D. (2002). *How to make collaborations work: Powerful ways to build consensus, solve problems, and make decisions*. San Francisco, CA: Berrett-Koehler.

Tometi, O., Garza, A., & Cullors-Brignac, P. (2015, January 18). Celebrating MLK Day: Reclaiming our movement legacy. *Huffington Post*. Retrieved from http://www.huffingtonpost.com/opal-tometi/reclaiming-our-movement-l_b_6498400.html

Van Velsor, E., & Wright, J. (2015). *Expanding the leadership equation: Developing next-generation leaders* [White paper]. Retrieved September 5, 2015, from http://insights.ccl.org/wp-content/uploads/2015/04/ExpandingLeadershipEquation.pdf

7

Common Purpose

Marybeth Drechsler Sharp and Alex Teh

> A single arrow is easily broken, but not ten in a bundle.
> —JAPANESE PROVERB

College students are often part of many groups—student organizations, sports teams, jobs in offices, or project groups in classes. Melanie Sava was an undergraduate student studying political science at Mount Saint Mary's University, Los Angeles, where she participated in the student government association, the leadership scholar program, and the commuter mentor program, and competed on the MSMU moot court and mock trial teams. Melanie wrote:

> Once I founded the Oxfam America Club and had recruited members to join the club, we all immediately realized the importance of developing a shared vision. While we were all passionate and determined to achieve success as a group, we all had different ideas of what that success would look like. It was only once we discussed those ideas and synthesized them that we were able to begin determining our shared goal and, through this, the goal of our new club as a whole.

As Melanie's quote illustrates, what it means to be a group emerges from the things that link group members to one another. Although possessing mutual interests and passions brought people together for the Oxfam America Club, identifying a clear and shared purpose unified and drove the group forward. Doing so required conversation, navigating different perspectives, and finding the path that worked for the whole.

The C for Common Purpose involves individuals working in groups with others to achieve shared visions. For example, project groups in classes are designed to foster learning about a certain topic. Similarly, many student organizations form to create a community for students with similar views or interests. To be successful, groups should be able to ask and answer questions that get at the heart of their shared purposes: why are we here, and what are we doing?

Think about specific groups you belong to as you examine the concepts in this chapter. Consider why those groups exist and what they hope to accomplish. Having a common purpose is a central component of groups—particularly those we discuss in relation to leadership and social change—that form, survive, and thrive.

The ensemble (Higher Education Research Institute [HERI], 1996) wrote:

> Common Purpose means to work with others within a shared set of aims and values. Having these shared aims facilitates the group's ability to engage in collective analysis of the issues at hand and the task to be undertaken. Common Purpose is best achieved when all members of the group share in the vision and participate actively in articulating the purpose and goals of the group's work. (p. 55)

CHAPTER OVERVIEW

This chapter examines three key components of Common Purpose: its occurrence within groups; its presence in shared values, vision, and aims; and its central role when working in community with others. Each component is intertwined with the others—just as each of the Cs within the SCM works with and is influenced by the rest—the components of Common Purpose cannot be separated completely from each other. The interactions among these components must be kept in mind when exploring what it means to be a part of a group, what it means to share a vision and values, and how people work with others to establish and sustain a group's Common Purpose.

DEFINING GROUPS

When thinking about the definition of Common Purpose, it is imperative to know exactly what a *group* entails. This is particularly important, because a group can take on myriad specific names—*committee, council, team, club,* or any number of others—or, similar to a group of friends, not have a tangible name at all. In the context of leadership, though, groups are more than just people who are in the same place at the same time. From a leadership perspective, groups are considered to be "three or more people 'interacting and communicating interpersonally over time in order to reach a goal'" (Komives, Lucas, & McMahon, 2013, p. 311). In the broadest sense, within the context of the Social Change Model, a group's visionary goal translates into the notion of Common Purpose.

Teams are specific types of groups, and literature written about teams can provide a better understanding of groups in general. Johnson and Johnson (2013) identified a team not in terms of a number of people but instead as interpersonal interactions organized to achieve agreed-on goals. "The essence of a team is common commitment," explained Katzenbach and Smith (1993), and "this kind of commitment requires a purpose in which team members can believe" (para. 12). The best teams are small groups of people who spend significant time shaping a purpose that they collectively own and then translating that purpose into specific performance goals for which they are mutually accountable (Katzenbach & Smith, 1993).

There are some overlapping themes in these group definitions. First, groups contain more than just a single person. Each definition mentioned either specifies a minimum number of people or indicates interactions that must necessarily include more than one person. Second, all of the definitions assert that the group has a purpose or a goal that it strives to achieve. Finally, each of the three definitions indicates some sort of interaction, cooperation, or commitment among group members to achieve the group's goal (see Chapter 6 on Collaboration).

The three parts of this definition of a group may sound familiar, because Common Purpose is very closely aligned with the way in which groups are defined and identified. With a clearer idea of what is meant when talking about a group, the meaning of having a shared vision or goal can be examined.

UNDERSTANDING SHARED VALUES, VISION, AND AIMS

Common Purpose addresses several main ideas that inspire and direct groups. If they have a true sense of Common Purpose, groups should be able to answer the question, "How do we, as organization members, agree to treat ourselves and others as we pursue our mission and vision?" (Komives et al., 2013, p. 369). This inquiry challenges groups to identify collectively agreed-on core values and leads to further discussion about vision and aims.

Often these elements of Common Purpose—values, vision, and aims—will continue to motivate a group when it hits a rough spot. No matter what relational or external problems arise, a group with a well-articulated, meaningful, and relevant Common Purpose will always have something linking its members together. The values, visions, and aims that are central to any group comprise salient aspects of Common Purpose, and it is imperative to examine fully these constructs of a group and how they came to be.

Values

Common values are a critical, foundational element of Common Purpose. They encompass the underlying, intangible things in which a group believes and by which it is defined. "Values convey a sense of identity, from boardroom to factory floor, and help people feel special about what they do" (Bolman & Deal, 2013, p. 249).

Values may be implicit or explicit, but groups with strong core values will manifest them through the ways members interact, the stories they share, symbols they embrace, and approaches to reconciling conflicts (Bolman & Deal, 2013). Valuing innovation, openness, or high-quality programs unites the efforts of group members and also provides direction for their collective endeavors. Communicating values can help build group buy in, shape their Common Purpose, and enhance the performance outcomes the group achieves. Although values may be discussed infrequently among group members, they are infused in the culture of an organization, illuminate how members make decisions together, and address how the group aims will be pursued.

A member whose own values and reasons for belonging to a particular group do not fit with the group's values will likely not enjoy the group. For example, one group might place a high value on organization, efficiency, and respect for how busy members are with other commitments. A second group might value social relationships and being able to have a laugh along with getting work done. The two group meetings would operate quite differently. A member from the second group might interpret the first group's efficiency as cold and lacking in fun, unless members from the first group were able to articulate that this behavior is rooted in a desire to show respect for others. An important leadership skill is recognizing indicators of group values and facilitating explicit conversations about them.

Vision

Possessing a vision is another important aspect of Common Purpose. Bolman and Deal (2013) explained, "Vision turns an organization's core ideology, or sense of purpose, into an image of the future" (p. 250). Through vision, a group paints a picture of its aspirations and ideals.

A group's vision is distinct from its purpose, aims, or goals. In business organizations, for example, the shared goal is to create profit for owners and shareholders and to produce an excellent product for customers. The vision, however, points to the future direction the organization aspires to. Kotter (1995) points out that even with well-defined goals, the lack of a unifying vision is often the downfall of otherwise successful companies. "A vision says something that clarifies the direction in which an organization needs to move" (Kotter, 1995, p. 63). A vision should go beyond numbers and logistical information to provide a clear representation of the future that will inspire and motivate everyone associated with an organization.

A vision that exemplifies transformational leadership results in "engendering enduring enthusiasm for a cause" (Denning, 2007, p. 54). The international aid organization Stop Hunger Now articulates a compelling overarching vision, or a "why," for the work they do. The "vision of a world without hunger" drives the efforts of this organization, uniting people across the globe to collaborate and contribute in various ways to ending world hunger. From the sweeping, future-oriented vision of Stop Hunger Now their aims and specific approaches emerge. Thus, the group provides avenues for direct and indirect service to interested individuals, communities, and like-minded organizations.

Aims

The aims of certain groups can clarify the differences between them. For a professional sports team, the Common Purpose may be to compete well and win games. For another team in a developmental league, the Common Purpose may be to continually build skills and teamwork, a goal that can be met regardless of who wins each game. For yet another team in a social or recreational league, the Common Purpose might be to meet people and have a fun social time. A Common Purpose clarifies why the group exists and what it is trying to achieve. Having a Common Purpose gives group members a feeling of confidence that everyone is in agreement about where the group is headed. It provides clarity about the group's priorities and values and helps to generate a high level of trust among group members and with other members of the community.

Clear aims, vision, and a set of core values are central to understanding your group's purpose. The things your group is working toward can often serve as unifying factors during rough times. Common Purpose provides clarity when the group has too many projects and needs to make priorities and choices and serves as a tool for periodically refocusing efforts. Even so, the origin of a group's Common Purpose influences how it is pursued and achieved. The following section explores how Common Purpose can be developed and facilitated through individual or shared processes.

DISTINGUISHING BETWEEN PERSONALIZED AND SOCIALIZED PURPOSES

For a group's purpose truly to be a Common Purpose, it must belong to the group and be supported by individual members. Two differing approaches to establishing a group's aims are through personalized vision and socialized vision (Howell, 1988). Personalized vision is created when the person in charge comes up with a dream or a plan and then passes that vision on to those in the group. People are sometimes hired into positional roles in an organization because of their vision of what the organization can and should be doing. An inspired personalized vision certainly can serve to recruit people to join a worthwhile effort.

Envision an ambitious student with a genuine passion for creating a healthier campus environment and promoting wellness who decides to launch an organization that pursues her vision; the purpose and aims evolve according to her perspectives and interests. When her like-minded peers arrive at the first group meeting, this founding student provides a detailed plan that includes everything she thinks the group should tackle along with a semester-long schedule that describes exactly how and when related projects will occur over the coming months. Some individual students may react positively to the structure and guidance provided, but others may feel forced into the individually determined approaches and stop participating because they were unable able to influence or shape the vision and aims.

However, a socialized vision is constructed when group members contribute to setting the broader direction for the group. Members of the group then contribute collectively to establishing aims and purposes. This approach recognizes people's tendency to support and remain invested in what they have helped to create. This does not necessarily mean that each person's personal vision is incorporated into the group vision but rather that everyone is involved in developing the group vision (Komives et al., 2013). It may be that some parts of the group vision are very different from parts of your personal vision, but through the socialized vision process group members are allowed to set priorities and have a say in the parts of the group vision to which each of them is best suited to contribute.

VOLS 2 VOLS Peer Educators engages many student groups and campus facilities at the University of Tennessee (UT) to promote health and wellness. Our programs are requested by various organizations on campus, such as University Housing, Multicultural Student Life, Greek Life, UT's Women's Coordinating Council, and freshmen seminars. We also collaborate with many of these student groups as well as the OUTreach Center, UT's LGBT and Ally Resource Center. All of our campus organizations share the common goal of supporting students and positively influencing their well-being and success, and we educate organizations on topics such as communication skills, maintaining healthy relationships, and bystander intervention. By pooling resources and sharing ideas with other organizations on our campus, we are able to contribute to this larger goal.

—Summer Watson is a former student at the University of Tennessee, Knoxville, where she served as the president of the VOLS 2 VOLS peer education program and mentored first-year students in the Chancellor's honors program.

Revisiting the previous example of a health and wellness organization, consider the real-life student group story from the University of Tennessee. The VOLS 2 VOLS group devised a socialized vision of creating a healthier campus community, and, rather than working independently to promulgate their goals, members collaborate in their groups and partner across campus with others who share their vision.

The preceding group scenarios demonstrate differences between what occurs when a group begins with a personalized vision or a socialized vision. The origin of the vision influences the way a group devises goals and aims. Common Purpose reflects how important it is that the values, vision, and aims are embraced by all members of a group rather than solely by a positional leader. Although a personalized vision can sometimes draw people to a worthwhile effort, allowing the group to collaborate and develop shared values, vision, and aims creates greater levels of investment and commitment to a Common Purpose. Commitment to the shared vision means that members will fulfill their responsibilities to the group, share resources with the group, and support fellow group members because they expect others to do the same and are invested in the greater goals. This is the process of developing Common Purpose, which is central to the SCM (HERI, 1996).

WORKING TOGETHER TOWARD A COMMON PURPOSE

Groups must transparently practice intentional processes that lead to building Common Purpose. Just as individuals grow and change, so do groups and organizations. Oft-cited research by Tuckman (1965; Tuckman & Jenson, 1977) revealed that the journey groups take in this process of development has a predictable path. It can be useful for group members to have awareness of that path, because some points along the way can seem like everything is going wrong when actually they are an indicator that the group is experiencing important stages of growth. Just as individual development refers to how individuals can develop their leadership skills in group settings, group development is how groups grow their leadership capacity by attending to the processes the group engages in to advance and expand their capacity to function well as a group.

Stages in Group Development

Tuckman and Jenson (1977; Tuckman, 1965) studied the evolving nature of groups and observed that they go through predictable stages of what they call *forming, storming, norming, performing,* and *adjourning.*

Forming

The forming stage occurs early in a group development process, when individuals come together around their shared purposes. During this phase, individuals focus on determining how the group can address their interests and needs, figuring out what their roles will be in the group, and deciding how engaged they will be in the life of the group.

Storming

As the group evolves, members identify differences of opinion about what process they will use and what their real purposes are; their individual expectations may conflict. In the storming stage, members may challenge each other and pull away from each other, the process, or the purpose. Members may also recognize storming as a stage in the group's process and encourage everyone to return to the group's purposes and find ways to work through their controversies.

Norming

Working through storming is called *norming*. The group establishes what they will expect of each other, determines how they will work together, and solidifies the culture of the group so all members know what to expect and how they can contribute.

Performing

As the group members settle into working together to accomplish their purposes, they begin truly performing and maintaining group processes. The group recognizes the need to bring in new members and incorporate them into the ongoing goals of the group.

Adjourning

At some point many groups end and disband—a class is over or a service project ends—which represents an adjourning of the group process. Often the structure of the group may continue (for example, a staff or student organization has a large turnover), but the group has to start over in this cycle and form again.

In order to work together effectively toward a Common Purpose, groups will navigate the aforementioned stages. In addition to how a group handles its leadership needs, how groups transmit their culture and values, sustain Common Purpose, communicate, and make decisions are central to their collective action.

Transmitting Group Culture

Groups develop around shared interests and goals of members, but they solidify as the shared purpose, culture, and norms are transmitted to present and future members. The means by which a group communicates its core values—and ultimately its Common Purpose—are essential to the leadership process. In order to make values, vision, and aims explicit to members, groups use myths, stories, and symbols that reinforce culture and Common Purpose.

Groups may employ legendary stories and symbols to reinforce group norms, values, and purposes. Symbols are essential ingredients of organizational culture. Manifested as a group's images, myths, heroes, and rituals, symbols convey values and meaning (Bolman & Deal, 2013). Logos can be displayed to demonstrate loyalty, an organizational hero may prompt a strong worth ethic, myths can evoke renewed motivation, and rituals may bond group members through communal experience. When used with intention, symbols are unifying for groups of people working toward Common Purpose.

Similarly, storytelling can be a powerful tool for reinforcing shared goals. Through stories, group members learn about their organizational history, guideposts, and legends. Groups may use storytelling to bring members together around shared values. According to Bolman and Deal (2013), stories "establish and perpetuate tradition" as well as instill confidence and build support within a group (p. 261). Akin to telling tales, groups may rely on metaphors and archetypes to create familiar feelings and cultivate understanding of complex ideas.

Symbols and stories are a few ways that groups communicate a shared sense of values and identity to cultivate new members and to keep existing group members on track. The Delta Delta Delta Fraternity, known also as Tri Delta, articulates that its purpose is establishing lasting friendships among members and promoting strong character; the legendary stories of the organization's founders reinforce that. Boston University seniors Sarah Ida Shaw and Eleanor Dorcas Pond created Tri Delta because they wanted a group of women friends focused more on character than appearance (Delta Delta Delta, 2016). More than 125 years later, the stories and rituals continue to guide Common Purpose and programs for Tri Delta members. For example, a present-day initiative of the group includes promoting healthy body image in college women using experienced alumni members.

In developing Common Purpose, some groups find it useful to schedule a retreat to create a formal mission statement or statement of core values. The climate in other types of groups may not lend itself to such a formal process, but this does not mean they should give up on having a conversation about the group's common purpose. The use of relevant icebreakers can kick off a conversation about why the group exists. Creating metaphors can be particularly meaningful. For example, imagine asking a group's members, "If this group were a consumer product, what would it be?" A response such as "a cassette tape player" might indicate feelings that the group's purpose has lost its relevance whereas a response such as "an artist's camera, because it captures the true reality of what is happening on campus and brings it to people's awareness," conveys quite a different message. Sometimes conversations about marketing and publicity can be common purpose discussions in disguise. Members are motivated to make decisions about what they want others to know about the group and what its purposes are. Carefully facilitated, decisions about what slogan to put on the group's T-shirt can start a meaningful dialogue about what the shirts will convey about the group's purpose and values.

Sustaining Common Purpose

To engender continual enthusiasm for a common purpose, four aspects of an activity's purpose must be evident to participants (Denning, 2007). First, participants should perceive the activity as intrinsically rewarding. According to Denning, "participants can see themselves making progress toward something that is good for its own sake, not primarily because it will lead to something else" (p. 57). Second, the challenge of an activity should be appropriate for the ability level of participants. Throughout an activity, participants must feel they are personally growing and receiving appropriate feedback about their performance. Third, participants will remain enthusiastic about the activity if they "see themselves as contributing to, raising the sights of, and enhancing the efforts of other people pursuing the same activity" (p. 58). Finally, participants should receive some positive external benefits for their engagement.

The kind of interaction necessary to develop Common Purpose in a group can be a vehicle for improving how members work together. Engaging in dialogue about individual experiences, balancing multiple perspectives, and making tough choices can be learning experiences for group members. Strong leaders facilitate this group development by encouraging members to reflect on how they collectively and collaboratively work. The group can emerge from creating Common Purpose better equipped to handle the future challenges. Establishing a group's common purpose enables a group to learn about itself, and ensuring the process is a constructive experience is a shared responsibility of group members.

Along with partners in a community organization, Robertson and Lubic (2001) co-taught an SCM-based course at San Diego State University dedicated to interventions in smoking and underage drinking. At the end of the semester, Janet, one of the college students in the course observed,

> We did not maximize what we learned from the class. There were times when some of the Seven Cs were used, but they were not reinforced as much as they should have been. One disappointment was when we did not follow one of the most important concepts as a group—Common Purpose. Although we had brainstormed ideas during our first meeting, our decision of the solution was not made together.

As a result, Robertson and Lubic reflected, "Learning, then, occurs by way of success and failure, but most importantly, it is negotiated through experience" (p. 97).

A dilemma that poses a problem for some groups is a regularly revolving membership. This can occur in voluntary organizations and community associations and poses a challenge for keeping the vision and common purpose alive and meaningful as old members leave and new members join. This dilemma is likely prevalent among college student organizations. Given that college students usually leave their institutions after some amount of time, many groups and organizations on campus exist well before and after any one group of students is a part of them. It is likely that these groups have preexisting purposes and at some point underwent the process of developing a common purpose. Student leaders should ask themselves how the purpose of each group they belong to applies to them and how they, as group members, can influence and maintain a group's vision. Intentional activities that ask new members why they want to join this group, acquaint new members with the current vision, and create time to discuss any discrepancies will let new members know their views matter to the future of the group and keep the group renewed and vibrant with these new ideas (Komives et al., 2013).

Effectively Communicating

Engaging in successful and sustainable group work toward a Common Purpose is very difficult without open communication among group members. Effective communication within a diverse group can make the difference between a frustrating, stagnating process and a synergistic, dynamic process. There is a strong relationship between communication and the group values of socially responsible leadership. When differences arise that block the flow of ideas, effective communication can help move groups through dissimilarities in such a way that builds trust and takes members toward creation of a shared vision and purpose and synergistic solutions. Personal communication and group communication skills are key to enacting leadership for social change and practicing socially responsible leadership. Four aspects of effective communication come into play when individuals engage as a group to build and sustain Common Purpose: common language, listening, conveying a message, and reflective and meaningful dialogue.

Common Language

Often groups do not develop and communicate in a common language. Even within families, members rarely have the same internal representation of various words. For example, to one person the word *run* translates to jogging and fun, for another person the word invokes images of shin splints and discomfort, and yet someone else perceives elections and politicians (Crum, 1987). For members of a group to communicate effectively with each other, they must ensure that the words, phrases, and gestures they are using carry the same meaning from sender to receiver. If they do not, group members risk coming to a perceived agreement on an idea when in fact individuals are each thinking of slightly different concepts.

Listening

In a diverse group, differences of opinion, vision, and meanings of words will inevitably arise. The Prayer of St. Francis recommends that when differences arise, it is best first to understand, then to be understood. A good place to start in developing one's personal communication skills is listening. Hearing and listening are two distinct processes. Hearing is the "physiological process, involving the vibration of sound waves on our eardrums and the firing of electrochemical impulses from the inner ear to the central auditory system of the brain" (Lucas, 2004, p. 56), whereas listening is our attempt to pay close attention to and really understand and make sense of what we hear. Most people only grasp about 50% of what they hear, even when they believe they are listening attentively (Lucas, 2004).

Numerous things contribute to poor listening. First, many people do not fully concentrate on the person who is speaking and his or her message, allowing their thoughts to wander instead of remaining focused on the conversation at hand (Lucas, 2004). Other people listen too hard, trying to remember every word that is being said and, in the process, lose track of the main message that the other person is trying to communicate. Other times, people jump to conclusions, thinking that they know what people are about to say and either finish their sentence for them or tune out their actual message. In either case, a preconceived notion of what people are about to say prohibits people from being able to truly understand what they are trying to communicate. Finally, it is easy to become distracted by the delivery of the message or the person delivering it, and in the process tune out the actual message (Lucas, 2004).

Much of the listening done in life is passive—half-listening to someone while being engaged in other activity: listening to music while doing homework, listening to a professor while checking social media, or having a conversation with a friend while cooking dinner. In each of these instances, only part of the individual's attention is focused on listening. Because listening is essential to understanding, which is in turn essential to the process of building trust, it is useful to spend some time thinking about how to improve one's listening skills.

People become better listeners by improving skills in active listening (Lucas, 2004). Active listening involves focusing one's undivided attention on the person speaking and putting forth a genuine effort to understand the content and feelings that he or she is trying to communicate. Effective active listening requires that individuals listen for the content and the emotion of a message, occasionally paraphrase the speaker's message and feelings back to him or her to be sure the message is being accurately understood, listen without interrupting or assuming what the person is about to say, probe for further information, and refrain from forming a response while the other person is still speaking. Active listening is especially important in diverse groups because it can help us to better understand individuals with communication styles different from our own.

Conveying a Message

In addition to developing skills in active listening, it is also important to learn how to clearly convey a message in a way that the listener can hear it. The language and tone that one uses to communicate a message will have a large impact on the listener's ability to hear the message. Rosenberg (1999) identified communication traits that can block the listener's ability or willingness to hear the message, including making statements that contain moralistic judgments about people or ideas and that deny personal responsibility. To clearly convey a message in a way that others will be able to hear it, Rosenberg recommends people communicate using observations rather than evaluations. An example of an observation would be, "David has missed the last three meetings," where the evaluation might be, "David isn't committed to this group." Second, individuals should learn how to name and express feelings to connect more easily with one another. Finally, people must learn how to make clear and specific requests about what they need from one another rather than demands that may back people into corners. In order for individuals to feel that they have ownership and shared power in a group, it is important for them to be able to enter into or decline a request freely.

Reflective and Meaningful Dialogue

Listening and clearly conveying a message are extremely important elements of successful communication. However, successfully collaborating in diverse groups requires a step further. In addition to talking and listening, group members need to develop their abilities to engage in reflective and meaningful dialogues to bring out deeper meanings and create shared understandings within groups. Juanita Brown, David Isaacs, and the World Café Community (2005) have developed a process of reflective communication aimed at achieving a deeper and more accurate understanding among group members. They offer suggestions for engaging in authentic conversations that help develop trust and harness the power of the group's collective intelligence. These suggestions include creating a climate of discovery in which new ideas are encouraged and explored, being careful to listen fully and suspend premature judgment, taking the time to explore underlying beliefs and assumptions held by individual members and the group as a whole, encouraging and creating space for a wide range of perspectives, and taking the time to reflect on and articulate shared understandings that the group comes to throughout the conversation process.

Decision Making in the Face of Challenges

Whether a group adheres to a personalized vision or creates its own socialized vision, it will at some point need to resolve exactly what that vision will be. There are several ways in which groups make decisions, in large part based on the types of challenges and decisions they face. Some groups put everything to a vote, allowing the majority to rule the process. Others seek to build consensus, and still others place a great deal of faith in their positional leaders to make decisions for the group. Many groups grapple with adaptive challenges that will steer them toward new paths for pursuing Common Purpose.

In most cases, whether or not a group has a formal, positional leader, it is important to recognize that more and more group members expect to be involved in group decision making (Komives et al., 2013). It is always advisable to engage in some amount of meaningful dialogue and listening within groups. Johnson and Johnson (2013) describe seven ways in which groups typically make decisions:

1. Decision by authority without discussion: a single positional leader makes a final decision without consulting group members.
2. Decision by authority after discussion: the positional leader consults group members for their perspectives and ideas but ultimately makes the final decision.
3. Expert member: the final decision is made by the group member who has the most knowledge or experience related to the issue or problem.
4. Average member's opinions: the decision is based on what is presumed to be the opinion of the most typical member.
5. Majority control: the decision is based on the opinion held by the majority of the group's members.
6. Minority control: the decision is made by a few key members often when the group is dealing with time pressures.
7. Consensus: group members continue to discuss and persuade each other until everyone agrees (or those who do not agree are willing to commit to the decision).

Each of these methods is valid in certain contexts, depending, for example, on the type of decision and the amount of time available to make it. Komives et al. (2013) suggest that for a decision as important as the group's purpose and shared values, groups should use consensus when possible.

During my freshman year at Bowling Green State University, my scholarship cohort was given the task to implement a fund-raiser. The only rules were (1) every decision had to be made only using consensus and (2) the fund-raiser had to be meaningful. With 25 people, it was hard to decide on one project. However, when we heard that one of our cohort members' family members was killed, we all knew that assisting with medical bills would be the focus of our project. For two months we put on smaller fund-raisers so that we could buy supplies for our bigger fund-raiser. After about six bake sales and ribbon sales, we worked with the local community to put on a carnival to raise funds to help pay the medical bills for her family. I learned that the power of common purpose can unite even the largest groups.

—Rayia Gaddy was a student at Bowling Green State University, where she was a President's Leadership Academy Thompson Scholar, Chi Alpha Epsilon Scholar, and vice president of leadership for Alpha Phi Omega Service Fraternity.

A consensus does not necessarily imply that everyone is satisfied with the decision or that even most group members believe that the best decision has been reached. A consensus is present, though, when all team members have had the opportunity to voice their concerns and are comfortable enough with the decision to support its implementation (Rayner, 1996). Make no mistake: consensus is not always an easy thing to achieve. Groups must have a decent amount of time and be skilled at active listening, compromising, handling controversy, and collaborative discussion in order to move toward consensus (Komives et al., 2013).

Four guidelines for reaching consensus within a group:

1. Clearly define the issue facing the team.
2. Focus on similarities between positions.
3. Ensure that there is adequate time for discussion.
4. Avoid conflict-reducing tendencies (e.g., taking a vote) (Rayner, 1996, p. 76)

Making decisions when times become difficult presents challenges to groups oriented toward a Common Purpose. As their contexts change, groups must continually retool and adapt the approaches to achieving a vision and goals. "The most effective leadership anchors change in the values, competencies, and strategic orientations that should endure in the organization" (Heifetz, Linsky, & Grashow, 2013, p. 25).

CONNECTION TO THE OTHER Cs

The Common Purpose element is central to the Social Change Model's approach to leadership and leadership development. In many ways, it is the common thread that links the three sets of values: individual, group, and society/community (HERI, 1996). Common Purpose is identified as a group value, but for it to be authentic to group members, each individual must connect on some level with the goals of the group.

The ensemble argues that Common Purpose is "predicated on the three individual values" of Consciousness of Self, Congruence, and Commitment (HERI, 1996, p. 57). Working toward a group's Common Purpose will give group members insight into themselves, make them more self-aware, and challenge them to be congruent. A clear sense of Common Purpose can also help renew people's energy for their commitments.

Of course, Common Purpose is closely linked to the other group values: Collaboration and Controversy With Civility. It may make sense to argue that a group must be collaborative in order to develop a shared vision or purpose, but the connection between these two elements works both ways. Although Collaboration certainly aids in developing Common Purpose, a well-developed Common Purpose can provide the basis for collaborative work within the group. Very much along those lines, the differences that are bound to exist among group members demand an ability to have Controversy With Civility within the group while its purpose is being developed, but Common Purpose again serves as a stabilizer and unifying force that makes Controversy With Civility possible.

CONCLUSION

The SCM revolves around the idea that leadership is a collaborative, values-based process. Common Purpose is one of three values essential to leadership at the group level. A group's ability to develop and sustain a Common Purpose is based on its intentional collaborative processes that connect individual members together to shape the group's goals and future. A group may need to be mindful to intentionally shape the group's development to become a thriving environment.

DISCUSSION QUESTIONS

1. Some ensemble members have described Common Purpose as the most challenging value in the Social Change Model. Do you agree? Why or why not?
2. A student once observed that a group would never come to agree on a Common Purpose if it could not work collaboratively. Do you think this is true? Why or why not?
3. Imagine you are part of a group and cannot tell what its mission or vision is. What evidence or indicators might give you a clue? What questions would you ask to find out?
4. What kinds of matters should you seek consensus on in groups and teams? How does one facilitate a consensus-oriented discussion about purpose and shared values?

ACTION AND REFLECTION

1. Think about a student organization or other student-based group that you are a part of. Where did its shared vision come from? In what ways did you connect or not connect with it? If you had the chance, how would you suggest altering that group's vision? How can new members learn about the group's vision and be involved in shaping the group's future? How often is the shared vision revisited? Who is part of that process?
2. Think about a group you are part of. Does it have a Common Purpose? If so, how would you describe the way in which that group arrived at its Common Purpose? If not, what could you do to begin that process?
3. What are the values of a group with which you are involved? What symbols or stories convey those values? How can you tell these values are shared by all?

4. Thinking about your own experience, what is the difference between embracing a predefined vision and participating in the formulation of that vision with others? How do the two different approaches affect your engagement with the group?
5. Select a few organizations you admire and look them up on the Internet to review their stated missions, visions, and goals. How does each organization convey its values in this context (e.g., logos, photo choices, or anecdotes)? What are those values?
6. Use the rubric in Table 7.1 to gauge your development on various dimensions of coming to Common Purpose. Reflect on how you could develop this aspect of your leadership capacity.

REFERENCES

Bolman, L. G., & Deal, T. E. (2013). *Reframing organizations* (3rd ed.). San Francisco, CA: Jossey-Bass.

Brown, J., Isaacs, D., & the World Café Community. (2005). *The World Café: Shaping our futures through conversations that matter.* San Francisco, CA: Berrett-Koehler.

Crum, T. F. (1987). *The magic of conflict: Turning a life of work into a work of art.* New York, NY: Touchstone.

Delta Delta Delta. (2016). *Explore our history: It began with friendship.* Retrieved from http://www.tridelta.org/about/history/

Denning, S. (2007). *The secret language of leadership: How leaders inspire action through narrative.* San Francisco, CA: Jossey-Bass.

Heifetz, R. A., Linsky, M., & Grashow, A. (2013). *The practice of adaptive leadership: Tools and tactics for changing your organization and the world.* Cambridge, MA: Harvard Business Press.

Higher Education Research Institute (HERI). (1996). *A social change model of leadership development* (Version III). Los Angeles, CA: University of California, Los Angeles, Higher Education Research Institute.

Howell, J. M. (1988). Two faces of charisma: Socialized and personalized leadership in organizations. In J. A. Conger, R. N. Kanungo, & Associates (Eds.), *Charismatic leadership: The elusive factor in organizational effectiveness* (pp. 213–236). San Francisco, CA: Jossey-Bass.

Johnson, D. W., & Johnson, F. P. (2013). *Joining together: Group theory and group skills* (11th ed.). Upper Saddle River, NJ: Pearson Education.

TABLE 7.1 Common Purpose Rubric

	Excelling	Achieving	Developing	Needing Improvement
Shared Vision	Believes having a shared vision in a group is critically important Understands the importance of a shared vision in creating positive social change Actively pursues a shared vision in a group setting by enacting leadership in group processes that establish the shared vision	Understands that a shared vision among group members helps the group to be successful Genuinely engages in processes that pursue shared vision within a group	Able to better understand and articulate personal values Occasionally interacts with group members to listen to others' visions for the group and share his or her own vision	Unable to articulate and discuss personal values with much complexity Does not understand the importance of establishing a shared vision in a group Believes group vision to always be decided on by a positional leader
Collaborative	Seeks input from group members when making decisions that affect the future of the organization and believes eliciting this feedback is an important part of creating change within the organization Views collaboration as a means to harness individual strengths and thus works with others in an affirming way	Able to find common ground among group members Listens to and engages with the opinions of other group members Values Collaboration among group members Contributes to the goals of the organization	Is willing to listen to the ideas of fellow group members Understands that he or she is not always right Does not see that groups are formed out of common values among members	Can work in groups with other individuals Focuses only on individual ideas Sometimes listens to others' ideas Avoids working in groups whenever possible
Understanding of Purpose	Understands the purpose and works toward developing the vision of the organization Is able to recruit new members who share the same organizational values	Is interested in helping to develop the purpose and mission of the organization Shares the mission with others Seeks to understand the organization's core purpose	Learns the purpose or vision of the organization, which resonates with him or her Wants to learn more	Knows that there is a reason why the organization exists but is a member of the group mostly for personal gains, not to further the organization's mission Unaware that a vision exists for the group(s) he or she is a part of
Group Membership	Wants to bring more people with similar beliefs into the group to sustain the organization past his or her graduation Sees a need for growing membership with people who have values that align with the organization's values	Builds strong, authentic relationships with others in the group Is able to see shared values among group members Appreciates others' unique perspectives on common issues facing the group	Realizes that fellow group members have more to offer outside of group meetings and programs Enjoys learning about fellow group members	Sees no reason to join a group other than to benefit oneself Joins a group for personal benefits including surface-level relationships Not interested in deeper, more authentic personal relationships with other group members

Source: Developed by Anna Haller and John Fink.

Katzenbach, J. R., & Smith, D. K. (1993, March). The discipline of teams. *Harvard Business Review, 71*(2). Retrieved from https://hbr.org/1993/03/the-discipline-of-teams-2

Komives, S. R., Lucas, N., & McMahon, T. R. (2013). *Exploring leadership: For college students who want to make a difference* (3rd ed.). San Francisco. CA: Jossey-Bass.

Kotter, J. P. (1995). Leading change: Why transformation efforts fail. *Harvard Business Review, 73*(2), 59–67.

Lucas, S. E. (2004). *The art of public speaking.* New York, NY: McGraw-Hill.

Rayner, S. R. (1996). *Team traps: Survival stories and lessons from team disasters, near-misses, mishaps, and other near-death experiences.* New York, NY: Wiley.

Robertson, D. C., & Lubic, B. J. (2001). Spheres of confluence: Non-hierarchical leadership in action. In C. L. Outcalt, S. K. Faris, & K. N. McMahon (Eds.), *Developing non-hierarchical leadership on campus: Case studies and best practices in higher education* (pp. 90–98). Westport, CT: Greenwood.

Rosenberg, M. B. (1999). *Nonviolent communication: A language of compassion.* Encinitas, CA: PuddleDancer Press.

Tuckman, B. W. (1965). Developmental sequence in small groups. *Psychological Bulletin, 63,* 384–399.

Tuckman, B. W., & Jensen, M. C. (1977). Stages of small group development revisited. *Group and Organizational Studies, 2,* 419–442.

Controversy With Civility

Cecilio Alvarez

> Out beyond ideas of wrongdoing and rightdoing, there is a field. I'll meet you there.
> —RUMI

During a class discussion in a sociology course about race and ethnicity, a few students shared some remarks and perspectives other students interpreted as biased, uninformed, and hurtful. Rather than avoid the discomfort of disagreeing with or challenging others' perspectives, several students in the course asked their peers to review the communication ground rules to which they agreed for the course and commit to an open discussion about the exchanges that occurred during class. With the common goal of seeking understanding, students engaged in multiple dialogues during which they shared honest feelings and perspectives, explored and challenged biases, claimed responsibility for the impact of their words, and extended understanding of one another. The dialogues helped strengthen students' relationships with each other, shaped constructive exchanges in future class sessions, and provided examples of positive approaches to engaging contrasting viewpoints in and out of class.

    The goal of Controversy With Civility is to create a group culture in which people feel safe and supported to share and explore diverse perspectives. In this scenario, students could have opted to ignore the remarks and opinions expressed by their peers; instead, they extended an invitation to engage and challenge those ideas by seeking to understand each other's perspectives. Although approaching disagreements is something many people in groups hesitate to do, people have the power to create environments that welcome a healthy exchange of differences. Despite the outcome, facilitating Controversy With Civility can have positive implications for self-awareness, interpersonal relationships, and behaviors.

The ensemble defined Controversy With Civility in this way:

> Controversy refers to the disagreements and disputes which arise when those holding contrasting perspectives and opinions are encouraged to share their views with the other group members. By committing themselves to understand the nature of the disagreement and to seek a satisfactory resolution "with civility," the group provides a "safe" environment for acting with congruence and for enhancing knowledge of self and of others. . . . Controversy, in short, is viewed as an inevitable part of group interaction, which can reinforce the other values in the Model if it occurs in an atmosphere of civility. (Higher Education Research Institute [HERI], 1996, p. 60)

CHAPTER OVERVIEW

The first part of this chapter outlines important distinctions between conflict and Controversy With Civility and helps the reader understand this C as a value of leadership, groups, socially responsible leadership, and the social change process. An important part of this chapter explores elements that may shape the practice of Controversy With Civility. Connections to other Cs of the Social Change Model for Leadership Development are explored. Finally, this chapter will prompt readers to reflect on their experiences engaging with controversy and consider opportunities for growth in this C.

DEFINING CONTROVERSY WITH CIVILITY

Much of the leadership literature uses the word *conflict* to describe the inevitable disagreements that occur within groups working together to enact change. The ensemble that developed the Social Change Model intentionally chose instead to use the term *Controversy With Civility* in order to emphasize the importance of groups creating a culture that is open to dissent, not just handling conflict if it occurs.

Distinguishing Controversy With Civility From Conflict

The ensemble who developed the Social Change Model (Higher Education Research Institute [HERI], 1996) understood the importance of distinguishing Controversy With Civility from conflict. Although controversy and conflict involve inevitable differences in perspectives within a group, each is characterized by unique elements that promote different cultures within a group. It is important to distinguish Controversy With Civility from conflict.

Conflict is characterized by an argumentative environment of power, debate, and competition. In conflict, group members defend opposing positions on an idea and are pressured to take positions. Alternatively, Controversy With Civility is characterized by a safe and supportive environment of trust, respect, and collaboration. Group members are invited to share different positions on an idea and seek an understanding of different positions from multiple points of view. Controversy With Civility provides the opportunity for group members to collectively generate a more developed position on an idea. Moreover, this C allows different positions on an idea to remain unresolved and does not call for a "winning" position. Understanding controversy within this framework requires acknowledging that differences in a group's environment and process contribute significantly to creating a culture distinctive from groups that engage with conflict. Additionally, it is equally important to acknowledge that although Controversy With Civility invites resolution of differences, the environment a group creates and the process it engages to consider differences are the primary outcomes of this C.

Understanding Civility

It is difficult to manage controversy and perhaps harder still to do so with true civility. From the time children begin to understand their relationship to others—as siblings, friends, or kids on a school playground—they are socialized to avoid controversy. For some, key messages of "no fighting" and "be nice" have shaped our behaviors. For others, getting what they want by fighting reinforces the use of power and the disregard of others. How many individuals interpret and approach conflict may be traced back to these early messages. People may have learned that they can either be strictly right or wrong, that one person's point of view is more valid than another's, and perhaps that disagreement is synonymous with fighting. It is no surprise, then, that many would want to avoid speaking up when they disagree. This is the message that has been learned and one that has been reinforced consistently through many life experiences.

Civility, however, is more complex than simply "not fighting" and "being nice." Although civility involves behavioral dispositions toward courtesy and politeness, it certainly does not require one to remain quiet when one disagrees, pretending that all is well when it is not. Instead, civility means learning how to voice disagreement and to respond to disagreement from others in a way that respects other points of view. In "The Virtues of Leadership," Sergiovanni (2005) describes civility as a virtue "that embraces diversity, encourages tolerance, and legitimizes controversy. Civility builds frameworks within which people can cooperate despite their divergent views and interests" (p. 117). To engage in controversy with true civility means to value difference and appreciate the ways in which disagreement can contribute positively to a group.

THE VALUE OF CONTROVERSY WITH CIVILITY

In effect, Controversy With Civility challenges group participants to discuss diverse opinions and perspectives while maintaining respect for other group members and their ideas. The consideration of diverse perspectives through multiple lenses is key to leadership, group development, and the social change process. Without regard for respect or consideration of others' ideas, group members can quickly lose themselves in the heat of controversy, preferring to win or give up and lose rather than truly understand ideas and work collaboratively to attempt to resolve differences. Creating a group environment in which various opinions are valued and explored, a group can promote constructive discourse in order to negotiate a favorable outcome.

Controversy With Civility and Leadership

Social perspective taking (SPT) "is the ability to recognize alternative perspectives and infer the thoughts and feelings of others is congruent with emphases in contemporary leadership theory on self-awareness, other-directedness, and process orientations" (Dugan, Bohle, Woelker, & Cooney, 2014, p. 3). As discussed in Chapter 1, SPT, a complex cognitive skill, requires group members to be self-aware and behave congruently with personal values (Dugan et al., 2014). One study with data from the Multi-Institutional Study of Leadership of more than 13,000 U.S. senior college students' capacities for socially responsible leadership support that SPT has a strong direct impact on group leadership values of Collaboration and Controversy With Civility, in large part because of its impact on individual leadership values of Consciousness of Self, Congruence, and Commitment (Dugan et al., 2014). The study also found that

> social perspective-taking serves as a critical mediator of development between the individual and group domain. Some students demonstrate an ability to apply individual capacities in a group context directly, but others need to acquire competence with social perspective-taking in order to do so. (Dugan, Kodama, Correia, & Associates, 2013, p. 28)

The ability to recognize other perspectives and empathize with others in an attempt to seek understanding facilitates the development and maintenance of social relationships critical to group processes (Galinsky, Ku, & Wang, 2005).

Controversy With Civility and Group Development

As noted in Chapter 7, controversy is an inevitable element of group development. Group members may experience interpersonal and intragroup controversy as a form of resistance to creating a group structure (Tuckman & Jensen, 1977). Controversy With Civility is critical to working through differences in respectful and collaborative ways. Although this C engages group members to consider multiple perspectives, it does not require the group to agree with every idea that is raised. Rather, each idea should be listened to with respect and considered while thinking through an issue or making a decision.

In addition to helping groups navigate the storming phase of group development, Controversy With Civility also supports managing group norms that may seem desirable but are a detriment to group development and decision making. Irving Janis (1982)—a social psychologist who studied the impact of group dynamics on foreign policy decisions—identified groupthink as a common norm "people engage in when they are deeply involved in a cohesive in-group, when the members' strivings for unanimity override their motivation to realistically appraise alternative courses of action" (p. 9). Janis identified eight symptoms of groupthink syndrome categorized by three main types, or features, observed in many cohesive groups: "overestimation of the group—its power and morality," which encourages risk and disregard for the consequences of group decisions; "closed-mindedness," by which members dismiss or minimize the value of information used to make decisions; and "pressures toward uniformity," through censorship, conformity, and pressure placed on members to protect group consensus (pp. 174–175). Consider the example of U.S. presidential elections. Throughout campaign season, the public is overwhelmed with rhetoric and media from groups for and against each candidate. Although we assume that people research and evaluate information about each candidate to make informed decisions, we find some people endorse candidates based on collective assumptions, beliefs, or convictions shared by groups to which they belong, such as their political party or religion. Group members may hold strong to their belief that whichever side they are on is the "best" side, may ignore or minimize information that challenges their beliefs and decisions to support particular candidates, and may place pressure on other group members to uphold firmly held beliefs about specific issues to remain aligned with candidates' positions on issues. Although a person may not agree with group members about certain perspectives, that person may prioritize group consensus and avoid sharing information or differences to "keep the peace." This false sense of harmony, anchored in a group culture that pressures members to maintain group cohesion above all else leads to a "deterioration of mental efficiency, reality testing, and moral judgment" (Janis, 1982, p. 9). Engaging in Controversy With Civility is a commitment to considering multiple perspectives because the group culture supports an open and respectful exchange of ideas, rather than silences differences.

Controversy With Civility and Social Change

As much as civility may be thought of as a great character trait, it is also an attitude, a behavior, and, in the social change process, a value. In "The Value of Civility?" Boyd (2006) challenges the narrow definition of civility—its "functional role in maintaining the peace and order of society"—to posit civility as "a moral obligation borne out of an appreciation of human equality" (p. 875). The active practice of civility serves a critical democratic purpose in helping us engage the "plurality of different beliefs, cultures, and identities" in society (p. 872). To this end, civility requires the belief that there is not just one "right" point of view but that each person will see an issue slightly differently, depending on one's background and previous experiences. Although group members may engage in Controversy With Civility with the goal to resolve differences, the process of dialoguing about difference provides benefits and serves a purpose across individual, group, and societal levels.

PRACTICING CONTROVERSY WITH CIVILITY

Controversy With Civility is not an episodic phenomenon but an ongoing one. To truly understand Controversy With Civility means to create and sustain a culture within the group in which people's different points of view and different ways of thinking about problems are sought, respected, and used for the betterment of the group. Healthy groups help controversies surface so the group can engage with all divergent views en route to considering a sound decision. The degree to which groups are able to create and sustain this culture may often determine their approach to addressing controversy. The following are four approaches groups can take to Controversy With Civility, depending on the degree to which a group's culture engages controversy and practices civility, as summarized in Figure 8.1.

FIGURE 8.1: Practicing Controversy With Civility

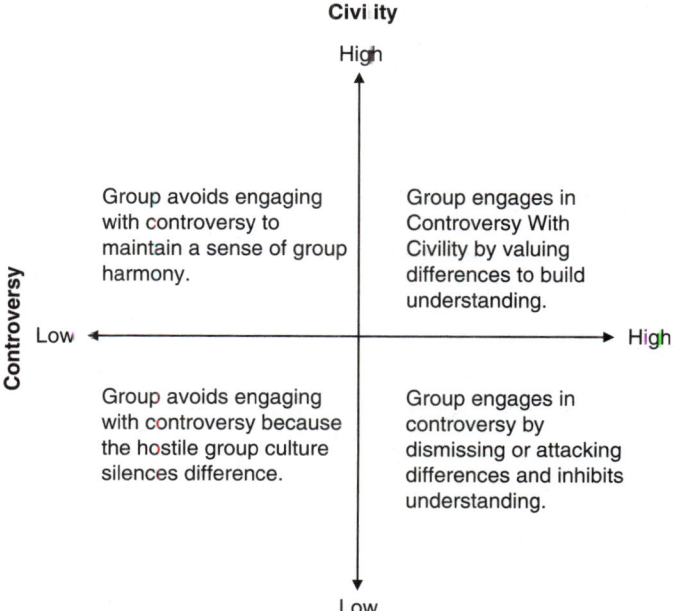

One approach is characterized by the group avoiding controversy because the group culture precludes members from engaging with differences. Combative and strained group dynamics dominate the group environment and force members to ignore or undermine differences. The risks of voicing controversy—for members and the group itself—far outweigh any possibility of a positive outcome. This approach signals there are more significant challenges and concerns regarding the group's development and functioning.

A second approach is to mistakenly try to maintain civility by avoiding controversy. Consider the example at the start of this chapter of the students in the sociology course. Students could have decided against discussing the comments some found to be biased and hurtful to prevent risking discord in class or out of fear of being ignored. This approach mistakenly prioritizes group harmony at the expense of considering and learning from multiple perspectives.

A third approach embraces controversy but without civility. In this group culture, members are not afraid of voicing opinions but are not able to do so in a way that respects or attempts to understand other views. In the example of students in class, a different opinion may have been attributed to lack of intellect or to a character flaw rather than to a difference in experience or perspective. Those with different opinions may have simply dismissed others' views as wrong or not worthy of comment. This approach mistakenly allows group members to express ideas without regard for others—a culture that inhibits differences from surfacing and works against building understanding.

Finally, a fourth approach is to promote Controversy With Civility. In this approach, group members are able to trust that others will not react negatively to disagreement. Rather than becoming defensive of their position, group members express appreciation for those with the courage to speak up and offer a perspective that has not been explored. Those with unique perspective or different ways of thinking through problems are valued for helping the group consider all the angles before making a decision. This does not mean every person's perspective is considered valid—reasoning based on credible evidence should always prevail—but all perspectives are given the consideration they are due. The students in the sociology course demonstrated a culture that promotes Controversy With Civility by committing to listen to others' perspectives and seeking and extending understanding to one another.

The extent to which any individual or group can engage effectively in Controversy With Civility depends on the development and practice of important skills. Interestingly, MSL research shows students self-report this as typically the least developed of the Cs (Dugan & Komives, 2007). To promote a group culture that values Controversy With Civility requires several elements that will be expanded on here: awareness of one's own worldview, awareness of others' worldviews, building trust, acknowledging and engaging with controversy, examining contexts and spaces, and fostering dialogue. The group must engage in a process that will develop these skills and establish a culture that values these approaches—that is, group development.

Awareness of One's Own Worldview

The perspectives one brings to relationships in a group or perspectives on what are important goals for the group to pursue come from one's own context influenced by the complexities of one's social identities: sex, gender, gender identity, age, race or ethnicity, religion or spiritual affiliation, abilities, socioeconomic class, sexual orientation, and other cultural and social dimensions of self. The same is certainly true for others. The perceptions or assumptions with which individuals approach any situation are known as *worldview*. Recognizing that individuals may have different worldviews enables one to be open to explore personal assumptions and understand the assumptions of others.

A person's worldview, or frame of reference, defines something much more complex than one's opinion or perspective on a situation. In Adlerian therapy, a type of counseling, the client's frame of reference is known as the person's "subjective reality" (Corey, 2005). "This 'subjective reality' includes the individual's perceptions, thoughts, feelings, values, beliefs, convictions, and conclusions" (p. 96). In essence, one's collective life experiences influence the ways in which one makes meaning of events in one's life. For example, one's experiences of working in groups could inform whether one would take on a similar or different role, adapt one's experience to reflect the things they enjoyed, or avoid the things one found frustrating with other groups. Similarly, people's attitudes and approaches to controversy are framed within a set of what they have learned and experienced. These frames are as complex as our thinking itself, but nonetheless can teach us about the way in which we perceive controversy.

Awareness of one's own worldview is necessary to be able to understand the lenses through which one perceives and makes assumptions about situations; however, this awareness is also paramount to critically evaluating those same perceptions and assumptions. A core element of practicing Controversy With Civility involves the willingness to consider, assess, and reevaluate different perspectives, including our own. As noted in Chapter 1, this process of critical self-reflection enables one to examine one's values, beliefs, strengths, abilities, and the myriad ways one's life experiences and identities shape one's approach to practicing Controversy With Civility.

Awareness of Others' Worldviews

Exploring Leadership (Komives, Lucas, & McMahon, 2013) states that "groups are made up of great diversity. Even if members are all of one sex or one race or one major, there are great differences in personality, learning preferences, and experiences" (p. 192). Group members' multiple frames or worldviews, essentially, make groups dynamic: together, they represent diverse thoughts, beliefs, and values that have been informed by different experiences and social identities. The ensemble felt that "effectively resolving opposing views and opinions requires an understanding of the individuals involved: their assumptions, their values, and their goals" (HERI, 1996, p. 61).

As mentioned previously in the chapter, SPT is a skill that can enable one to recognize and empathize with others' perspectives. As an orientation to others, SPT invites understanding in "discerning the thoughts, feelings, motivations, and points of view" of others (Gehlbach & Brinkworth, 2012, p. 2). Although SPT can be reduced to the empathic idea of putting oneself in "someone else's shoes," the practice can involve a number of strategies through which one can use available information or gather information to understand how others perceive situations (Gehlbach & Brinkworth, 2012).

One of the ways by which we seek understanding in groups is to ask questions. Inquiry involves the process of critical thinking characterized by

> (1) identifying the assumptions that frame our thinking and determine our actions, (2) checking out the degree to which these assumptions are accurate and

valid, (3) looking at our ideas and decisions (intellectual, organizational, and personal) from several different perspectives, and (4) on the basis of all this, taking informed actions. (Brookfield, 2011, p. 1)

Consider how the following questions may help group members develop an understanding and appreciation for others' points of view:

What are the different perspectives emerging within the group?
What do you perceive those involved may be thinking or feeling?
What do you know about others' identities and experiences that you perceive may be informing their perspectives?
What assumptions may be operating within different perspectives? Have these been evaluated?
What information is available in support of others' perspectives? Is additional information needed? (adapted from Browne & Keeley, 2011).

It is important to clarify that although this process involves critical questions, the process of learning about, exploring, and evaluating other perspectives remains grounded in a civil approach that invites difference and understanding. In *Asking the Right Questions: A Guide to Critical Thinking,* Browne and Keeley (2011) advise that the manner in which one demonstrates critical thinking communicates one's purpose. By thinking critically, we "move us all forward toward some better understanding of who we are" (p. 203).

By practicing and learning to ask these critical questions, group members can evaluate alternative perspectives. Equally important, group members can begin to understand others' worldviews and the social and cultural contexts through which differences are considered. Understanding these contexts is critical because all of our experiences take place against a backdrop of complex social systems that privilege or marginalize our social identities in different ways. This use of the concept of "critical" means analyzing and interpreting assumptions, not making disapproving comments. As a value of social change, Controversy With Civility facilitates understanding of others' worldviews through these critical lenses to support the group's collective action to effect change.

 One of the primary challenges facing the Peer Support Network (PSN) at McGill University is our volunteers come from . . . myriad . . . backgrounds, perspectives, and knowledge about what providing support entails. A lot of our training focuses on helping people develop their own self-awareness, biases, attitudes, and stereotypes in order to move past them and provide support for others. A crucial part to being able to accomplish this involves collective, open, and honest discussions within the team. The discussions emphasize being present in the moment to really listen to and understand what someone else is saying. Many of the volunteers have commented on the fact that within the PSN environment, there's a widespread willingness to listen to one another, regardless of what is being said.

—Michael Dougan was a student at McGill University, where he served as the chair of the Peer Support Network.

Building Trust

Having the confidence to voice an opinion that is different from the rest of the group requires trust. Trust, as noted in Chapter 6, may be characterized by the degree to which group members have confidence that a person can be relied on to behave in a predictable way. Group members must be able to trust that although others may not share their opinion, they will respect that it comes from a person with a valid perspective and will take it into consideration.

Kouzes and Posner (2012) identified several important things one can do to create a climate of trust in an organization:

- Invest in trust. Nurture an environment "that allows people to freely contribute and innovate" and supports "an open exchange of ideas and truthful discussion of issues" (p. 222).
- Be the first to trust. Model the vulnerability and self-confidence to open up. When members risk opening up to each other, sharing what they value and what they hope for, they demonstrate a willingness to trust each other. Demonstrate actively your trust in others.
- Show concern for others. Listen to others, pay attention to their ideas, help others solve problems, and be "open to their influence" (p. 224).
- Share knowledge and information. To foster competence, contribute what you know and involve others to do the same.

In addition to trusting others, engaging in Controversy With Civility requires trusting the group's process. Encouraging dissent and differing opinions means a loss of control over where the group is going. This can feel risky and creates a certain degree of vulnerability. It is important to trust that the process of sharing multiple perspectives and working through differences will help the group arrive at a resolution. Trusting the process means realizing that when controversy emerges, it is not a sign that something has gone wrong with the group. Rather it is a sign that the process is working and multiple points of view are ferreting out potential problems or helping the group to be more inclusive.

Acknowledging and Engaging With Controversy

Although controversy can be simplified to mean the sharing of "a difference of opinion," the definition used by the SCM emphasizes "the process in which individuals holding contrasting perspectives in a group are encouraged to engage with one another across these differences" (HERI, 1996, p. 60). Similar to dissonance in music, when a group of musical notes creates a disquieting sound, the feelings and thoughts associated with controversy may seem unsettling.

According to Festinger (as cited in Matz & Wood, 2005), dissonance is a psychological discomfort or an aversive drive state that people are motivated to reduce, just as they are motivated to reduce hunger. Most people are quick to want to resolve disagreements, and perhaps even avoid them, without thinking about or understanding how they occur. "Festinger's original dissonance theory did not specify the origins of cognitive inconsistency beyond the general notion that inconsistency arises when one cognitive element does not follow from another, as occurs when others in a group disagree" (Matz & Wood, 2005, p. 23). In effect, people attribute dissonance to a "difference of opinion" rather than attempt to understand how various elements of human interaction may shape disagreements.

Controversy With Civility challenges one to grow comfortable with and embrace differences of opinion rather than attempt to avoid or reduce them. Controversy that results from the differences in values and ideas that members have should be recognized as a normal and healthy part of groups being groups. It is unrealistic and detrimental for groups to ignore or discourage controversy because it risks forging and perpetuating a false harmony. Groups should establish a process to bring controversies into the conversation in civil and productive ways. In the example at the start of the chapter, students in the sociology course relied on communication ground rules to which they agreed collectively for support in engaging with controversy.

Examining Contexts and Spaces

The space in which controversy occurs will certainly affect a group's ability to approach controversy civilly. Physical, social, and cultural environments can shape the conditions, norms, and process through which a group engages with controversy. In a study of 476 members of the Association for Conflict Resolution—the national organization of mediators, arbitrators, and conflict resolution practitioners in the United States—Anthony Purvis (2012) outlined 12 environmental aspects that participants identified can affect the process of building consensus: symbolic meaning; personal space; space planning; materials and finishes; windows and views of nature; lighting; indoor air quality and odor; ambient temperature; sound and noise; auxiliary spaces; security, safety, and surveillance; and environmental control. To engage productively in Controversy With Civility, it is important for groups to consider how elements of various spaces can contribute to a group's process.

Undeniably, technology has opened the doors for people to engage in controversy beyond physical spaces in online environments. These opportunities, however, can be overshadowed by the challenges associated with online disagreement. For instance, although a great tool, social media is replete with examples of people engaging publicly and, at times, destructively with controversy. In 2013, Justine Sacco—then a senior director of corporate communications—posted an incredibly offensive message on her Twitter account before boarding an 11-hour flight to South Africa. When she landed in Cape Town, Justine was shocked to find tens of thousands of responses to her message. "The furor over Sacco's tweet had become not just an ideological crusade against her perceived bigotry but also a form of idle entertainment" (Ronson, 2015, para. 11).

Data from Civility in America: An Annual Nationwide Survey to "gauge American's attitudes toward civility in a variety of areas impacting American society and daily life" demonstrate that 7 out of 10 Americans "agree that the Internet encourages uncivil behavior" (Weber Shandwick, Powell Tate, & KRC Research, 2014). Millennials—identified in the survey as people born between 1981 and 1996—"overwhelmingly identified social media in general and individual social networks as uncivil" (Weber Shandwick et al., 2014). Social media, part of many online platforms for communication, can be a valuable asset to groups. It is important to understand, however, one's responsibility in engaging with controversy in online environments. Table 8.1 summarizes important practices for engaging with civility online.

TABLE 8.1 Practices for Engaging with Civility Online

Practice	Description
Take time to process information	It can be easy to react to e-mails, comments, posts, and other forms of online communication. Spend some time away from the information and reread it later.
Solicit feedback	Discuss feelings and thoughts about the communication and a planned response with someone outside the situation who may be able to offer alternate perspectives.
Practice perspective taking	Consider the experiences, values, beliefs, and identities that may be shaping a person's worldview and perspective.
Choose if and how to respond	Recognize we have the choice to engage with controversy and that choice can be shaped by assessing one's and others' ability to engage with controversy in a civil manner. Decide whether the response should be a private message to the sender or a reply that others can read.
Craft a civil response	Respond thoughtfully and responsibly by using "I" statements, which contribute to a positive tone.
Articulate goals of a response	Communicate what you intend in a response. Whether it is resolution or understanding, it is important to orient a response to a specific outcome.
Seek and offer clarification	Invite clarification from others about what they meant in their message and extend the same to others.

Source: Adapted from Munro (2002).

Fostering Dialogue

Dialogue skills may be the critical answer to many leadership problems in group and community settings. "The purpose of dialogue is not to convince or influence the other person but to understand his or her perspective, concerns, values, emotions, assumptions and goals" (Kazepides, 2012, p. 920). Bohm (2004) describes dialogue as coming to a shared meaning or new understanding. Table 8.2 illustrates the contrast between dialogue and debate.

TABLE 8.2 Distinguishing Between Dialogue and Debate

Dimensions	Dialogue	Debate
Premise	Multiple points of view are valid.	There are right and wrong arguments.
Purpose	To explore different perspectives and develop a shared understanding of the issue	To win the argument by challenging and ultimately defeating the opposition, defending one's position as the best
Environment	Collaborative, characterized by trust and an appreciation of difference	Combative, characterized by opposing sides trying to prove the other is wrong
Behaviors	Listening to learn about and find value in others' perspectives, seeking commonalities, identifying and evaluating assumptions	Critiquing the other side, hearing only for opportunities to discredit or find flaws in other arguments, treating assumptions as truth
Outcomes	New, informed understanding rather than resolution of the issue	Ends with the best or most strongly argued side declared the winner

Source: Adapted from "Comparing Debate, Discussion, and Dialogue" (2008).

Being able to dialogue is perhaps the most important skill in achieving Controversy With Civility. Many college campuses are now using a process called *intergroup dialogue*—facilitated learning experiences that bring together students from different social identity groups (e.g., lesbian, gay, and bisexual students and heterosexual students; students of color and White students; men and women)—to engage students in exploring differences, social inequalities, and opportunities to work together for equality and justice (Gurin, Nagda, & Zúñiga, 2013). In a three-year, U.S. multi-institutional study of intergroup dialogue courses, students who participated in intergroup dialogue "demonstrated significant change in awareness of group inequalities (intergroup understanding), empathy and motivation to bridge difference (intergroup relations), and frequency and confidence in taking action individually or with others (intergroup collaboration)" (Lopez & Zúñiga, 2010, p. 38).

Controversy With Civility promotes the kind of group culture characteristic of intergroup dialogues in which members "create understanding through exploring meaning, [identify] assumptions that inform perspectives, and [foster] a willingness to reappraise one's thinking in light of these exchanges" (Gurin et al., 2013, pp. 44–45). Although they exist for a specific purpose, often to engage students in learning about difference, privilege, and structural inequalities, their design can be adapted to help other types of groups learn to use the dialogue process. Intergroup dialogues often use a four-stage design:

Stage 1: The group members form relationships and build trust and respect through intentional team-building activities. The group learns about the concept of dialogue. The structured activities and discussions about dialogue serve to help the group establish guidelines for engaging with one another in a learning community.

Stage 2: With the foundation for dialogue, group members explore social identities and inequalities. The purpose of Stage 2 is to understand how social identities develop, their place within social structure of power and privilege, and "to discover how group-based identities are implicated in relationships that emerge within the dialogue itself" (Gurin et al., 2013, p. 63).

Stage 3: Group members engage in dialogue about controversial topics. Stage 3 helps students to "examine their perspectives on issues and listen to those of others with curiosity and openness to broaden their thinking" (Gurin et al., 2013, p. 67). Understanding the issues is emphasized, and defending any one position as "right" or "wrong" is discouraged.

Stage 4: Based on the whole group's improved understanding, the group collaborates to create an action plan that advances social justice. The goal of this stage is to connect explicitly dialogue and action (Gurin et al., 2013, pp. 60–72).

Incredibly, over nearly 10 years of studies, findings from the Multi-Institutional Study of Leadership consistently show that "socio-cultural conversations with peers are the single strongest predictor of socially responsible leadership capacity for students across demographic groups" (Dugan et al., 2013, p. 9). These types of dialogues about differences and across groups of individuals from different identities

> may impact leadership development because they require students to clarify and articulate their own perspectives; seek a better understanding of others' world views; comprehend how personal values fit into larger social structures; and discern how to work with different communities to initiate positive change. (Dugan et al., 2013, p. 9)

CONNECTION TO THE OTHER Cs

As mentioned in previous chapters, all of the Cs are linked such that improving effectiveness in one C will positively affect one's ability to practice the other Cs, and vice versa. It is no less true with Controversy With Civility. This C engages Consciousness of Self by prompting one to be aware of and evaluate one's worldview. Engaging with controversy challenges one to act in Congruence with one's values and priorities. Working with others through differences of opinion, values, or ideas provides opportunities to practice Commitment to the group's cause, even when the going is not easy.

Controversy With Civility also influences the other group Cs. Creating a group culture that welcomes differences of opinion and supports group members to work through them with civility drives a group's ability to Collaborate and come to a Common Purpose. Finally, Controversy With Civility is a critical skill to effective local or global Citizenship. As an active community member working toward change, one will inevitably encounter controversy. Maintaining civility means being socially responsible and working across differences for the betterment of a community.

CONCLUSION

As one of the Seven Cs, Controversy With Civility acknowledges disagreements are inherent in a process that strongly emphasizes and encourages collaboration. The practice of Controversy With Civility, however, differs from traditional conflict management approaches by focusing on creating a group culture that values and embraces difference. By understanding oneself and others, fostering group trust, recognizing and engaging with controversy, maintaining a civil approach within the different spaces in which controversy occurs, and practicing effective dialogue, one can continue as a social change agent and work effectively across differences.

DISCUSSION QUESTIONS

1. A key element of Controversy With Civility is that resolution of differences is not always an outcome. How does practicing Controversy With Civility still

contribute to a group's process, even when the group does not reach a conclusion or point of agreement?
2. Controversy With Civility encourages one to develop an awareness of others' worldviews. What are ways in which individuals and groups can support and sustain this practice?
3. What do you think may contribute to a person's approach to engaging with controversy online versus the way in which they might engage with controversy in person?

 ACTION AND REFLECTION

1. In a group setting this week, practice perspective taking by asking yourself the questions listed in the "Awareness of Others' Worldviews" section. How did what you learned help inform your own perspective?
2. Identify a personal or public example of groupthink and false harmony. What were the outcomes? How could practicing Controversy With Civility have shaped those outcomes?
3. Take the time to think about the many dimensions of your identity that have shaped the person you are today. What experiences, values, beliefs, or identities have shaped or changed your approach to controversy? Can you remember a time when you approached controversy differently than you do now?
4. What have been your experiences with controversy online? How have these experiences shaped your approach to engaging with controversy online and in person?
5. What skills have you developed that you feel can help you engage effectively in Controversy With Civility? What skills would you like to develop further? Use the rubric in Table 8.3 to gauge your development on this C. Reflect on how you could develop this aspect of your leadership capacity.

TABLE 8.3 Controversy With Civility Rubric

	Excelling	Achieving	Developing	Needing Improvement
Respect for and Courtesy to Others	Actively engages and participates with others Reciprocates respect of values and opinions Models a civil atmosphere and encourages others to do so	Shows respect for others most times and actively helps to facilitate a civil atmosphere	Begins to engage with others beyond his or her interests and understands that own actions can affect how others feel Occasionally shows limited courtesy	Only engages in conversations related to his or her interests Expresses negative attitudes Speaks over and interrupts others Frequently disrespectful to others
Ability to Work Cooperatively	Engages with a win-win philosophy and shared purpose Actively supports and works with others collaboratively	Works effectively as a team member Actively shares in discussions different from own opinions	Interacts with hesitancy Helps with work rather than engages At times lets conflict slow process	Does not engage as a member of the community Focuses only on individual actions and input
Trust	Asks intelligent questions aimed at starting good conversations with the purpose of seeking understanding, solving problems, and making decisions	Seeks out opinions of others even if they differ from his or her own	Begins to open up to others and share thoughts while using space to hear others' opinions Questions about others' ideas seem superficial or fake	Shows physical and verbal signs of distrust for group Does not share opinions or thoughts but expects to hear from others
Dialogue Skills	Always participates in constructive conversation Understands that others' views might help in developing his or her own ideas as well as those of the group	Frequently participates in constructive conversation Analyzes ideas fully and coherently before sharing with the group	Attempts to understand why he or she has arrived at thoughts Some difficulty in expressing own ideas to others	Does not seek to help explain his or her ideas to group or try to understand why he or she has come to these ideas
Controversy Versus Conflict	Fully embraces controversy as important tool of sharing in group problem solving and decision making	Begins to challenge others' opinions in a nonhostile manner No longer sees controversy as a negative impact on collaborative process	Begins to understand how controversy can help group process Sometimes struggles with conflict	Does not understand the difference between controversy and conflict Sees conflict as a hostile environment with no positive attributes
Awareness of Worldviews	Shares own values fully Deeply values others' worldviews and perceptions	Actively shares values and ideas most times Understands alternate viewpoints are inevitable and part of the creative process	Begins to share own perspectives with others Limited acceptance of others' views as being constructive	Does not value the perspectives of others Only sees own views as constructive and does not evaluate own perspectives

Source: Developed by Heather S. Baruch and Christopher R. Boyle.

REFERENCES

Bohm, D. (2004). *On dialogue.* New York, NY: Rutledge Classics.

Boyd, R. (2006). The value of civility? *Urban Studies, 43,* 863–878. doi:10.1080/00420980600676105

Brookfield, S. D. (2011). *Teaching for critical thinking: Tools and techniques to help students question their assumptions.* San Francisco, CA: Jossey-Bass.

Browne, M. N., & Keeley, S. M. (2011). *Asking the right questions: A guide to critical thinking* (10th ed.). Upper Saddle River, NJ: Pearson Prentice Hall.

Comparing debate, discussion, and dialogue. (2008). Retrieved from http://eoa.oregonstate.edu/sites/default/files/comparing_debate_discussions_dialogue.pdf

Corey, G. (2005). *Theory and practice of counseling and psychotherapy* (7th ed.). Belmont, CA: Brooks/Cole.

Dugan, J. P., & Komives, S. R. (2007). *Developing leadership capacity in college students: Findings from a national study.* A report from the Multi-Institutional Study of Leadership. College Park, MD: National Clearinghouse for Leadership Programs.

Dugan, J. P., Kodama, C., Correia, B., & Associates. (2013). *Multi-Institutional Study of Leadership insight report: Leadership program delivery.* College Park, MD: National Clearinghouse for Leadership Programs.

Dugan, J. P., Bohle, C. W., Woelker, L. R., & Cooney, M. A. (2014). The role of social perspective-taking in developing students' leadership capacities. *Journal of Student Affairs Research and Practice, 51,* 1–15. doi:10.1515/jsarp-2014-0001

Galinsky, A. D., Ku, G., & Wang, C. S. (2005). Perspective-taking and self-other overlap: Fostering social bonds and facilitating social coordination. *Group Processes & Intergroup Relations, 8*(2), 109–124. doi:10.1177/1368430205051060

Gehlbach, H., & Brinkworth, M. (2012). The social perspective taking process: Strategies and sources of evidence in taking another's perspective. *Teachers College Record, 114*(1), 1–29.

Gurin, P., Nagda, B. A., & Zúñiga, X. (2013). *Dialogue across difference: Practice, theory and research on intergroup dialogue.* New York, NY: Russell Sage Foundation.

Higher Education Research Institute (HERI). (1996). *A social change model of leadership development* (Version III). Los Angeles: University of California, Los Angeles, Higher Education Research Institute.

Janis, I. L. (1982). *Groupthink: Psychological studies of policy decisions and fiascoes* (2nd ed.). Boston, MA: Houghton Mifflin.

Kazepides, T. (2012). Education as dialogue. *Educational Philosophy and Theory, 44,* 913–925. doi:10.1111/j.1469-5812.2011.00762.x

Komives, S. R., Lucas, N., & McMahon, T. R. (2013). *Exploring leadership: For college students who want to make a difference* (3rd ed.). San Francisco, CA: Jossey-Bass.

Kouzes, J. M., & Posner, B. Z. (2012). *The leadership challenge: How to make extraordinary things happen in organizations* (5th ed.). San Francisco, CA: Jossey-Bass.

Lopez, G. E., & Zúñiga, X. (2010). *Intergroup dialogue and democratic practice in higher education* (New Directions for Higher Education, no. 152, pp. 35–42). doi:10.1002/he.410

Matz, D. C., & Wood, W. (2005). Cognitive dissonance in groups: The consequences of disagreement. *Journal of Personality and Social Psychology, 88*, 22–37. doi:10.1037/0022-3514.88.1.22

Munro, K. (2002). Conflict in cyberspace: How to resolve conflict online. In J. Suler (Ed.), *The psychology of cyberspace*. Retrieved from http://truecenterpublishing.com/psycyber/psycyber.html

Ronson, J. (2015, February 12). How one stupid tweet blew up Justine Sacco's life. *New York Times Magazine*. Retrieved from http://www.nytimes.com/2015/02/15/magazine/how-one-stupid-tweet-ruined-justine-saccos-life.html?_r=0

Purvis, A. J. (2012). *Conflict resolution and the interior built environment: Design considerations for consensus building*. Unpublished thesis. Retrieved from http://purl.flvc.org/fsu/fd/FSU_migr_etd-5122

Sergiovanni, T. J. (2005). The virtues of leadership. *The Educational Forum, 69*(2), 112–123. doi:10.1080/00131720508984675

Tuckman, B. W., & Jensen, M.C. (1977). Stages of small-group development revisited. *Group & Organization Studies, 2*, 419–427.

Weber Shandwick, Powell Tate, & KRC Research. (2014, October 21). Civility in America 2014: Five generational differences. [Infographic]. Retrieved from http://www.webershandwick.com/news/article/civility-in-america-2014-forecast-bleak-but-with-hope-for-millennials

PART 4

Society/Community Values

> Community is the binding together of diverse individuals committed to a just, common good through shared experiences in a spirit of caring and social responsibility.
> —NATIONAL LEADERSHIP SYMPOSIUM

> All that is necessary for the triumph of evil is that good [people] do nothing.
> —EDMUND BURKE

Membership in any group brings with it the rights of membership and the responsibilities to serve the good of the group. These groups are the communities each individual engages with in daily life—from the smallest unit, such as the community of one's family, residence hall suite, seminar class, work staff, campus, religious institution, local neighborhood, professional colleagues, to the nation and world. Feeling responsible to those communities and moving those communities positively to address change in the arenas they influence is a responsibility of membership. This indeed is the inherent nature of being a citizen of those communities. Communities must "continually participate in conversations about the questions 'Who are we' and 'What matters?'" (Wheatley & Kellner-Rogers, 1998, p. 17). The process of that engagement is Citizenship.

Former secretary of Health, Education, and Welfare and president of Common Cause John Gardner (1997) viewed communities as networks of responsibility:

> All citizens should have the opportunity to be active, but all will not respond. Those who do respond carry the burden of our free society. I call them the Responsibles.
>
> They exist in every segment of the community—ethnic groups, labor unions, neighborhood associations, businesses—but they rarely form an effective network of responsibility because they don't know one another across segments. They must find each other, learn to communicate, and find common ground. Then they can function as the keepers of the long-term agenda. (p. 5)

In Part 4, the Social Change Model examines leadership development from the society/community perspective. This section examines the importance of people coming together through groups, organizations, and coalitions in community to address their shared needs and address shared problems. The ensemble asked, "Toward what social ends is the leadership development activity directed? What kinds of service activities are most effective in energizing the group and in developing desired personal qualities in the individual?" (Higher Education Research Institute [HERI], 1996, p. 19). The value explored in the society/community perspective is Citizenship.

REFERENCES

Gardner, J. (1997). You are the responsibles. *Civic partners*. Charlottesville, VA: Pew Partnership for Civic Change.

Higher Education Research Institute (HERI) (1996). *A social change model of leadership development* (Version III). Los Angeles: University of California, Los Angeles, Higher Education Research Institute.

Wheatley, M. J., & Kellner-Rogers, M. (1998). *A simpler way*. San Francisco, CA: Berrett-Koehler.

Citizenship

Jennifer Bonnet

> We have the power within us to create the world anew. We can begin by doing small things at the local level, like planting community gardens or looking out for our neighbors. That is how change takes place in living systems, not from above but from within, from many local actions occurring simultaneously.
> —GRACE LEE BOGGS

Chelsea Mason was a student at Georgia State University, where she studied Spanish and psychology. She served as a resident assistant and tele-counselor for the University Welcome Center. Chelsea wrote:

> Growing up I was always aware of the social problems that many people face around the world; however, I always felt like a bystander. I felt like there was little to nothing that I could do because I was just one student among many. As a double minority (African American female) I really felt like my voice would never be heard—that is until I participated in a leadership program where I learned about the Seven Cs of the Social Change Model and in particular citizenship. I learned that every person has a duty to make a difference whether it be big or small to their school, community, or nation. I learned that as a leader I possess the skills to make this difference. Learning this enabled me to have the confidence to make these "small differences" by volunteering in the local homeless shelters and advocating for educational excellence through tutoring in the psychology department.
>
> The awareness that each of us is part of a larger community—whether our campus, hometown, state, country, or the world—brings an opportunity to connect meaningfully with others to address issues that could make this a better shared world.

DEFINITION OF CITIZENSHIP

In the context of the Social Change Model, Citizenship centers on active community participation resulting from a sense of responsibility to the communities in which people live. Former Indiana University president Tom Ehrlich (2000) was describing a perspective in alignment with the ensemble's definition of Citizenship when he wrote that "civic engagement means working to make a difference in the civic life of our communities and developing the combination of knowledge, skills, values and motivation to make that difference. It means promoting the quality of life in a community" (p. vi).

The ensemble described Citizenship in the following way:

> Since "citizenship" can have several different meanings, it is important to understand the special sense in which it is being used as a component of the Social Change Model of Leadership Development. To speak of an individual as a "citizen" requires us to think in terms of multiple communities, large and small, to which the individual belongs. But "citizenship," in the context of the model, means much more than mere membership; rather, it implies active engagement of the individual (and the leadership group) in an effort to serve that community, as well as a "citizen's mind"—a set of values and beliefs that connects an individual in a responsible manner to others. Citizenship, in other words, implies social or civic responsibility. It is the value that responsibly connects the individual and the leadership group to the larger community and society. (Higher Education Research Institute [HERI], 1996, p. 65)

CHAPTER OVERVIEW

This chapter presents an overview of citizenship through the lens of the Social Change Model of Leadership Development. The Social Change Model highlights key leadership qualities of informed, committed, and conscientious community members. Citizenship within this model emphasizes civic-mindedness and engagement as well as accountability to the communities in which people participate. Several facets of citizenship will be explored, including the definition of Citizenship within the SCM, the historical roots of civic engagement in the United States, the importance of community involvement, and emerging approaches to civic participation in today's world. How groups within a community can work effectively together—community development—is also explored.

Civic Roots in the United States

The United States has a long history of people working together as citizens to address their common needs. In the 1830s, French historian Alexis de Tocqueville traveled throughout the United States and wrote about his surprise at the extent to which Americans worked together to solve their common problems. "Americans of all ages, all conditions, and all dispositions constantly form associations.... Wherever at the head of some new undertaking you see the government in France, or a man of rank in England, in the United States you will be sure to find an association" (de Tocqueville, 1835/1956, p. 198). de Tocqueville observed communities forming associations to create hospitals, schools, and places of worship, and to provide entertainment such as musical groups and community theaters. He believed that community building was one of the keys to making a democratic society work.

Associated Living

In 1916, educator and philosopher John Dewey defined what it meant to live in a democracy: "A democracy is more than a form of government; it is primarily a mode of associated living ... each has to refer his own action to that of others, and to consider the action of others to give point and directions to his own ..." (p. 87). At a fundamental level, Dewey's concept of democracy referred to people working together so that communities could function. Such essential functions might include volunteer fire departments, community youth programs, the chamber of commerce, or the parent-teacher association.

A century after Dewey's publication, we are now striving to achieve associated living on a global scale by recognizing how our actions affect one another—whether that involves our impact on the environment and shared global resources, the world economy, opportunities for safe working situations, or other human rights issues. Governments, corporations, and nonprofit organizations have a better understanding of how we can collaborate across sectors in associated living—it is not just about the volunteer association anymore.

Collective Responsibility

Prominent cultural historian Ronald Takaki (1993) pointed to an extensive history of communities of color working together to build strong communities. Active citizenship in these communities developed, in part, from a cultural expectation that one should support fellow community members the way one would support a family member. Underscoring this idea, Juana Bordas (2012) referred to the Cherokee tradition of acknowledging others as "all my relatives" and the Lakota greeting *Mitakuye oyasin*, which means "We are all related" (p. 164). Similarly, she described the concept of *la familia* in various Latina/o cultures as an elastic one that stretches beyond the nuclear family to include honorary aunts and uncles, godparents, good friends, and community members, all of whom can expect to give and receive support from their extended kinship network. According to Bordas, strong community connections are also present among many African American communities, wherein a person's identity is not fully understood in isolation from those with whom they share their lives. In a similar vein, many Asian American communities value collaborative leadership efforts and attention to group needs over individual desires (Liang, Lee, & Ting, 2002). In all of these situations, importance is placed on community members' helping one another, being responsible for the welfare of others, and standing stronger by standing together (Takaki, 1993).

This sense of collective responsibility is growing. The president's Council of Economic Advisors (2014) reported that young people born between 1980 and the mid-2000s place greater value than previous generations on community participation and closeness with family and friends. This generation has even been dubbed the "We generation" in surveys of the fastest growing subset of the U.S. population (Greenberg & Weber, 2008; Kielburger & Kielburger, 2014) amid a lively debate on the degree to which millennials are more or less engaged in civic duties than previous generations (Public Affairs, 2014).

What Citizenship Looks Like

Even when defined as working with others to make a positive difference in one's communities, what that work looks like might be different from person to person. For some, this means becoming informed of issues that affect society and holding elected officials accountable to their constituents. This is often achieved through political engagement, such as online petitions, advocacy on social media platforms, attendance at protest marches, or participation in local and national elections. For others, it means being an active member of community organizations. For still others, the term *good citizen* harkens back to the days of elementary school, when the "good citizen award" went to the student who helped a classmate in need, remembered to recycle the milk cartons, or followed the rules. As adults, we now connect these approaches to citizenship with our awareness of our larger impact on communities, for example, by participating on one's residence hall floor, volunteering with Habitat for Humanity, donating to a local blood drive, or boycotting clothing made in sweatshops. This section further illustrates the SCM's approach to Citizenship through community development and engagement.

Following a series of thefts and assaults in off-campus apartment properties, students at Arizona State University responded by working with university staff members and city police to create the "Be a Good Neighbor Program." The program included generating and distributing public relations announcements and publications to better educate and inform students and community members of safety and security issues. In addition, a series of town hall meetings was held. To this day, there is a biannual safety campaign that highlights community safety tips, thanks to these engaged students, community members, university and city police, and university staff members.

Community Defined

If citizenship is approached as working with others in one's communities to make a difference for the common good, then it is important to explore what is implied by the word *community*. Community typically refers to people associated with one another through shared interests, perspectives, attitudes, or goals, but in addition to this affiliation, *community* implies a shared responsibility toward achieving something bigger than the individual. Educational theorist Etienne Wenger (2006) provides a relevant framework in his discussion of communities of practice (CoPs), or social systems built around common interests, which are strengthened when individuals interact with, learn from, and are accountable to one other. In this conceptualization, there are various dimensions of community that comprise not only the physical location where a group of people live (or take part in a joint activity) but also reflect shared experiences, cooperative and intentional engagement among members, and a diversity of participation and expertise.

A student in an American Indian leadership course at the University of Maryland wrote:

> A community is a group of people tied together through some defining link such as ethnicity or geographical region. I belong to the University of Maryland community, the College Park community, the upperclassman community, the

Prince George's County community, the activist community, and the American Indian student community.

Another student in that course noted:

Citizenship is reflected through my participation in student groups on campus, through my voting in elections, when students become actively involved in the classroom by participating in class, building relationships with professors, and working with classmates in or out of class. This happens any time I take part in an academic or extracurricular activity.

Political scientist Melissa Williams (2005) underscores this notion of citizenship, which she dubbed "membership in a community of shared fate" (p. 209). In her description of communities, Williams asserted that there is not simply one place where individuals or communities are "supposed" to engage in citizenship; rather, it can be practiced anywhere. For example, a student may belong to Circle K International, a student organization whose mission is to foster "responsible citizens and leaders with a lifelong commitment to service" (Circle K International, 2015). This student may participate in community service on a regular basis as a member of this organization; however, this type of action is not the only defining feature of civic engagement, nor is this the sole organization through which a student can participate in civic activities. As members of the Black student union, several students may promote a campus movie series about the history of civil rights and segregation at their land-grant institution, thus serving their campus community through educational programming. In current dialogues on climate change adaptation, students around the globe are working on awareness campaigns regarding environmental stewardship and sustainable practices through campus divestment initiatives. Williams's definition of citizenship emphasizes a key element of the Social Change Model of Leadership Development: everyone has the capacity to engage in their communities and to practice Citizenship.

 I always thought a good citizen voted for the president. Through my introductory leadership class, I realize that I'm also a good citizen when I help my roommate with her math homework or when I volunteer for freshmen orientation.

—A junior criminology major

> In response to proposed budget cuts to the California State University (CSU) system several years ago, CSU Channel Islands students and staff members collaborated to form a statewide organization called "Access Denied?" which organized a rally on the capital, resulting in an increase of funds into the CSU system.

The Processes of Community Engagement

People have the opportunity to engage in their communities in many different ways. Table 9.1 presents a range of forms of engagement that support communities and their needs.

Engaging in Citizenship

Citizenship is not often an activity undertaken on one's own. The fact that citizenship involves working with others is what links citizenship and leadership so closely. Although anyone can be involved in his or her community for the common good, there are skills and knowledge that can make that involvement more effective. Key factors include an understanding of social capital, awareness of community history, empowerment and privilege, social perspective taking (SPT), and coalition building.

Social Capital

Alexis de Tocqueville believed the strength of democratic communities in the United States was the frequency of citizens working together in community associations (Tocqueville, 1835/1956). Indeed, the principles of democracy or associated living rely on the social contract of shared responsibility. More than 150 years later, social scientists can confirm this belief with empirical research. Whether aims are better schools, a safer college campus, effective government, or economic development, a community's chances at success are more likely to improve if citizens are actively engaged with each other (Putnam, 2000). Harvard professor Robert Putnam (1999) defined the outcomes of this type of engagement as social capital, that is, the value derived from "networks, norms, and social trust that facilitate coordination and cooperation for mutual benefit" (p. 573). Communities with social capital have citizens who have worked together, socialized together, and who know and trust each other. Citizens who build social capital belong to local organizations, attend public

TABLE 9.1 Forms of Individual Civic Engagement

Direct Service	Giving personal time and energy to address immediate community needs; examples include tutoring, serving food at a shelter, building or repairing homes, and neighborhood or park cleanups
Community Research	Exploring a community to learn about its assets and how it is being affected by current social problems; this form of civic engagement provides knowledge that other efforts can build on
Advocacy and Education	Using various modes of persuasion (e.g., petitions, marches, letter writing) to convince government or corporate decision makers to make choices that will benefit the community; raising public awareness of social issues by giving speeches to community groups, distributing written materials to the general public, or providing educational activities in schools
Capacity Building	Working with the diverse constituencies of a community, building on existing assets, to solve problems and make it a better place; creating a space for everyone in the community to have a say in what the community should be like and how to get there
Political Involvement	Participating in processes of government, such as campaigning and voting; this includes keeping informed about issues in the local, national, and global communities in order to vote responsibly and engaging in discourse and debate about current social issues
Socially Responsible Personal and Professional Behavior	Maintaining a sense of responsibility for the welfare of others when making personal or professional decisions; using one's career or professional training to benefit the community; this category describes personal lifestyle choices that reflect commitment to one's values: recycling, driving a hybrid car, or bicycling to work; buying or not buying certain products because of unjust corporate policies; or choosing to work for companies with socially just priorities
Philanthropic Giving	Donating funding or needed items, organizing or participating in fund-raising events
Participation in Associations	Participating in community organizations that develop the social networks that provide a foundation for community-building efforts, including civic associations, sports leagues, church choirs, and school boards

Source: Owen, J. E., & Wagner, W. (2010). Situating service-learning in the contexts of civic engagement and the engaged campus. In B. Jacoby (Ed.), *Establishing and sustaining the community service-learning professional: A guide for self-directed learning.* Providence, RI: Campus Compact. Used with permission of the authors.

meetings, and serve on voluntary committees. They participate in community sports, choirs, book clubs, professional societies, fraternal groups, faith-based groups, or service clubs. Neighbors in such communities shovel snow from each other's sidewalks, invite one another over for meals, and lend and borrow items when someone is in need.

Putnam (2000; Putnam & Goss, 2002) described two key dimensions of social capital: bonding and bridging. Bonding refers to social interactions that are limited to people who are similar to one another, such as an all-women's book club or a student organization for business majors. Exclusive social groups such as these have many benefits for those who are in them and can be a particularly meaningful source of support and strength for members. However, they can also be limiting. These types of groups sometimes emphasize an "us" and "them" attitude that can reduce opportunities to expand with those with whom individuals associate and from whom they draw experience and knowledge. Bridging refers to social interactions among more diverse groups of people. An example is the student government association that brings together students of all majors and backgrounds to address common concerns for the campus. Bridging social capital tends to have many benefits for individuals and the community. In fact, bonding has been described as useful for getting by, but bridging is what is needed to get ahead (Putnam, 2000).

Examples of social capital exist in all communities and can easily be found on the college campus. Compare a residence hall floor where neighbors do not interact with one that has a vibrant social events committee, a floor-sponsored intramural sports team, active participation in floor meetings, or neighbors who tend to eat together. Residents who regularly interact with one another are more likely to trust each other, help each other, and more easily resolve their common problems. As Putnam (1999) noted, "life is easier" (p. 573) for those who are living in communities that have worked to foster social capital.

Awareness of Community History

Staying informed about a community and its issues is an integral part of the Citizenship value. This includes making conscious decisions to engage in awareness-building activities such as reading the news, following relevant groups or organizations through social media, or participating in in-person or online discussions about important topics.

An essential aspect of keeping informed is to educate oneself about a community's history as well as how it currently functions. When a fraternity struggles with decisions about some of its existing programs, it is useful for the group to remember why they were created and what the group's mission and vision are. Understanding the nature of the ongoing relationships between individuals in the community is also worthwhile in order to better understand the dynamics, needs, and future directions of the group. When college students across the United States learned that a young Black man was shot and killed by a police officer in Ferguson, Missouri, a number of them chose to spend their spring break meeting members of the Ferguson community, learning about efforts to improve neighborhood policing, and working alongside local residents to register voters. Through this experience, students broadened their awareness of systems of oppression as well as ways that they could become engaged in local government in their home communities.

Empowerment and Privilege

When working with others to shape community, it is important to keep in mind that some members of a community may feel empowered (i.e., feel free to try something new or to try again if a previous effort failed), and others disenfranchised (i.e., feel less able to effect change). This can have real consequences when envisioning the possibilities and limitations to community development. For example, a group of undergraduate student parents may collaborate with their office of graduate student affairs to draft a well-intentioned and thoughtful proposal to start a campus daycare center for students with children. Although these students may be hopeful for support from the university, they may also assume that establishing the center is an impossible and unrealistic goal because of issues of space or financial resources. When examining their reactions to the change process, this group may realize that they hold some empowering beliefs that could move them forward (seeing the value of the center, optimism for success), as well as constraining beliefs that could inhibit their progress (assumptions of failure or of a lack of resources or interest from other students).

Table 9.2 illustrates some of the constraining as well as the empowering beliefs that many students embody. Being aware of these viewpoints will be important as students work through differences and attend to power structures in order to be thoughtful, inclusive, understanding, and collaborative in building campus communities.

Part of empowerment work within a community involves a commitment to a plurality of voices, life experiences, skills, and abilities. There are several essential questions to consider when developing oneself as an engaged, conscientious member of a community. The following questions have been adapted to reflect this type of growth (Banks, 2001; Bettez, 2011; University of Kansas, 2015):

TABLE 9.2 Constraining and Empowering Beliefs in Campus Community Building

Constraining Beliefs		
Individual Internal Beliefs	Individual External Actions	Implications for Individual Development
I don't have time to get involved. Faculty members don't value my contributions. I don't have anything to offer student organizations. Other students don't support my interests.	Individual students are not engaged in campus life. Individual students are passive learners. Individual students self-select out of student organizations.	Individual students are not viewed as major stakeholders or change agents and are therefore overlooked for opportunities to develop community. Individual students are less self-aware of their talents and opportunities to be part of campus life.
Group Internal Beliefs	Group External Actions	Implications for Group Development
This campus doesn't care about students. Students do not have enough experience to engage in major campus community–building efforts.	Students and student groups are not involved in shared responsibilities for effecting growth. Fragmentation exists among student groups.	Students do not learn collaborative models of community building that embrace • Shared purpose • Inclusion • Commitment • Group learning • Coalition building • Working with diverse populations
Empowering Beliefs		
Individual Internal Beliefs	Individual External Actions	Implications for Individual Development
I can manage multiple roles and tasks so that I can make a difference on campus. As a campus citizen, I have a responsibility to help shape matters that affect me and my peers. Individual students have the ability to shape their futures. Each student has the capacity to engage in community building.	Individual students are engaged in a wide array of activities inside and outside the classroom. Individual students take the initiative to become involved in the life of the campus.	Individual students have opportunities for community development through formal and informal programs and experiences.

(continued)

TABLE 9.2 continued

Group Internal Beliefs	Group External Actions	Implications for Group Development
Students are viewed as major stakeholders. Students are viewed as change agents. Student community building can make a difference on campus.	Students build coalitions with other campus groups to advance a shared vision and purpose. Students actively participate in shared campus governance. Students involve and prepare other students for community responsibilities.	Students and student groups model collaborative leadership. Students learn how to work interdependently to effect change. Students learn how to influence and shape the future of their campuses.

Source: Adapted from Astin and Astin (2000, pp. 24–25).

1. Who gets to participate in the group or community? Who feels welcome in the community?
2. Whose voices are heard or listened to? Who does the listening?
3. To whom does the community belong? Who defines the boundaries of the community?
4. What is the community's history? How knowledgeable are community members of this history?
5. Who benefits from the community?
6. Who is held accountable to the community? How does this work?
7. What groups have formed effective networks or coalitions to share community issues?
8. Who makes the decisions in how the community develops, and redevelops, itself?
9. How does the community redevelop when some within the community feel alienated or marginalized?

These are critical questions for leaders to contemplate when examining the groups in which they participate, the diversity and inclusiveness of those groups, and the members who feel empowered and who feel powerless.

Use these questions as guidelines for observing existing student groups, such as classes, clubs, student organizations, athletic teams, committees, or work groups, in which you participate. How did each of these questions influence the communities in which you were involved?

In collaboration with other local universities, Rachel Osuna, a student at the University of San Diego, organized a regional conference called C.A.S.E.: Collaborative for Action, Service, and Engagement. Each year for three years the group picked a topic and created a community project to raise awareness of its significance. In her senior year, that issue was educational inequity. As community volunteers, they saw the gap that existed between low- and high-income public schools and sought to empower students and parents to speak up for change. Rachel shared:

> Often when discussing issues of educational reform, parents, school officials, and politicians talk about what should be done to "fix" the problem, but they rarely ask the children what they would change. That night, the voices of the children were heard.

Social Perspective Taking (SPT)

Williams (2005) complemented her definition of citizenship with philosopher Seyla Benhabib's assertion that "an enlarged mentality" (p. 237) is necessary to understanding one's place in the greater community. This approach points to the concept of SPT, or the ability to identify and understand how others are thinking or feeling. Research has begun to explore connections between SPT and socially responsible leadership values within the Social Change Model (Dugan, Bohle, Woelker, & Cooney, 2014), yet a key question persists: how does a community develop SPT? One approach is to look to Williams's discussion of empathy, which she described as (1) a capacity developed through its exercise, which (2) depends on experiences with diverse practices and beliefs and (3) is cultivated through "discursive exchange between different perspectives, that is, through dialogue with different others" (p. 237). It is often through the free discourse of ideas, including those that conflict, that communities seek shared solutions (see Chapter 8 on Controversy With Civility).

Coalition Building

When situating Citizenship within the larger SCM framework, it may be useful to think of group leadership as having an internal and external component. Leadership that pays attention to internal issues may focus on developing members' own capacity for participation in a group or on working collaboratively toward common goals. However, leaders of successful groups also need to pay attention to external issues—what is happening in our communities? What do our communities need from us (us as individuals and us as a group)? What do we need to better understand about our communities to be effective participants and leaders? Who else should our group be working with? In more complex organizations, formal positions are sometimes structured around these two tasks, with the chief executive officer (CEO) handling external leadership issues and the president handling internal leadership issues.

When several distinct organizations decide to formally join together around a common goal, a coalition is born. A coalition allows groups to join resources and expertise in order to solve problems they share, while letting each organization retain its autonomy. Organizations in coalitions each preserve their unique missions, identity, and values. In fact, sometimes organizations within a coalition may disagree on many issues, but they do not let those disagreements deter them from uniting on the issues they do agree on (Mizrahi & Rosenthal, 1993).

Coalition building is an important aspect of Citizenship because most community problems are too complex to be solved by one approach or one group acting alone. Forming coalitions also encourages communities to reach out to groups with diverse perspectives and experiences in order to strengthen their efforts at success.

A student intern from Illinois Wesleyan University worked with a neighborhood in Bloomington, Illinois, to create a community garden. In order to succeed, the student partnered with neighbors, the Boys & Girls Club, a local corporation, and the community's historical society. The resulting garden was a welcome addition to the natural beauty of the area, and it served as an educational tool for local children.

Community development specialist Thomas Wolff (2001) outlined several salient characteristics of an effective coalition:

> It is composed of community members. . . . It addresses community needs, building on community assets; it helps resolve community problems through collaboration; it is community-wide and has representatives from multiple sectors; it works on multiple issues; it is citizen influenced if not necessarily citizen driven; and it is a long term, not ad hoc, coalition. (p. 166)

This statement reflects the growing trend for communities to build on members' strengths to develop well-functioning communities (Morse, 2004).

EXPANDING FORMS OF CITIZENSHIP

Citizenship is evident in many forms of engagement of a person in their communities of practice. Today's communities are evident in cyberspace, protest movements that span great distances, and as a bond among people who share the same profession. New community contexts require us to consider what responsible citizenship looks like in those settings.

Digital Citizenship

Students increasingly use technology to voice their concerns or take action on local and global issues, whether through online petitions, e-mail campaigns, personal or organizational websites, or social media. Social media is particularly fertile ground for student engagement. According to a survey from the Pew Research Center, a large percentage of young adults are inclined to seek information about sociopolitical issues as a result of what they read on social media, and "the youngest American adults are more likely to engage in political behaviors on social networking sites than in any other venue" (Smith, 2013). Examples of such efforts intended to effect social change include the University of Missouri Students Association Social Justice Committee on Facebook, Michigan State University's Students for Fair Trade group on Twitter, or the "Feminist Thought Bubble" on Instagram (created and maintained by a 20-year-old college student).

In recent years, hashtag activism has become a frequently used phrase to describe campaigns initiated on social media that are intended to educate and mobilize supporters. Examples include #RapeCultureIsWhen, #JeSuisCharlie, and #NotYourAsianSidekick. Students have become ardent supporters of these forms of expression and engagement, as evidenced by the #BlackLivesMatter movement, which is not only active on Facebook, Twitter, Tumblr, and Instagram but also on photo-sharing sites such as Flickr. Building on this momentum, there is an increasing number of campaigns related to selfies for a cause, such as Radford University's #RecyclingSelfie campaign for America Recycles Day.

Questions remain regarding the extent to which digital activism translates to deeper engagement on a social issue or to social change itself. Consider the commonly used term *clicktivism*, which refers to a demonstration of support for a cause through the click or tap of a button. Examples include retweeting, clicking a like or join button, sharing someone's post on social media, or signing an online petition. Technology critic Evgeny Morozov (2009) calls this form of engagement *slacktivism*, emphasizing the passive nature of providing support on an issue without much effort, a sense of accountability, or follow-through. Others suggest that clicktivism is more than simply endorsing a cause; it is also an organizing tool, an opportunity to change minds, and a means for facilitating active participation in larger community initiatives such as boycotts or crowdsourced projects (Clicktivist.org, n.d.). A recent study of the clicktivism phenomenon found that, as a group, "low-commitment participants" have the capacity to spread important information that can galvanize supporters and influence people's thinking on an issue, with the potential to incite further action (Barber et al., 2015).

Consumer Activism

Research has found that young adults aged 18 to 34 are more actively engaged than other generations in consumer activism (PR Newswire, 2010). This study refers to two such activities: *boycotting* and *buycotting* products and services. *Boycotting* involves opting out of certain purchases or services because of the conditions in which they were made or provided. For example, a student may choose to not purchase products from a campus food retailer that engages in discriminatory hiring practices and may petition such companies to change their policies. *Buycotting* refers to intentionally purchasing products or services that are distributed by companies that share the consumer's social and political values. Research has shown that young people take the lead in cause-based purchasing (Palmer, 2010; Stetzer, 2011) and younger consumers are consistently more likely to pay more than older generations for products and services from businesses they consider socially responsible (Marketing Charts, 2012; Nielsen, 2014). This may mean purchasing coffee from a vendor who sells free-trade coffee, supporting microlending firms that provide loans to entrepreneurs in developing countries, or purchasing gasoline from companies that are working toward reducing carbon emissions and developing green technologies. Boycotting and buycotting support the idea that the everyday decisions people make have an impact on others, at home and abroad.

CONNECTION TO THE OTHER Cs

Citizenship as the societal component of the Social Change Model of Leadership Development draws on the interconnectedness of the individual, group, and societal Cs. The ensemble (HERI, 1996) stated that "Citizenship thus acknowledges the interdependence of all who are involved in or affected by these efforts" (p. 23), that is, individual, group, and societal attempts to effect change.

Attention to the Citizenship C builds capacity in the other Cs as well. Experiences with Citizenship often challenge people to make choices that require them to clarify their Commitments, consider their values through Consciousness of Self, and examine whether their choices are Congruent with their beliefs. In addition to the individual-level Cs, the group-level Cs are positively affected by Citizenship. When actively participating in community endeavors, people have opportunities to practice Collaborating with others, reaching a Common Purpose, and learning to work through Controversy With Civility. Just as experiences with Citizenship build capacity to engage in the other Cs, experiences with the other Cs improve one's ability to engage in Citizenship.

CONCLUSION

According to an East African proverb, "The person who has not traveled widely thinks his or her mother is the only cook [the best cook]." The final outcome of the Social Change Model is, unsurprisingly, Change, which involves asking critical questions of oneself and others, as well as engaging in new and varied experiences that strengthen one's capacity for ethical leadership. The metaphor of traveling widely echoes this sentiment and directs the change agent to seek an increased understanding of internal and external leadership factors. This includes challenging one's own worldview, engaging in conversations across difference, and taking risks that involve trying new things and meeting new people.

Throughout this chapter, the Citizenship value of the Social Change Model has been discussed in its various dimensions. As the ensemble (HERI, 1996) recommended, one way to visualize these different levels of citizenship is to imagine a set of concentric circles with the smallest (most interior) circle representing the individual, the next one representing the group, the next one the institution, and so on, with the largest (most exterior) circle representing the society at large (p. 63). In this context, long-term, effective Citizenship will ideally intersect all circles in the set. Similar to understanding the individual, group, and societal levels of citizenship, Komives (1994) encouraged her readers to continually ask themselves three questions: "How am I like no one else here? How am I like some others here? And how am I like everyone here?" (p. 219). As you continue to learn and apply the Seven Cs of Change, you are encouraged to personally reflect on where you and your communities enter the value of Citizenship, to think critically about how you and groups with which you are affiliated see yourselves using the model in your communities, and to ask questions along the way.

DISCUSSION QUESTIONS

1. The term *Citizenship* has different meanings to different people. How do you define it?
2. What do you believe are the indicators of "good" Citizenship?
3. Which of the forms of Citizenship and active community involvement appeal to you most? Are there any forms described in this chapter that you have never done?

ACTION AND REFLECTION

1. What communities can you consider yourself a part of? What does Citizenship in those communities mean to you? How do you actively involve yourself in these communities?
2. Within the communities named in Question 1, how might you go about developing social capital and increasing your awareness of the issues in those communities? How would you increase the bonding form of social capital? The bridging form?
3. In a group you participate in, look around at who is part of the group this week, who participates in discussion, and whose opinions are recognized and affirmed. Pay attention to how decisions are made and consider how inclusive these discussions are.
4. Consider a group you are a part of. Who else in the community (individuals or groups) share similar aims? How might you approach them to build a coalition?
5. Use the rubric in Table 9.3 to gauge your own development within the Citizenship value. Reflect on how you could develop this aspect of your leadership capacity.

TABLE 9.3 Citizenship Rubric

	Excelling	Achieving	Developing	Needing Improvement
Acceptance of Social Responsibility	Frequently participates in community-based activities Views service to community as a mutually beneficial activity	Sometimes participates in community-based activities Views service to community as an activity of charity	Rarely participates in community-based activities Views self and community as separate, unrelated entities	No participation in community-based activities General unawareness of the larger community in which one lives
Confidence (of Self and of Communication Skills)	Enjoys sharing ideas and does so frequently Believes she or he can make a positive impact in any community	Regularly shares ideas with others Believes she or he can make a positive impact in the immediate community and sometimes in the extended community	Sometimes shares ideas with others Sometimes believes she or he can make a positive impact in the immediate community	Does not attempt to share ideas with others Does not believe she or he has the ability to make a positive impact in any community
Appreciation of Diversity	Embraces societal and individual differences Advocates on behalf of others Demonstrates cross-cultural competence Works well with diverse populations	Accepts societal and individual differences Willing to advocate on behalf of others Some cultural awareness	Acknowledges societal and individual differences Acknowledges the importance of advocacy Minimal cultural awareness	Unaware or not accepting of societal and individual differences No cultural awareness
Embracing of Change and Challenges	Believes that she or he can make a difference in his or her community Challenges general assumptions Welcomes ambiguity Values opportunities to create and harvest change despite obstacles	Believes that an individual can make a difference in his or her community Questions general assumptions Content with ambiguity Values the need for change	Aware of changes going on in community Aware of general assumptions Apprehensive or uncomfortable with ambiguity	Unaware of changes going on in community Unaware of any held assumptions Ignores ambiguity

Source: Developed by Jordan Draper and Kylie Goodell.

REFERENCES

Astin, A., & Astin, H. (2000). *Leadership reconsidered: Engaging higher education in social change*. Battle Creek, MI: W. K. Kellogg Foundation.

Banks, J. A. (2001). Citizenship education and diversity: Implications for teacher education. *Journal of Teacher Education, 52*, 1–13. Retrieved from http://jte.sagepub.com/cgi/reprint/52/1/5.pdf

Barber, P., Wang, N., Bonneau, R., Jost, J., Nagler, J., Tucker, J., & González-Bailón, S. (2015). The critical periphery in the growth of social protests. *PLOS-One*. Available at http://journals.plos.org/plosone/article?id=10.1371/journal.pone.0143611

Bettez, S. C. (2011). Critical community building: Beyond belonging. *Educational Foundations, 25*(3–4), 3–19. Available at http://files.eric.ed.gov/fulltext/EJ954978.pdf

Bordas, J. (2012). *Salsa, soul, and spirit: Leadership for a multicultural age* (2nd ed.). San Francisco, CA: Berrett-Koehler.

Circle K International. (2015). *CKI facts*. Retrieved July 25, 2015, from http://www.circlek.org/AboutUs/ckifacts.aspx

Clictivist.org. (n.d.). Home page. Retrieved December 15, 2015, from http://www.clicktivist.org/what-is-clicktivism

Council of Economic Advisors. (2014). *15 economic facts about millennials*. Retrieved July 25, 2015, from https://www.whitehouse.gov/sites/default/files/docs/millennials_report.pdf

de Tocqueville, A. (1956). *Democracy in America* (Heffner R. D., Trans.). New York, NY: Penguin Books. (Original work published 1835)

Dewey, J. (1916). *Democracy and education: An introduction to the philosophy of education*. New York, NY: Free Press.

Dugan, J. P., Bohle, C. W., Woelker, L. R., & Cooney, M. A. (2014). The role of social perspective-taking in developing students' leadership capacities. *Journal of Student Affairs Research and Practice, 51*(1), 1–15. Retrieved from http://dx.doi.org/10.1515/jsarp-2014–0001

Ehrlich, T. (2000). Preface. In T. Ehrlich (Ed.), *Civic responsibility and higher education* (pp. vi–x). Washington, DC: Oryx.

Greenberg, E., & Weber, K. (2008). *Generation we: How millennial youth are taking over America and changing our world forever*. Emeryville, CA: Pachytusan.

Higher Education Research Institute (HERI). (1996). *A social change model of leadership development* (Version III). Los Angeles, CA: University of California, Los Angeles, Higher Education Research Institute.

Kielburger, C., & Kielburger, M. (2014, April 8). From generation me to generation we: How millennials are changing business. *Huffington Post*. Retrieved July 15, 2015, from http://www.huffingtonpost.ca/craig-and-marc-kielburger/millennial-business_b_5112689.html

Komives, S. R. (1994). Increasing student involvement through civic leadership education. In C. C. Schroeder, P. Mable, & Associates (Eds.), *Realizing the educational potential of college residence halls* (pp. 218–240). San Francisco, CA: Jossey-Bass.

Liang, C.T.H., Lee, S., & Ting, M. P. (2002). Developing Asian American leaders. In M. K. McEwen, C. M. Kodama, A. N. Alvarez, S. Lee, & C.T.H. Liang (Eds.), *Working with Asian American college students* (New Directions for Student Services, no. 97, pp. 81–90). San Francisco, CA: Jossey-Bass.

Marketing Charts. (2012). Most prefer socially conscious cos., but many balk at paying them more. Retrieved August 29, 2015, from http://www.marketingcharts.com/uncategorized/most-prefer-socially-conscious-cos-but-many-balk-at-paying-them-more-21668/1346151867000

Mizrahi, T., & Rosenthal, B. S. (1993). Managing dynamic tensions in social change coalitions. In T. Mizrahi & J. Morrison (Eds.), *Community organization and social administration: Advances, trends and emerging principles* (pp. 11–40). New York, NY: Haworth.

Morozov, E. (2009). Foreign policy: Brave new world of slacktivism. Retrieved January 5, 2016, at http://www.npr.org/templates/story/story.php?storyId=104302141

Morse, S. M. (2004). *Smart communities: How citizens and local leaders can use strategic thinking to build a brighter future*. San Francisco, CA: Jossey-Bass.

Nielsen. (2014). Investing in the future: Millennials are willing to pay extra for a good cause. Retrieved August 29, 2015, from http://www.nielsen.com/us/en/insights/news/2014/investing-in-the-future-millennials-are-willing-to-pay-extra-for-a-good-cause.html

Owen, J. E., & Wagner, W. (2010). Situating service-learning in the contexts of civic engagement and the engaged campus. In B. Jacoby (Ed.), *Establishing and sustaining the community service-learning professional: A guide for self-directed learning*. Providence, RI: Campus Compact.

Palmer, S. (2010). Mothers and young people are most likely to buy products tied to a cause. *The Chronicle of Philanthropy*. Retrieved August 29, 2015, from https://philanthropy.com/article/MothersYoung-People-Are/226131

PR Newswire. (2010). Voting with their wallets: New research finds younger Americans, liberals and West Coast consumers most likely to report boycotting and "buycotting" based on values. Retrieved January 15, 2016, from http://www.prnewswire.com/news-releases/voting-with-their-wallets-new-research-finds-younger-americans-liberals-and-west-coast-consumers-most-likely-to-report-boycotting-and-buycotting-based-on-values-91533949.html

Public Affairs. (2014). The next America. *Trust.* Retrieved August 25, 2015, from http://magazine.pewtrusts.org/en/archive/summer-2014/the-next-america

Putnam, R. D. (1999). Bowling alone: America's declining social capital. In B. Barber & R. M. Battistoni (Eds.), *Education for democracy* (pp. 573–577). Dubuque, IA: Kendall/Hunt.

Putnam, R. D. (2000). *Bowling alone: The collapse and revival of American community.* New York, NY: Simon & Schuster.

Putnam, R. D., & Goss, K. (2002). Introduction. In Robert D. Putnam (Ed.), *Democracies in flux: The evolution of social capital in contemporary society.* Oxford, UK: Oxford University Press.

Smith, A. (2013). Civic engagement in the digital age. Retrieved June 15, 2015, from http://www.pewinternet.org/files/old-media/Files/Reports/2013/PIP_CivicEngagementinthe-DigitalAge.pdf

Stetzer, A. (2011). All talk, little action: Study reveals how cause marketing can move consumers from talk to purchase. Retrieved August 29, 2015, from https://www.ketchum.com/pt-br/news/all-talk-little-action-study-reveals-how-cause-marketing-can-move-consumers-talk-purchase

Takaki, R. (1993). *In a different mirror: A history of multicultural America.* Boston, MA: Little, Brown.

University of Kansas. (2015). Work Group for Community Health and Development Community toolbox (ch. 27, section 11: Building inclusive communities). Retrieved from http://ctb.ku.edu/en/table-of-contents/culture/cultural-competence/inclusive-communities/checklist

Wenger, E. (2006). Brief introduction to communities of practice. Retrieved June 15, 2015, from http://wenger-trayner.com/wp-content/uploads/2012/01/06-Brief-introduction-to-communities-of-practice.pdf

Williams, S. (2005). Citizenship as identity, citizenship as shared fate, and the functions of multicultural education. In K. McDonough & W. Feinburg (Eds.), *Citizenship and education in liberal-democratic societies* (pp. 208–248). Oxford, UK: Oxford University Press.

Wolff, T. (2001). Community coalition building—contemporary practice and research: An introduction. *American Journal of Community Psychology, 29,* 165–172.

PART 5

On Change

Leadership = conviction in action.
—DENNIS C. ROBERTS

Dennis C. Roberts (2007), a member of the Social Change Model (SCM) ensemble and author of *Deeper Learning in Leadership*, believes that "leadership = conviction in action" (p. 98). Putting all the Cs together mobilizes individuals to understand themselves and come together in collaborative ways to accomplish change particularly social change.

One's commitments to action embody the very leadership the SCM values. Author Jennifer Louden (2008) calls this an "inner approach with outer impact." Indeed, *Leadership Reconsidered* authors (Astin & Astin, 2000) assert:

> Consistent with the notion that leadership is concerned with change, we view the "leader" basically as a change agent, i.e., "one who fosters change." Leaders, then, are not necessarily those who merely hold formal "leadership" positions; on the contrary, all people are potential leaders. (p. 8)

Roberts (2007) encourages students to

> start at a place where you can reasonably determine that you will be effective—think big and bold for a better future, constantly check your purposes and those of others on whom you rely, regenerate ideas and resources to continue your progress, and cherish the opportunity to be a constant student of leadership and your own experience. (p. 129)

Become mindful of yourself engaging with others and hold high expectations that you can make a difference with your actions. Today's times need new approaches to leadership. Former college president Lorraine Matusak (1996) observed, "Commitment, courage, caring service, collaboration, broad inclusive visionary thinking, and a deep respect for the gifts of others are the key concepts for the new breed of leader needed for the twenty-first century" (p. 12). Deciding that you will do something to make a difference to advance your commitments and that you will work with others in socially responsible ways is to be a change agent.

The final C in the Social Change Model is Change. Part 5 is devoted to understanding and implementing change. Chapter 10 unpacks the complexities with how change occurs and how people engage with change. Chapter 11 digs deeper into the concept of social change with examples that illustrate how students can engage in social change in college. Chapter 12 ties the previous chapters together with a focus on how readers can implement the Social Change Model in their own leadership.

REFERENCES

Astin, A. W., & Astin, H. S. (2000). *Leadership reconsidered: Engaging higher education in social change.* Battle Creek, MI: W. K. Kellogg Foundation.

Louden, J. (2008). *Being a change agent: An inner approach with outer impact.* Retrieved July 11, 2008, from http://www.selfgrowth.com/articles/Louden22.html

Matusak, L. R. (1996). *Finding your voice: Learning to lead anywhere you want to make a difference.* San Francisco, CA: Jossey-Bass.

Roberts, D. C. (2007). *Deeper learning in leadership: Helping college students find the potential within.* San Francisco, CA: Jossey-Bass.

10

Change

Wendy Wagner

> Give me a place to stand and a lever long enough and I will move the world.
> —ARCHIMEDES

Mark has become overwhelmed by the work involved in being the publicity chair of the program board. The students on his committee were active and helpful at the beginning of the year, but after a few months he has found himself doing nearly all the work. He made several attempts to use deadlines and incentives, but the other committee members still submitted sloppy work. Recognizing that this ongoing problem indicated a need for group change, he began to ask committee members what they thought needed to shift for everyone to start sharing the workload. The responses surprised him, "I worked really hard on the first few flyers I made, and you changed almost everything about them. I guess I figured you knew what you wanted already so I just started submitting the basic information knowing you would change the look of the flyer yourself anyway." Another student said, "I drew up our new T-shirt design and even though everyone really liked it, you created a new one. I'm not mad about it, but I'm really busy. I don't have time to work on things that aren't going to happen anyway." Mark realized that perhaps the change that was needed started with him. Although he thought he believed in delegation, he needed to explore the reasons why he was not yet comfortable letting others have control of their tasks.

LEADERSHIP AND CHANGE

The Social Change Model of Leadership Development provides a framework for facilitating the growth and leadership development for individuals, groups, and communities. The ultimate goal of leadership is to enact the values at each of these levels to influence intended change. As the opening anecdote illustrates, in order to effectively influence community change, groups must be capable of change. In order for groups to be capable of change, the individuals in them need to capable of personal change.

As a model of leadership development, the Social Change Model is grounded in the assumption that successful leadership achieves goal and process outcomes. Did the group meet its task objective? Did the leadership initiative facilitate growth in the group members' Consciousness of Self, Congruence, and Commitment? How did it help the group continue to develop its ability be Collaborative, engage in Controversy With Civility, and hone in on its Common Purpose? How did the initiative help the community learn to be more effective by fostering greater social capital or building trust through new coalitions?

Change, as outlined by the ensemble, does not refer only to how goals are implemented but also how individuals, groups, and communities experience growth and development as a result of quality leadership processes. As depicted in Figure 10.1, change

FIGURE 10.1 The Social Change Model and Change

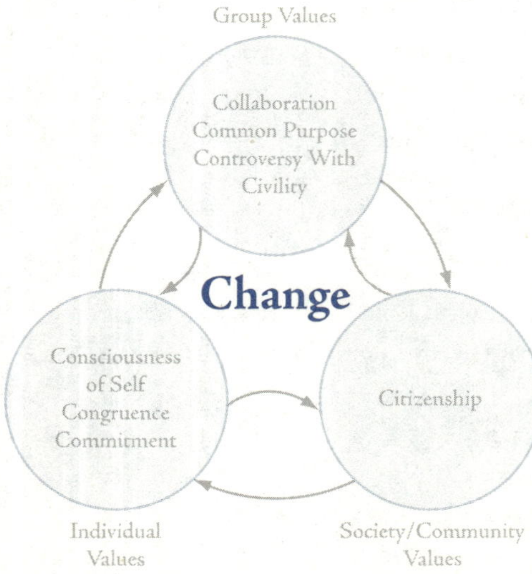

is the heart of the Social Change Model and is the purpose of leadership. Exploring the complex nature of change, as well as the implications of how we conceptualize change at the individual, group, and community level, is the subject of this chapter.

Change is the hub of the Social Change Model and focuses on making "a better world and a better society for self and others" (Higher Education Research Institute [HERI], 1996, p. 21).

CHAPTER OVERVIEW

As indicated by its framing and naming, the Social Change Model of Leadership Development is a model in which change at every level is of central concern. The audacious goal of this chapter is metacognitive: to examine how we think about change. The chapter explores the features of an organic conceptualization of change and what these new ideas about change mean for the role of leadership.

CHANGE AT THE INDIVIDUAL, GROUP, AND COMMUNITY LEVELS

The conceptualizations of change in this chapter are the result of decades of research across several academic disciplines. There is remarkable overlap of ideas, despite the different contexts of the scholarship. Individual-level change is informed by the work in developmental psychology and sociology (Brown, 2015; Kegan & Lahey, 2009). Group- and community-level change are informed by scholars from management science, organizational development, leadership studies, political science, psychology, and sociology (Allen & Cherrey, 2000; Heifetz, 1998; Heifetz, Grashow, & Linsky, 2009; Kotter, 1996; Senge, 2006, 2014; Stroh, 2015; Vaill, 1996; Wheatley, 1999). These scholars, representing many perspectives, have concluded that an important role of leadership is to facilitate good change processes—individual, group, and society/community change.

Change in this chapter does not refer to simple, surface-level shifts but to the complex changes that require examination of our individual and collective ways of being. One way to clarify this distinction is articulated by developmental psychologists Kegan and Lahey (2009):

> The challenge to change and improve is often misunderstood as a need to better "deal with" or "cope with" the greater complexity of the world. Coping and dealing involve adding new skills or widening our repertoire of responses. We are the same person we were before. (pp. 11–12)

Real personal (and, arguably, group- and community-level) change requires that we go deeper than *adding* knowledge of facts or theories. Learning new skills, terminology, or techniques is not the same as change. A better goal than *adding* is *developing*, which means gaining more complex ways of thinking and being, affecting how we perceive and interpret our experiences (Kegan & Lahey, 2009). The result of this development is that we can thrive within the complexity of our context rather than simply cope with it. Table 10.1 has examples of developmental change at each level of the Social Change Model.

TABLE 10.1 Examples of Developmental Change at Each Level of the Social Change Model

Individual-Level Development	• Learning to trust others so delegation is more successful • Learning to monitor one's emotional response in order to benefit from criticism and feedback • Learning to be a more reliable team member, such as addressing procrastination or lateness
Group-Level Development	• Changing the group's collaboration processes in order to use the talents and strengths of group members (see Chapter 6) • Collectively learning how to challenge false harmony and respond appropriately to those who disagree (see Chapter 8) • Learning to integrate information and tasks across subgroups or committees, such as event planning, publicity, and member recruitment • Replacing long-standing norms that do not align with group values, such as new member orientation that does not involve hazing • Building a more supportive community for learning leadership and the applied tasks of the group's work
Community-Level Development	• Collectively creating a community with a sense of shared responsibility and individual and group empowerment • Increasing social capital, building relationships or coalitions among individuals and groups • Collectively learning how to create an inclusive community in which everyone has a sense of belonging, appreciation, and way to contribute

AN ORGANIC CONCEPTUALIZATION OF CHANGE

In recent decades, the scholarship on leadership and change has shifted. More traditional thinking about change came from the context of hierarchically controlled organizations. Traditional models are described as being based on the assumption of a stable, predictable, controllable world (Allen & Cherrey, 2000; Stroh, 2015; Uhl-Bien, Marion, & McKelvey, 2007). Traditional approaches to change call on leaders to identify the solution to the problem and implement it through command and control. Some of these traditional approaches are still useful in certain contexts; however, when they don't work it is ineffective to continue to try the same approach when new thinking is needed.

Today's scholarship on leadership and change takes into account the unpredictability and complexity of modern leadership contexts. This view is referred to as an *organic* conceptualization of change because examples from nature illustrate that the real world is dynamic, not stable, controlled, or artificial. Change is not initiated by an authority, but is a constant. There is always momentum toward growth or decay and while that change cannot be controlled, it can be influenced if the forces at work are understood well. An organic perspective of change calls on leaders to have very different roles than does the traditional approach. Table 10.2 summarizes many of the core differences between traditional and organic approaches to change described by this body of literature (Allen & Cherrey, 2000; Senge, 2006, 2014; Stroh, 2015; Uhl-Bien et al., 2007; Vaill, 1996; Wheatley, 1999).

Individuals, groups, and communities do have qualities represented by the traditional view of change. They also have qualities that resemble the organic view of change. It is imperative to attend to both. Using the traditional view of change, leaders might address problems with solutions such as implementing standardized operating procedures and more efficient processes of communication and task sharing. These changes do help create the sense of stability and predictability that individuals, groups, and communities need in order to do their best. Stability is critical for teams to have solid ground to work from. But stability is not change; change is organic.

The organic nature of change has four important characteristics that will be explored further here. Each characteristic has implications at the individual, group, and society/community level. Organic change occurs in systems not compartments, is ongoing not episodic, is exponential not linear, and can be influenced but not controlled.

TABLE 10.2 Traditional and Organic Conceptualizations of Change

Assumptions of Traditional Change	Assumptions of Organic Change
Orderly structures are clear; the relevant facts are known; certainty and predictability are achievable.	Order exists, but it is complex and often difficult to see. Change is influenced by so many interdependent factors that certainty and awareness of all the relevant information is not possible. Outcomes are considered probable but not predictable.
With good planning, it is easy to predict outcomes. Perfect execution and efficiency are realistic expectations.	Ongoing experimentation and assessment, and the need to shift course and realign, is expected. Inefficient detours occur but can offer valuable insights. Goals are often achieved but do not look exactly as envisioned. Unintended consequences are known to occur, so outcomes must be monitored carefully.
Leaders can control the implementation of change with policies, procedures, and clear reporting structures. Top-down control from authorities ensures quality of process and outcome.	Control is not possible, but change can be influenced by aligning the small efforts of individuals and groups across the system. Influence is multidirectional and insights from all levels of the network are valued. Rather than delegation of tasks, individual initiative, guided by the group's shared values and vision, is valued and generates greater commitment.
Collaboration requires efficient sharing of information. Effective solutions from one team can be shared with others in order to apply them in other contexts.	Collaboration results in the creation of knowledge and new insights through shared understanding of perspectives. Creative solutions incorporate the unique characteristics of the context.
The problem can be understood by breaking it into separate parts, changing just the parts that need to be fixed.	The problem exists in a context of interdependent parts. Understanding the issue requires examining the whole system. The relationships between the parts are as important as the functioning of the parts themselves.
Leaders work to determine the solution to the problem, creating a clear plan to implement.	Problems have multiple causes and need multiple partial solutions, implemented by many individuals and groups across the network. Each act changes the context such that additional goals or shifts to the plans will be needed.

Organic Change Occurs in Systems Not Compartments

Traditional approaches to change use compartmentalized analysis, meaning that leaders examine only the part of the issue believed to be problematic. If a person has recurring headaches, a compartmentalized approach would only look at the head.

Taking an aspirin might seem to be a great solution because it solves the problem in the moment. However, if the person continues to get headaches, more complex analysis is needed. Systems thinking examines the multiple influences and contributors to the issue and how they interconnect. The headaches are likely a sign of several problems: stress, lack of sleep, unhealthy food, or dehydration. Each of these factors individually can cause recurring headaches, but systems thinking reveals the interconnections among these factors. Stress can be a cause of the headaches and can also contribute to lack of sleep, another cause. Lack of sleep can contribute to overuse of coffee, which can contribute to dehydration and further lack of sleep. The causes of the problem form an intersected web. One can see why dependency on aspirins might appear to be a simpler solution than addressing the larger system. But in the long term, the easy solution is rarely the final solution. As Senge (2006) wrote, "The easy way out usually leads back in" (p. 60).

Systems Thinking Results in Multiple-Part Solutions

Traditional approaches to change seek a simple cause-effect solution; when A happens, do B, and C will result. However, in the real world, there are multiple influences on A and B, making C difficult to predict as an outcome. A compartmentalized approach to address a problem does not consider other influences or stakeholders, so leaders are not aware that their simple solution produces problems in other parts of the system. These problems are referred to as unintended consequences and are often the result of quick fixes (Stroh, 2015).

Senge (2006) uses the analogy of a rug with a large bump in it. Stepping on the bump solves the problem and removes that particular bump, but the bump immediately reappears in another part of the rug. In this analogy, sometimes the bump is a problem that is "solved" by intentionally making it someone else's problem. More often, however, leaders truly believe their solution resolved the problem, without realizing that it created an entirely new problem somewhere else in the system. A compartmentalized approach to change results in leaders across the system continuing to pass bumps around the rug without ever addressing the problem in a way that works for everyone. "Today's problems come from yesterday's 'solutions'" (Senge, 2006, p. 57).

The gentrification of many urban areas in the United States is a community-level example of this challenge. In gentrified neighborhoods, inner-city poverty has been replaced by beautiful upscale, walkable neighborhoods. But this approach does not really address poverty or improve the city, it only moves the challenges associated with poverty to the inner suburbs. Families and senior citizens who are forced to leave their homes, schools, and neighborhoods because of the increases in rent certainly do not experience this change as a solution.

Systems thinking reveals the many influences that contribute to the continuation of the problem. An effective change strategy must examine how to interrupt each of those influences. A single large-scale change cannot be as effective as a strategy with multiple solutions, implemented across the system in a coordinated way. These small coordinated nudges are carefully chosen to have the most leverage (Allen & Cherrey, 2000; Senge, 2006, 2014; Stroh, 2015).

Systems Thinking Reveals the Power of Networks and Relationships

Systems thinking and an understanding of the need for multipart solutions reveal the ill fit of top-down hierarchical structures for influencing change in complex systems. Organizations do need an organizing structure to facilitate the division of labor, specialization of skills, and communication. However, a group that recognizes the complexity of systems will encourage influence to be initiated from anywhere in that structure rather than assuming that all ideas and instructions flow from the top to the bottom of the hierarchy.

Multipart solutions are initiated more effectively when all stakeholders in the system understand the wholeness of the system, are aware of how their actions affect others in the system, and are empowered to seek out their unique potential for influence on the system given their position in it. Systems thinking reinforces the relational leadership of the Social Change Model. Relationships are critical for effective leadership in a complex system—no one person can have all the perspectives needed to truly understand the problem. Similarly, one person cannot have an influence in all the areas across a complex system. Systems thinking helps identify the stakeholders needed for collaboration and coalition building (Stroh, 2015).

Systems Thinking Reveals How We Unintentionally Contribute to the Problem

When leaders go beyond the simple cause-effect understanding of change and recognize the multiple influences on the system, another outcome is the realization that their own behavior may also be contributing to the problem. The anecdote introducing this chapter is a group-level example of this principle. Using a compartmentalized analysis, Mark sees the problem as committee members who do not follow through on their work. Typical responses to this problem are based on the assumption of laziness or incompetence of committee members. To Mark's credit, he instead sought to understand the problem from others' perspective, which revealed his own problem with delegation. When leaders do not expect other members to be as committed or competent, they do not delegate the most meaningful tasks. Group members do not find their involvement meaningful, so they prioritize other groups and involvements. The leaders see these small tasks blown off, completed late or with poor quality, and conclude their assumption about the members' commitment was correct. This is a common pattern revealed by systems thinking, called a *reinforcing feedback loop*: an action produces a result that influences more of the same action, whether or not the action has the long-term desired effect (Senge, 2006; Stroh, 2015). In the headache example previously presented, taking the aspirin can also be considered a contributor to a reinforcing feedback loop. When the person takes the aspirin, the headache goes away—along with the motivation to discover or address what causes the recurring headaches in the first place. The feedback reinforces aspirin as the solution, even though it is not the answer to addressing recurring headaches in the long term, and the problem continues unresolved.

Systems Thinking Reveals Which Changes Will Yield the Most Impact

When the existing system does not create the results the individual, group, or community wants, then systems thinking can help identify the shifts needed to achieve the desired outcome. Always assume that the system exists to achieve something. If it is not resulting in the outcome you want, it helps to identify what the current system does achieve and for whom.

 I was admitted into the honors program of Universidad de Monterrey. I was part of a diverse group who shared the same goal: to be change agents. We capitalized on each other's strengths, which was key to the success of our project. My team's project was to educate others of the negative effects of plastic bags and encourage the use of reusable bags. We participated in various social events and created connections with local government and the business sector to promote this initiative.

—Aurora Guillén Graf is a graduate physician at Monterrey University, Mexico, where she is an instructor in clinical investigation. She was involved in the honors program, JÄLPEM, Free Books, and the Medical Student Society.

Organic Change Is Ongoing Not Episodic

Not only does change occur in complex networked systems with many interrelating parts but also the context of those systems is dynamic and constantly shifting—not fixed (Drath & Palus, 1994). Change was once thought of as an experience with a beginning, middle, and end. Whether initiated by the leader or by unexpected external shifts, it was thought that changes could be responded to one issue at a time. In fact, a popular, classic model for navigating organizational change suggested that organizations attend to three stages: (1) unfreeze the status quo by preparing the organization for the period of uncertainty ahead, (2) make the change, and (3) refreeze such that the organization once again achieves stability with the new change in place (Lewin, 1947).

Perhaps this model is less applicable because of our fast-paced modern times and the rapid exchange of information in the Internet age, or perhaps a view of change as episodic has always been overly simplistic. Either way, models with an organic conceptualization describe change as a constant state rather than happening in individual episodes (Drath & Palus, 1994; Senge, 2006, 2014; Vaill, 1989, 1996). Peter Vaill (1989) aptly described this ongoing state of change as feeling similar to *permanent whitewater.*

> Most managers are taught to think of themselves as paddling their canoes on calm, still lakes.... They're led to believe that they should be pretty much able to go where they want, when they want, using means that are under their control. Sure there will be temporary disruptions during changes of various sorts—periods when they'll have to shoot the rapids in their canoes—but the disruptions will be temporary, and when things settle back down, they'll be back in the calm, still lake mode. But it has been my experience... that you never get out of the rapids! No sooner do you begin to digest one change than another one comes along to keep things unstuck. In fact, there are usually lots of changes going on at once. The feeling is one of continuous upset and chaos. (p. 2)

Interestingly, Charles Palus, a senior fellow at the Institute for Creative Leadership, actually happens to enjoy kayaking in his spare time and was able to take Vaill's analogy a step further (Palus, Horth, & Ill, n.d.). Palus clarifies that although whitewater appears chaotic and unpredictable, learning to read the river is an early lesson in kayaking. People can learn to see patterns and use them to their advantage. What may look to the untrained eye like a shift off course is actually a move right into a current that will shoot the kayak down the river quickly. Palus finds the same to be true for navigating the constant change of organizational life. Today's leaders should not expect to control a step-by-step process leading them back to stability. Unpredictable conditions will send us off in unexpected directions; however, those who take the time to learn can see the patterns in the system and occasionally use the unexpected to shift them closer to their goals. Again, the result of a more complex view of change is the ability to not only cope with our context but also thrive in it.

Two key attributes, applicable to individuals, groups, and communities, contribute to the ability to be successful in the ongoing whitewater of change: the ability to do systems thinking and the ability to learn (Palus, Horth, & Ill, n.d.; Senge, 2006, 2014; Vaill, 1989, 1996). Again using an analogy, Vaill (1989) contrasts being convinced of one's certainty with having the attitude of a learner:

> It is the nonexplorers who rather naively assume that once they have a clear sharp picture in mind of where they are going, they can trust that picture through to the end. To be an explorer is to not know where, precisely and concretely, one is going.... The explorer feels your uncertainty and your fear and even sometimes your fury. However, he or she does not think these states of mind can be escaped. Instead, they are part of what the explorer explores. (p. 45)

This is not to say that leaders do not identify their aims, but in today's constantly shifting environment, it is more effective to have clear purposes and to be open about what it might look like to make our way there.

Peter Senge, a scientist researching organizational systems at MIT, has concentrated much of his career on examining how organizations can enhance their ability to learn collectively. He agrees that our rapidly changing organizational environments require leaders and organizations themselves to be flexible and adaptive—*nimble*. Senge (2006) believes all people have the capacity for continual learning but that many organizational environments are not conducive to the creative experimentation and reflection that would support it. Senge's ongoing work on the creation of *learning organizations* has identified important elements of such organizations, including the belief that learning at the individual and organizational levels are ongoing processes rather than an occasional event, that organization members must have a commitment to the shared vision and see themselves as a part of it, and that systemic thinking is key (Senge, 2006).

Organic Change Is Exponential Not Linear

A linear conceptualization of change assumes that the pace of change is steady and relative to the magnitude of the effort. Given this assumption, harder work should result in more change. For example, imagine a person has an idea and wants it to spread. With a linear conceptualization of change, the person might hope the idea spreads to, say, 10 new people every minute. In 10 minutes, 100 people would have seen the idea. To spread the idea faster, the person should work harder and tell 20 new people every minute.

Anyone who has observed a meme going viral on the Internet knows this is not how ideas actually spread. Organic change is not linear, it is exponential. Every minute 10 people each tell 10 friends, and those 100 people each tell 10 friends. If it were possible for that pace to continue for 10 minutes, the idea would reach one billion people. Harder work does not result in more change, but smarter work does: choosing the right 10 people from the start and sharing a message that captures people's attention.

Stroh shared a riddle occasionally used in algebra classes that illustrates several important aspects of exponential change:

> Imagine a lily pond where the lily plant doubles in size every day, and the pond is totally covered by the lily in thirty days. When is the pond half covered? The answer, . . . is day twenty-nine: Half of the pond is covered just one day before the pond is completely blanketed by the lily. How much of the pond is covered in fifteen days? The answer here is 0.0025 percent. In other words, halfway into the month the lily is barely noticeable. (p. 48)

The barely noticeable progress of the lily 15 days into its growth shows how self-defeating it can be to expect change to happen in linear fashion. Leaders who do not see enough early evidence of change from their efforts may stop the project too soon or fail to appreciate how their small achievements contribute to a larger trajectory of growth toward a complex goal.

Many social movements offer examples of leaders creating change by harnessing the momentum of exponential growth. One such example is the 1955 Montgomery, Alabama, bus boycott. As is often true with organic change, most of the facts people remember from this historic event did not occur until the "water lily" had already been growing for many years. The story actually begins much earlier, when

Black citizens in Montgomery, Alabama, boycotted the segregated streetcar system from 1900 to 1902 (Meier & Rudwick, 1969; Theoharis, 2013). Self-organized ride sharing in privately owned carriages and horse-drawn wagons emerged across the city (Meier & Rudwick, 1969). After two years of significant financial hardship from the boycott, the Mobile Light and Railroad Company decided to simply stop enforcing the city's segregation law. At least one streetcar conductor was arrested. Unfortunately, the city did not repeal segregation laws and enforcement gradually returned (Meier & Rudwick, 1969).

During the 1940s and 1950s segregation laws reached a peak. In 1944, Viola White was beaten and arrested for refusing to give her seat to a White woman. In 1953, a bus boycott in Baton Rouge, Alabama, was successful in addressing some segregation restrictions. Claudette Colvin, a Montgomery teenager, refused to give up her seat to a White woman and was arrested in 1955 (Theoharis, 2013).

Meanwhile, Rosa Parks had joined her local NAACP and had been active for 12 years, including serving on the executive board. In the summer of 1955 she attended a 10-day training session on labor and civil rights organizing at the Highlander Center, where she met many of the previous generation of civil rights leaders and learned about the success of the streetcar boycotts from 1900 to 1902. Following Colvin's arrest, Parks joined Martin Luther King Jr., E. D. Nixon, and other Black leaders in a meeting with Montgomery city administrators to discuss bus segregation policies, with few results. A few months later, Mary Louis Smith, another Montgomery teenager, refused to give up her seat to a White woman and was arrested (Theoharis, 2013).

Finally, on December 1, 1955, Rosa Parks refused to give up her bus seat to a White man and was arrested. The next day, the Women's Political Council announced their call for a 1-day bus boycott to occur on December 5 in protest. Although a 60% boycott was expected, 90% to 100% (estimates vary) of the Black community participated. Black leaders met and created the Montgomery Improvement Association (MIA), with Dr. Martin Luther King Jr. elected president. The MIA presented a list of demands to the city of Montgomery, which they refused, so the bus boycott was extended (Theoharis, 2013).

The bus boycott continued for a full year, during which time the homes of E. D. Nixon and Dr. King were bombed, and more than 80 boycott leaders were arrested and indicted by the city under "anti-conspiracy" laws. The MIA and other community members implemented carpool systems and other alternative sources of transportation, some of which were challenged by city officials. In November 1956, the Supreme

Court ruled against required racial segregation of buses and in December, when new policies were implemented in Montgomery, the boycott ended (Theoharis, 2013).

This example of community-level change demonstrates the importance of multiple influences from across the system, relationships and connections among those influences, and the experience of exponential rather than linear growth once the conditions are right. A year-long bus boycott across an entire city required empowerment and initiative from every person's sphere of influence, not followers waiting for directives from an authority figure.

This example also demonstrates a reality regarding who receives the credit for success. Many skilled and hard-working Black leaders contributed to the success of the Montgomery bus boycott, going back to the early boycott in 1900. Parks, Nixon, and King are the civil rights leaders the general public has heard of because they were doing the work when the change went viral. This point is not to diminish the importance of their influence but rather to generate an equal amount of appreciation for the leaders who kept the faith during the early years when the results were small and the movement had less momentum. Paul Loeb (2010), in his book *Soul of a Citizen,* said of Parks, "Parks' decision didn't come out of nowhere. Nor did she single-handedly give birth to the civil rights movement. Rather, she was part of a longstanding effort to create change, when success was far from certain and setbacks were routine" (p. 2).

Sensitivity to Initial Conditions

Exponential growth can result in such rapid change that it becomes more difficult to have influence on the outcome toward the end. The early choices that set the direction of the change are therefore very important. This concept is referred to as "sensitivity to initial conditions" (Komives, Lucas, & McMahon, 2006, p. 63). It is easy in the first stages of growth to control where the water lily will be, but once exponential growth has led to the point that the water lily's spread is noticeable (half the pond is covered), it is much more difficult to influence the direction of that growth. Similarly, when working in groups, setting the tone for trust, collaboration, and inclusion at the beginning of group formation is easier than responding to widespread hostility later on. Beginning with the assumption of trust, group members will find many early opportunities to share ideas and demonstrate teamwork. These experiences confirm and deepen the group's belief in their ability to trust and work together. The right initial conditions make it much easier to leverage exponential growth in the group's ability to trust and collaborate.

Broken Windows Theory

Exponential growth also applies to changes we do not want, so it is important to address small problems early on before the change momentum is beyond what we have the power to influence. Stroh (2015) offers a reminder here of what is known as the broken windows theory. Communities who attend to smaller problems such as fixing a broken window or keeping litter off the streets are able to keep their neighborhoods clean and safe by not allowing individuals to see a space where littering appears to be the norm. One can imagine how a problem like this could escalate quickly in a busy community. Recent research links sensitivity to initial conditions to interpersonal disputes as well. Some police forces are taking on community-building roles, helping neighbors build positive relationships in order to prevent small interpersonal disputes from growing into violence (Cloutier, 2015).

Organic Change Can Be Influenced but Not Controlled

With so many factors exerting influence on the outcomes of a system, particularly once exponential growth has gained momentum, it becomes apparent that it is not possible to force change or control the change process. Vision, influence, and power do not come from one point in the system. Although having a sense of control gives comfort to some leaders, it is more productive to understand that we do not have control over what happens, but we do have influence. If we are smart, we also build relationships with people who can influence the system in areas that we cannot.

Alexis Ohanian, the cofounder of Reddit, explained the importance of understanding influence without control by describing a social movement that was greatly influenced by the Reddit online community (Ohanian, 2009). Greenpeace had a goal to stop the Japanese government from a whaling expedition that would hunt endangered humpback whales. One aspect of the initiative was to place a tracking chip inside one humpback whale so the prey, if not the expedition's predators, could be tracked. Hoping to leverage increased public awareness and support, they decided to put a more personal "face" on their initiative and distributed an online poll to choose a name for the whale with the chip. Several symbolically meaningful names were suggested, but following some viral enthusiasm on Reddit, 70% of the votes were in favor of naming the whale, Mister Splashy Pants.

Greenpeace was not thrilled with this outcome, so they extended voting for a week, hoping another name would win out. Online voters pushed back in full force. Reddit and several other online news aggregators changed their logos to encourage votes for Mister Splashy Pants, Facebook pages were created, and the message spread widely. In the end, more than 19,000 people voted, 78% of the total, for Mister Splashy Pants. By then, Greenpeace had learned their lesson and used the (by now quite popular) Mister Splashy Pants logo to raise money by selling T-shirts and pins (Ohanian, 2009).

The primary lesson learned by Greenpeace was to let go of what they could not control in order to take advantage of the momentum that they could at least influence. By letting go of the name itself but allowing the meme to go on its own uncontrolled momentum, they reached an audience thousands larger than they would have otherwise. Although the specific name chosen was very different than what they imagined, they wildly exceeded the expectations of their original goal, which was spreading public awareness about the hunting of whales by Japan. (The Japanese government ended the whale-hunting expedition, by the way.) As Ohanian concluded, "You can do a lot online, but no longer is the message going to be controlled from the top-down. If you want to succeed, you've got to be OK with losing control" (Ohanian, 2009). Interestingly, at the time of this writing, the story is repeating itself, with British government officials refusing to accept the results of an online poll to name their new $300-million Antarctic research ship "Boaty McBoatface" (Friedman, 2016).

Examining health from a diversified perspective was vital while conducting water conservation research in Kimana, Kenya. I identified a sub-village, Ichalai, whose borehole had dried up because of a recent drought. After pinpointing the factors that were preventing the community from drilling a new source of water, I obtained funding through a service grant to drill a new borehole in closer proximity to the Maasai Boma. Upon receiving the grant, the women of Ichalai were able to access 20 liters of water in less than 30 minutes, as opposed to 4 hours. By analyzing population deterrents through the lens of a public health professional, an environmentalist, and alongside community stakeholders, I was able to impact a community's ability to obtain clean water.

—Colby Halligan is a 2015 graduate of Elon University, where she participated in Periclean Scholars, Elon Cycling, and the Watson and Odyssey Fellowship. While at Elon, she was an active member of the international and national fellowship department securing the Udall and the Ward Family Learning in Action awards.

ORGANIC CHANGE AND ADAPTIVE LEADERSHIP

Leadership scholar Ron Heifetz (Heifetz & Linsky, 2002) shares examples of evolutionary adaptation to help people in organizations learn to think about change in a new way. One such example is of peppered moths in England during the Industrial Revolution. Peppered moths in that particular region had light colored speckled wings that blended in with the lichens covering the trees. When the area industrialized and pollution killed the lichen, the light-colored moths now became quite visible against the dark-colored tree trunks and were eaten by predators. The few dark moths survived and bred and today peppered moths are known to have dark-colored wings. The lesson of adaptation is to learn to examine when it is no longer useful to try to change the environment, because what we need to change in order to succeed is ourselves—our own mind-set and approach.

Technical or Adaptive Change

Heifetz (Heifetz et al., 2009; Heifetz & Laurie, 1997; Heifetz & Linsky, 2002) makes a distinction between two types of problems: technical and adaptive. Technical problems are those that can be resolved by applying existing strategies. The procedures, skills, and processes we have learned to use in one context can often be applied to solve new problems. When the information and strategies needed to solve the problem are already known, technical solutions work. However, when the problem persists or resurfaces, this is a sign that the problem requires adaptation. Adaptive problems require an adjustment in mind-set: changing how we think about the problem, how we interpret the situation, or how we understand ourselves in relation to it. Adaptive change responses result from the realization that learning is needed—often shifts in values, attitudes, or habits of behavior are also required. The ability to do this shift requires becoming aware of what our existing mind-set is—also called our *mental model*.

Senge (2006, 2014) described mental models as deeply ingrained assumptions people have that lead them to make generalizations about how things are. They are our thinking frameworks, based on previous experiences and beliefs, which help us make connections and draw quick conclusions. George Roth (2006), a colleague of Senge's, used the image in Figure 10.2 to demonstrate mental models at work, in this case in interpreting visual information. Note that there is neither a triangle nor

FIGURE 10.2 Mental Models

a circle in this image, but most people's previous experience with these basic shapes leads them to see connections in order to identify those patterns.

Mental models help us understand situations quickly. For example, when we work with someone who expresses a preference for meetings with an orderly agenda and we observe that he or she keeps a very organized calendar, our mental models help us to predict that this person is also likely to have a high value for meetings that begin and end on time. Sometimes however, mental models are not accurate and lead us to see patterns that do not actually exist. For example, a person with a fear of being left out will have a mental model that interprets the slow response to a text message differently than a person who does not.

Mental models are neither good nor bad in and of themselves. However, we spend most of our time perceiving situations, interpreting them, and problem solving without any conscious awareness that we have a mental model at work. So when our mental models are leading us to make connections that do not exist, we do not think to question our assumptions but instead may keep trying to force solutions that are not a fit for the context.

It is often not until our technical solutions continue to fail that we realize we have a mental model at all and that it is based on assumptions that are not accurate. Consider young children learning to understand math by counting on their fingers. They can add 2 + 3 by holding up two fingers in one hand, three fingers in the other, and by counting all the fingers, arrive at the right answer: 5. However, when the context shifts, and the problem is to add 8 + 7, the mental model no longer works.

Continuing to apply their known strategy, they might invite friends to share their fingers, a technical solution, but ultimately the existing finger-counting strategy no longer works. This is an adaptive problem. The solution lies in changing their mental model for how to add.

Adaptive challenges are those in which we realize the problem lies in our own faulty mental models. In other words, the problem is not *out there*; it is *in here*. The positive outcome of accepting the need to adapt is not only that it paves the way to change that actually works but also that the formation of more accurate mental models represent learning and development that expand our capacity to solve future problems. A really good problem is one we don't solve; it solves us.

Individual-Level Adaptive Change

There are many examples of using technical solutions to foster individual change. We set goals and plan rewards for reaching them. We change our environment to make "bad" behavior less automatic. We attend workshops to add leadership skills. These approaches work when the problem is, in fact, a technical one. When technical solutions do not work, we often blame ourselves for not having enough self-discipline or for starting well but not sticking with it. However, much of the individual development needed for leadership involves not adding skills or changing the external environment but addressing our mental models about leadership.

Kegan and Lahey's (2009) research on individual-level change suggests that adapting our mental models is a cornerstone issue. "Distinguishing adaptive challenges from technical ones again brings our attention back from the 'problem' to the 'person having the problem' (p. 29). Kegan and Lahey explain that adaptive personal change requires the individual to make what they call a *subject/object shift*. Being unaware of the mental models we use to make sense of experiences makes us subject to them. Similar to seeing the world through glasses that we don't know we are wearing, we are subject to the mental models that affect what we notice and what we interpret it to mean. Similar to the addition problem previously described, we often become aware of having a mental model only when it no longer works. Awareness of a mental model means we are no longer subject to it, it becomes an object—something we can examine and question, accept or reject. According to Kegan and Lahey, this is how individuals become capable of achieving real personal change.

Kegan and Lahey's (2009) research provides a memorable example. One study participant was continually forgetting to take his heart medication every morning. He had tried several technical approaches to change, such as keeping the pill bottle with his toothbrush to align it with an existing daily habit. Still, he regularly forgot to take it. Through the research interview, it was revealed that the man had a mental model that connected taking morning pills with being very old, in fact he shouted at the researcher that he is nothing like his elderly father who takes pills each morning. No technical change was going to get this middle-aged man to adopt a daily practice he equated with old age. His subconscious was protecting him from having to identify as "elderly." Once this mental model, "if I take morning pills, then I'm an old man" shifted from subject to object, he was able to examine that assumption, consciously disconnecting "taking pills" from "being an old man."

Although protecting one's identity from accepting an older sense of self may not resonate for many readers just yet, this example bears a clear resemblance to college students who struggle with personal change goals such as being on time or having a regular bedtime because their subconscious mental models connect "responsible adult behavior" with the need to shed their "cool," carefree, youthful sense of self.

In the anecdote introducing this chapter, Mark's openness to feedback revealed that he is not able to delegate as well as he thought he was. Although there is a chance that implementing some technical changes will help Mark learn to delegate effectively, as long as he is subject to a mental model that does not allow him to trust the quality of others' work, the technical approaches are unlikely to be successful in the long term. To facilitate an adaptive approach, Mark can begin by asking himself why he changed his committee members' work. Perhaps his mental model for leadership involves demonstrating control over subordinates. Perhaps he fears becoming irrelevant if the committee is able to succeed without him. Perhaps he believes that quality and perfection are the same thing. Any number of mental models may be revealed by personal reflection, and they will vary even among individuals who share the same personal change goal. This is why the work of individual change is called *personal* development: it isn't possible for others to truly know what Mark's mental models are.

The thoughtful reader will have already noted at this point that the research on individual-level change is in direct alignment with the values of the Social Change Model. An adaptive rather than technical approach to individual change requires deep reflection on issues of consciousness of self and congruence. Although Mark may say he wants the committee members to be empowered and to contribute to the work, his actions clearly demonstrate competing values that he is not consciously acknowledging. Once he is aware of having these assumptions (consciousness of self) he will be able to examine them and figure out how to adapt his mental models in a way that will maintain his feelings of being needed and his belief in allowing group members to be empowered to do some of the work themselves. Arriving at this adaptive solution may require some creativity and experimentation, but it will not only have a better result for this specific committee it will also result in an important aspect of lifelong leadership development for Mark: the ability to trust others.

Group-Level Change

Just as Kegan and Lahey (2009) address the distinctions of technical and adaptive change at the individual level (described previously), other scholars, notably Heifetz (1998; who coined these terms) and Senge (2006) have described the same issues applying at the group level. The concepts are the same but the mental models are collectively held and the reflection involves group dialogue as well as individual introspection. When groups have trouble with members being accountable for their work, the first response is typically a technical one: create rules, set minimum requirements, require reports, and other accountability processes. This may result in improvements the group is satisfied with. However, having members meet minimum standards is not the aim of the group values of the Social Change Model. Greater aims would involve generating the sense of collective responsibility and empowerment that result when people consistently go above and beyond. This kind of change requires a deeper examination of group and individually held mental models. What needs to shift for all members to feel that their contributions are central rather than marginal to the group?

For example, one common challenge for student organizations, as well as community associations and nonprofit boards, is the annual turnover of elected officers. Sometimes it seems that just as the group is making progress, new leadership comes in with a steep learning curve and interests that take the group in a different direction than it had been heading. Technical solutions work for some groups: officer transition manuals or executive board transition retreats. However, even with these changes in place, sometimes groups are continually disappointed by the extent to which officer transition disrupts the group's momentum. An adaptive solution would have the group members examine the collective mental models that might be at the heart of this ongoing problem. Perhaps it is time for the group to think about why the general membership is so in the dark about what elected officers do. How could the vision, tasks, and ongoing decisions of executive officers become more transparent to all the members? How can more be delegated to regular members so when those members eventually become the elected leaders, they have a clearer idea of what the work involves, already understand the campus policies that affect them, and already have relationships with the people on campus who can help them do the work?

Community-Level Change

Facilitating adaptive change at the community level continues the same themes. The role of leaders is to engage whole communities in examining collectively held mental models and asking challenging questions about commonly held values and the gap between espoused values and behaviors.

For example, Americans almost uniformly value "equal opportunity" and believe anyone can succeed if he or she is willing to work hard. However, there are many policies and practices in place that are incongruent with those espoused values. Educational funding is one example of such a policy: education is not funded centrally so that every school receives the same amount of funding per child taught. Rather, schools are funded locally through property taxes, meaning children who already have the benefit of coming from a wealthy family also will attend a school with more financial resources available than children from low-income neighborhoods. Technical solutions have been attempted, such as busing lower-income children to better-funded schools outside of their own neighborhoods. However, this problem of inequity in education will continue until community members are challenged to examine their mental models about which children "deserve" quality education, and whether it really is "inevitable" that the children of parents with financial means and political connections will receive an education that will keep them ahead of their peers. Bringing the shared mental models into the collective consciousness, where they can be questioned and challenged, is a first step toward a shared process of generating adaptive community-wide solutions. Many of the issues related to facilitating change at the community level are discussed in Chapter 11.

 Community involvement has definitely taught me the importance of keeping an open mind. I once conducted an independent research project for a study abroad course in Djerba, Tunisia, where a school had recently been constructed to support the education of girls. Until then, the few girls in the community who received a secular education only did so until their early teens, after which they stayed home to preserve traditional values. Given what I already knew about this community, I began my research assuming that the Orthodox Jewish population there had probably been against the construction of a school for girls. However, I learned that they loved the school. The adults felt more comfortable knowing where the girls were during the day and the girls were happier learning than running errands for their households. I continue to wonder about how to support education for girls in a way that aligns with the values and traditions of people in the local community.

—Karina Lichtman is a recent graduate of The George Washington University as a major in human services and social justice. She continues her interests as a Peace Corps volunteer in Cambodia.

Distinguishing the Difference Between Technical and Adaptive Problems

It is very important to be clear that not every change requires an adaptive response. There is nothing wrong with technical solutions, when they work. As a species, the peppered moths adapted themselves to have dark wings instead of light because they did not have the capacity to change industrial pollution. If they did, perhaps that solution would have worked.

To facilitate change at any level, the ability to distinguish between technical and adaptive problems is an important leadership capacity (Heifetz & Linsky, 2002; Kegan & Lahey, 2009). Adaptive responses are indicated when leaders realize they need to shift focus away from the problem and toward the way they are thinking about the problem.

Heifetz has identified two primary indicators that a change requires an adaptive solution. The first is that technical solutions have been tried and they did not work. Perhaps a different technical solution could be attempted—it has already been emphasized that in organic change, experimentation and ongoing learning is an important value. But when continued attempts to apply new rules or procedures only work temporarily, then it is likely that the change requires adaptation.

The second indicator is to question whether it is people's habits and behaviors that need to change or if it is their core beliefs and values. For example, will enforcing a policy against alcohol consumption in campus housing reduce drinking if students' core beliefs about the "normal" college experience are still grounded in binge drinking? Stroh (2015) suggested that one outcome of systems thinking is that it makes our mental models explicit—we become consciously aware of our assumptions. Systems thinking in this example would help campus leaders identify other parts of the system they can influence (in addition to campus housing policies) in order to educate students and shift campus culture. Key questions to ask in identifying the need for an adaptive change are "Whose values, beliefs, attitudes, or behaviors would have to change in order for progress to take place? What shifts in priorities, resources, and power [are] necessary? What sacrifices would have to be made and by whom?" (Heifetz & Laurie, 1997, p. 126). When we recognize the shift needed is in our own thinking, rather than continuing to blame external influences, then adaptive leadership has begun.

RESISTANCE TO CHANGE

Whether approaching a technical or adaptive change, some involved in the change process may resist the change. Allen and Cherrey (2000) use another metaphor from nature to illustrate the outcome of trying to force change rather than influencing organic growth: wet sand. Have you ever been at the beach right at the water's edge and noticed that if you forcefully stamp your foot into the wet sand it meets hard resistance? Wet sand is composed of silicone and saline, which form a hard, temporary bond under that pressure. But if you just stand in wet sand, eventually your foot sinks into it. People and organizations also meet change with resistance—often resisting with a force equal to what they feel is being thrust on them. Change requires readiness. Understanding the organic nature of change helps us remember that we will get further, faster, by slowly working our way in.

Resistance to change can be either consciously, actively done, such as blocking, blaming, or sabotage, or as Kegan and Lahey's (2009) research demonstrated, unconsciously done, by not following through or procrastinating. This is true at the individual, group, and society/community levels. The temptation for leaders to walk away in frustration is strong, but it is that sort of resistance that most requires leaders to stay, listen, and understand. When resistance is strongest, we need to ask ourselves whether this is because we are stamping our feet in the sand rather than staying in the sand to work our idea in. Are we listening to others' ideas or are we too attached to our own? Are we open to the idea that the resistors may have a point? Are we assuming that change comes from one place in the organization or community or are we using the system to create coordinated nudges? Are we too invested in taking credit for the change?

IMPLICATIONS FOR LEADERSHIP

An organic conceptualization of change creates different expectations and roles for leaders. Individuals and groups must pay attention to the ever-changing environment, be connected to others in the community system, and be able to adjust course quickly to make the small, well-timed, coordinated nudges that leverage the potential for exponential growth. They must be capable of seeing mental models (theirs, others, their group's, their community's) and be willing to challenge them in order to adapt when necessary. All of these things require individuals and groups to develop more complexity of thinking and working together.

> In the world in which we *used to* live, it was enough in most cases if people were good team players, pulled their weight, were loyal to the company or organizations where they worked, and could be counted on to follow conscientiously the directions and signals of their bosses.... [Today] we are calling upon workers to understand themselves and their world at a qualitatively higher level of mental complexity. (Kegan & Lahey, 2009, pp. 24–25)

Facilitate Learning and Development for Individuals, Groups, and Communities

The work of implementing technical solutions is often done by people in positions of authority. The role of leaders is to know the appropriate response to the problem and either enact it or delegate that action. An adaptive response, however, requires inner work by the people with the problem, which changes the role of leadership. The work of leadership is no longer to have the vision and delegate tasks but to facilitate the group's process of questioning mental models, to help individuals, groups, and communities adapt their way of understanding themselves in relation to the problem. A key role for adaptive leaders is to facilitate learning and development (Heifetz 1998; Heifetz & Linsky, 2002; Kegan & Lahey, 2009; Senge, 2006). "Leadership, seen in this light, requires a learning strategy. A leader, from above or below, with or without authority, has to engage people in confronting the challenge, adjusting their values, changing perspectives, and learning new habits" (Heifetz & Laurie, 1997, p. 134).

Facilitate Inner Work

Rather than the doing the personal work of challenging strongly held core beliefs and mental models, it is much easier to just have an authority figure tell us what to do. Heifetz calls this *work avoidance*. Leaders can learn to recognize the signs of work avoidance in their groups. For example, group members are avoiding the work of adaptive change when they insist on using the same traditional approaches even though these methods fail to work, blame an authority figure or other scapegoat for not implementing the technical change well, deny the problem exists, use a different problem as a distraction, or draw conclusions too quickly in order to avoid going deeper (Heifetz, 1998; Heifetz & Linsky, 2002). The leadership capacity that will set 21st-century leaders apart is the ability to get individuals and groups to do this inner work—challenging them to wrestle with values and incongruence, identify their mental models, and question their assumptions (Heifetz 1998; Heifetz & Linsky, 2002; Kegan & Lahey, 2009; Senge, 2006).

Optimizing Stability and Disequilibrium

"Adaptive change is distressing for the people going through it. They need to take on new roles, new relationships, new values, new behaviors, and new approaches to work" (Heifetz & Laurie, 1997, p. 124). The foundational literature on learning and development is clear that development occurs through an optimal balance of stability and disequilibrium (Kegan, 1998; Sanford, 1962). In stability, people are comfortable, confident, know what to expect, and know what is expected of them. To generate the motivation to change requires disequilibrium—the unsettling feeling when the status quo is no longer working. The role of the leader is to create a balance of stability and disequilibrium.

Heifetz and Linsky (2002) liken the achievement of this balance to controlling the temperature of the holding environment. If it is too cool (too much stability), the group will continue work avoidance: demanding simpler technical solutions, blaming external circumstances, or insisting that authority figures just tell them what to do. In this case the leader needs to raise the heat:

- Encourage conflict to come to the surface rather than allowing false harmony.
- Ask tough questions: are we avoiding an issue because it makes us uncomfortable?
- Facilitate a discussion identifying hidden mental models and assumptions.

Sometimes, however, the temperature gets too high and the anxiety that results is not conducive to either development or collaboration. In these cases, leaders should cool things off:

- Temporarily define the problem and make decisions for the group.
- Support and maintain current group norms to reintroduce stability.
- Create a technical solution in the short term, while continuing to explore adaptive work.

Rather than taking the time and effort to *do the work*, challenging their assumptions and changing how they work with others, some group members would rather have a leader just make a rule or decision and enforce it. Less-confident leaders may succumb to the resulting criticism: "If you were a real leader you would lead us. Just tell us what to do." But Social Change Model assumptions about leadership expect all group members to engage in the leadership process. This requires that everyone develop that capability and efficacy. The leader's role is not to provide solutions but to help the group become capable of working collaboratively to create their own solutions, taking advantage of the variety of perspectives and wisdom available in the group. The key to helping individuals and groups learn to adapt is to always "give the work back to the people" (Heifetz & Laurie, 1997, p. 52).

Reconsider and Embrace Power

Power properly understood, is the ability to achieve purpose. It is the strength required to bring about social, political, or economic changes. In this sense power is not only desirable but necessary in order to implement the demands of love and justice. One of the greatest problems

of history is that the concepts of love and power are usually contrasted as polar opposites. Love is identified with a resignation of power and power with a denial of love. What is needed is a realization that power without love is reckless and abusive and that love without power is sentimental and anemic. Power at its best is love implementing the demands of justice. Justice at its best is power correcting everything that stands against love.
—MARTIN LUTHER KING JR.

A leader's evolving philosophy about how to influence change must include reflection about his or her attitude toward power and an assessment of the sources of power. One of the challenges of the concept of power is that it has been conflated with authority. Many leaders and groups do not spend enough time thinking strategically about the sources of power they have, either because they believe only people in positions of authority have power or because they have negative associations with power. In order to be effective, leaders need to work from an awareness of where and how they can have the most leverage in an organic change system. Two frameworks for understanding power are presented here with interesting implications given the new conceptualizations of change presented in this chapter. The first is the classic five bases of power developed by French and Raven (1959; Raven, 1993); see Table 10.3.

It is important to recognize how the bases of power intersect. For example, a group's community service coordinator has legitimate power from holding the position and may also have access to coercive power (the power to enforce the number of service hours required for all members). The same leader could also exercise reward power by implementing awards for members who participate in service projects.

The second framework for power was first developed by Mary Parker Follet, who was a social worker and scholar of organizational behavior in the early 1900s (Tonn, 2003). One of her groundbreaking concepts was a framework for power that contrasts *power over* and *power with*. Power over describes a relationship in which one person, group, or community exercises domination and coercion over the other in order to achieve the desired outcome. Power with describes a greater ability to achieve goals that results from collaboration and co-creation. Power with requires that everyone involved understands everyone else's goals and interests so the group can work together to arrive at solutions that represent a positive outcome for everyone. Power with requires transparency, individual and group capacity building, and the ability to see how each person's and group's actions influence everyone else's (systems thinking). Follet also noted that although power over requires continued reinforcement, power with naturally grows stronger with use.

TABLE 10.3 French and Raven's Bases of Power

Power	Source
Expert	From having knowledge or expertise that is valuable given the current context. Others in the group respect the ideas and opinions of the expert. Expert power has great influence on decision making and how the group takes action.
Referent	From having positive interpersonal relationships with others in and out of the organization. This power refers to the influence that charismatic, "popular" people have on others and also to the connections the person has to others who have power.
Legitimate	From a position held in the organizational hierarchy. It gives the person influence on the organization's procedures, for example, the authority to create or cancel meetings, as well as select who will and will not attend them. *Note:* French and Raven used the term *legitimate* to describe this power because it is only effective when others perceive that the person has earned the position in the organization legitimately.
Information	From having the access and the ability to share information that others want. Access to information gives a person's opinions more weight and influence.
Coercive	From the perceived ability to punish, threaten, or create conditions others do not want. This power includes the ability to influence the behavior of others by enforcing rules and policies. It is also represented by those who can restrict others' sense of belonging by leveraging the norms of the group's culture (the unwritten rules).
Reward	From the perceived ability to provide incentives or conditions that others want. This power gives the ability to reward groups or individuals with awards, incentives, positive recommendations to others, and other motivations.

CONCLUSION

This chapter opened with a quote from Archimedes, the ancient Greek physicist and engineer. Using a lever and fulcrum in the right place, small nudges can result in big changes. The concepts emerging from an organic view of change suggest the same is true for individuals, groups, and communities. Being capable of understanding leadership through the lens of organic change helps us determine where and how our efforts can have the most influence. We need to learn to do systems thinking, take advantage of exponential growth, and gain comfort with having influence—rather than control—in a process that engages multiple stakeholders through small nudges of influence in the right places. The implication for leaders then is to develop the capacity of individuals, groups, and communities to think and lead *together* by expanding their collective ability to think with more complexity and empathy and to act with more intentionality.

 ## DISCUSSION QUESTIONS

1. This chapter uses many analogies and metaphors for change. What other analogies might you use to describe your experience with change? Does that analogy describe a traditional or organic view?
2. To what extent does the description of the whitewater of ongoing change accurately describe the experience of leadership?
3. Is the concept of exponential growth in organic change encouraging given the great amount of change that can be leveraged through small influences, or is it threatening given how quickly small outside forces can overwhelm the progress of a group's intentional plans?

 ## ACTION AND REFLECTION

1. Consider a personal change goal that you have tried to make but did not maintain. What mental models might be at work that you should address?
2. Consider a change goal you would like to make at the group or community level. Depict the systemic influences on that issue through a drawing such as a mind map.
3. Consider the last experience you had in which you were intentionally working to influence change at the group or community level. Would you describe the attempt as a technical or adaptive solution? What mental models were at work? Who held them?

REFERENCES

Allen, K. E., & Cherrey, C. (2000). *Systemic leadership: Enriching the meaning of our work.* Washington, DC: University Press of America.

Brown, B. (2015). *Rising strong: The reckoning. The rumble. The revolution.* New York, NY: Spiegel & Grau.

Cloutier, C. (2015). Boston researchers' study raises questions about "broken windows" theory of policing. *Boston Globe.* Retrieved May 10, 2016, from https://www.bostonglobe.com/metro/2015/09/11/boston-researchers-study-raises-questions-about-broken-windows-theory-policing/DVrmqE6BiFIVhucAWnKt5L/story.html

Drath, W. H., & Palus, C. J. (1994). *Making common sense.* Greensboro, NC: Center for Creative Leadership.

French, J.R.P., & Raven, B. H. (1959). The bases of social power. In D. Cartwright (Ed.), *Studies in social power* (pp. 150–167). Ann Arbor, MI: Institute for Social Research.

Friedman, U. (April 21, 2016). False promise of democracy. *The Atlantic.* Retrieved May 1, 2016, from http://www.theatlantic.com/international/archive/2016/04/boaty-mcboatface-britain-democracy/479088/

Heifetz, R. A. (1998). *Leadership without easy answers.* Boston, MA: Harvard Business School Press.

Heifetz, R. A., Grashow, A., & Linsky, M. (2009). *The practice of adaptive leadership: Tools and tactics for changing your organization and the world.* Boston, MA: Harvard Business Press.

Heifetz, R. A., & Laurie, D. L. (1997). The work of leadership. *Harvard Business Review, 75,* 124–134.

Heifetz, R. A., & Linsky, M. (2002). *Leadership on the line: Staying alive through the dangers of leading.* Boston, MA: Harvard Business School Press.

Higher Education Research Institute (HERI). (1996). *A social change model of leadership development* (Version III). Los Angeles: University of California, Los Angeles, Higher Education Research Institute.

Kegan, R. (1998). *In over our heads: The mental demands of modern life.* Boston, MA: Harvard University Press.

Kegan, R., & Lahey, L. L. (2009). *Immunity to change: How to overcome it and unlock potential in yourself and your organization.* Boston, MA: Harvard Business Press.

Komives, S. R., Lucas, N., & McMahon, T. R. (2006). *Exploring leadership: For college students who want to make a difference* (2nd ed.). San Francisco, CA: Jossey-Bass.

Kotter, J. P. (1996). *Leading change.* Boston, MA: Harvard Business School Press.

Lewin, K. (1947). Frontiers in group dynamics concept, method and reality in social science: Social equilibria and social change. *Human Relations, 1*(1), 5–41.

Loeb, P. R. (2010). *Soul of a citizen: Living with conviction in challenging times* (2nd ed.). New York, NY: St. Martin's Griffin.

Meier, A., & Rudwick, E. (1969). The boycott movement against Jim Crow streetcars in the south, 1900–1906. *The Journal of American History, 55*(4), 756–775.

Ohanian, A. (2009, November). *Alexis Ohanian: How to make a splash in social media* [Video file]. Retrieved from https://www.ted.com/talks/alexis_ohanian_how_to_make_a_splash_in_social_media?language=en

Palus, C. J., Horth, D. M., & Ill, S. H. (n.d.). Leadership in permanent whitewater: Playing with the metaphor. Retrieved from http://www.leadingeffectively.com/leadership-explorer/leadership-in-permanent-whitewater-playing-with-the-metaphor/

Raven, B. H. (1993). The bases of power: Origins and recent developments. *Journal of Social Issues, 49*(4), 227–251.

Roth, G. (2006, July). *Leadership and learning organizations.* Presented at the National Leadership Symposium, Richmond, VA.

Sanford, N. (1962). *The American college.* New York, NY: Wiley.

Senge, P. M. (2006). *The fifth discipline: The art and practice of the learning organization.* New York, NY: Doubleday/Currency.

Senge, P. M. (2014). *The dance of change: The challenges to sustaining momentum in a learning organization.* New York, NY: Crown Publishing Group.

Stroh, D. P. (2015). *Systems thinking for social change: A practical guide to solving complex problems, avoiding unintended consequences, and achieving lasting results.* White River Junction, VT: Chelsea Green Publishing.

Theoharis, J. (2013). A timeline of the Montgomery bus boycott. Retrieved from http://www.beaconbroadside.com/broadside/2013/12/a-timeline-of-the-montgomery-bus-boycott.html

Tonn, J. C. (2003). *Mary P. Follett: Creating democracy, transforming management.* New Haven, CT: Yale University Press.

Uhl-Bien, M., Marion, R., & McKelvey, B. (2007). Complexity leadership theory: Shifting leadership from the industrial age to the knowledge era. *The Leadership Quarterly, 18*(4), 298–318. doi:org/10.1016/j.leaqua.2007.04.002

Vaill, P. B. (1989). *Managing as a performing art: New ideas for a world of chaotic change.* San Francisco, CA: Jossey-Bass.

Vaill, P. B. (1996). *Learning as a way of being: Strategies for survival in a world of permanent white water.* San Francisco, CA: Jossey-Bass.

Wheatley, M. J. (1999). *Leadership and the new science: Learning about organization from an orderly universe* (2nd ed.). San Francisco, CA: Berrett-Koehler.

Examining Social Change

Wendy Wagner

> If you have come here to help me, you are wasting your time. But if you have come because your liberation is bound up with mine, then let us work together.
> —ABORIGINAL ACTIVISTS GROUP

College students across the country are finding many ways to make a positive difference on their campuses, in their communities, and in the world.

- Every year, hundreds of students from the University of Alabama partner with Impact America to complete the training needed to assist low-income families in preparing their tax returns, particularly identifying any tax credits owed to them. In 2015, more than 9,000 families received assistance, collectively claiming over $15.6 million in tax refunds. Student volunteers describe a transformative new perspective on the realities of working families in the United States, coming face-to-face with the costs of childcare and health care, while getting to know the parents who work multiple jobs to cover expenses (Impact America, n.d.).
- Students in a first-year leadership studies course at the Staley School of Leadership Studies at Kansas State University studied the recent increase of community service vacations and "orphanage tourism" in particular. In cooperation with child-protection organizations around the world, they created a public awareness campaign about the harm inflicted by orphanage tourism, offering ethical alternatives. With the values of the Social Change Model of Leadership Development

as a reflective guide, the students learned to advance their individual and collective leadership capacity (Hartman, 2016).

- Students in George Mason University's Sustainable Living Learning Community learned about the value of rain gardens from their course work and decided to create one outside their residence hall. Rain gardens are a combination of plants and layers of soil and gravel that filter out the oil and heavy metals that rainwater collects as it rushes over roofs and parking lots. In addition to getting their hands quite dirty, the students' project involved acquiring grant funding and forming partnerships with the university through the facilities department and the office of housing (Piedmont/Tidewater Rain Garden, n.d.).

Many of the social issues that matter to us most are also the most complex and seemingly insurmountable. Social change involves coordinated work with many people on many fronts and often a sustained effort is needed before any tangible results are achieved. Maintaining hope and commitment can be hard when visible signs of success are not immediate and when the role one plays in the greater effort seems small in comparison to the problem.

However, important contributions to address social problems are made every day by leaders just like us. These examples are true stories of students who are creating positive changes in their communities. The work may involve community service, raising awareness about social issues, advocating for policy change, or conducting community-based research to inform action. Regardless of the form, all social change efforts stem from a set of foundational assumptions, which will be discussed in this chapter.

The ensemble that developed the Social Change Model wrote this about change:

> Leadership is ultimately about change, and . . . effective leaders are those who are able to effect positive change on behalf of others and society. (Higher Education Research Institute [HERI], 1996, p. 10)
>
> "Change . . . is the ultimate goal of the creative process of leadership—to make a better world and a better society for self and others" (HERI, 1996, p. 21).

CHAPTER OVERVIEW

The leadership concepts in this book are useful for a variety of contexts and goals; however, there is a unique set of values for leaders whose goals are connected to social change. This chapter addresses several of those key values. First the chapter will identify the distinguishing characteristics and values of social change and the implications for leadership. Then it will explore the potential pitfalls of doing work that is intended for the public good and how to avoid them. For readers whose context is not embedded in a social change effort, their way of practicing leadership in groups is still improved by the values of the SCM. Examples of this kind of socially responsible leadership are discussed here as well. The chapter closes with a discussion about the mutually reinforcing nature of social change experiences and leadership development.

ATTRIBUTES OF SOCIAL CHANGE

In the early 21st century, the United States faces a widening gap between the rich and poor, an education system that is failing children who live in less affluent school districts, concerns about whether the planet can continue to sustain our modern lifestyle, deep divisions within governing bodies at all levels, and many other public challenges. For many, the interest in addressing these or other social problems is the driver that brings them to an interest in leadership. There are many ways to engage in the community to address these problems. Change at this level is, of course, informed by the principles of organic change described in Chapter 10. Change in community contexts should be grounded by additional values.

Henry David Thoreau (1908) said, "There are a thousand hacking at the branches of evil to one who is striking at the root" (p. 57). To be the ones who can effect real change, it is critical to understand the true nature and aims of social change. The following section describes four key attributes that distinguish social change from other ways of addressing community problems:

- Is aimed at creating change
- Addresses the root causes of social problems
- Is collaborative
- Is not simple

Social Change Is Aimed at Change

This element may seem to be stating the obvious, but the intent to make change is what distinguishes social change from other community engagement. In fact, some efforts have a mitigating effect, meaning they reduce the severity of the impact, but they do not end the problem. Although these initiatives have the best of intentions, many argue that this work ultimately serves to sustain the status quo. When people see a situation as "not as bad as it used to be" it becomes easier for them to accept things as they are rather than doing more to address the systemic causes of the problem and end it (Mitchell, 2008).

It may come as a surprise to some that Millard Fuller, cofounder of Habitat for Humanity, had serious concerns about the legacy of his organization. Habitat had gained worldwide fame and respect for addressing the issue of unsafe, substandard housing for people living in poverty. Despite three decades of unprecedented success using volunteer labor to build quality housing for low-income families, Fuller knew that in fact, more low-income families lived in substandard housing than when Habitat for Humanity was founded. Fuller was concerned that Habitat volunteers were leaving their work sites not with greater awareness and outrage about housing conditions but instead feeling satisfied that they had done their part (S. Black, personal communication, April, 2016). Fuller began making important changes, and the organization has since been recognized as a model of excellence for intersecting direct service with public education and policy advocacy (Crutchfield & Grant, 2012). Now, in addition to building quality housing, Habitat for Humanity also educates the public about substandard housing issues and advocates for policy changes on its website. Volunteers who work on Habitat build sites are encouraged to continue the work by educating their neighbors and contacting their representatives about better polices for providing safe housing for all.

Another great voice for social change is Robert Egger, author of *Begging for Change* (2010). Similar to many people, Egger had an experience volunteering at a "soup kitchen," handing out cups of lentil soup in the streets of Washington, DC

(Moore, 2014). Rather than feeling the satisfaction those around him felt, Egger was annoyed. It bothered him that the work did not result in any lasting changes for the people they served. As long as people felt satisfaction for having handed out soup, they didn't feel obligated to question why the need for soup continued to exist. "Too much of what we call 'charity' is more about the redemption of the giver than the liberation of the receiver" (p. 20).

Egger also worked in the restaurant industry, and his soup kitchen volunteer experience made him keenly aware of the amount of food waste occurring in DC's restaurants. The project that resulted from Egger's frustration and expertise, despite everyone telling him it could not work, is now a nationally known model called DC Central Kitchen. The organization provides culinary skills training to people who were formerly incarcerated or homeless, using the otherwise wasted food from restaurants and grocery stores to provide meals that are distributed by schools and nonprofits. To date, more than 1,700 people have graduated from the program with a food handler's license and 90% of them have jobs. DC Central Kitchen staff, graduates, and volunteers are vocal advocates against city policies, cultural norms, and hiring practices that trap former offenders and people experiencing homelessness into a cycle of poverty (Moore, 2014).

Although well-intended involvement in our communities feels rewarding, the key *aim for change* value of social change means always asking hard questions:

- What is the long-term impact of our plan?
- What unintended consequences could result?
- Is our presence here actually maintaining the structures of inequity by mitigating the impact of the problem?

The aim for change implies that in addition to attending to the community's immediate needs, the root causes of those needs must be understood and addressed.

Social Change Addresses the Root Causes of Problems

Social change agents often refer to a parable that tells the story of a group of people living by a river who notice one day that there is a baby floating downstream, drowning. As it is being rescued, other drowning babies come into view. The people organize and work together to save as many babies as possible, but more continue to float down the river. One day someone finally decides to go upstream to stop whoever is putting the babies in the river in the first place.

Although it carries a valuable message about understanding the root causes of social problems, this story greatly oversimplifies their nature. As has been discussed in Chapter 10, the factors that influence social problems cannot be understood by seeking a linear cause-effect relationship but by learning to understand the whole system. It is doubtful there is any single evil person or group putting babies in the river (to continue the analogy). It is more likely that a number of people and organizations are all contributing to the problem in small ways. None of them are evil, but they are responding to their own pressures and working toward their own goals, without consideration of the impact of their actions on others. Many in that system will believe someone else is responsible for the babies. Some will understand how their own behavior contributes to the problem, but they will believe their influence is small compared to others and will be reluctant to change.

Systems thinking helps reveal the complexity of the root causes of social problems. Mark Rank, a leading researcher on poverty, inequality, and social injustice, uses the children's game of musical chairs as an analogy to illustrate the need to look beyond simple root causes.

> Picture a game with ten players, but only eight chairs. When the music stops, who's most likely to be left standing? It will be those who are at a disadvantage in terms of competing for the available chairs (less agility, reduced speed, a bad position when the music stops, and so on). However, given that the game is structured in a way such that two players are bound to lose, these individual attributes only explain who loses, not why there are losers in the first place. Ultimately, there are simply not enough chairs for those playing the game. (Rank, 2011, p. 19)

Some believe they have found the root cause of the problem when they ask, "What does this individual need to be able to get his or her own chair next time?" However, Rank makes clear that the problem will still persist for others until we examine the shortcomings of a social system (or economic, educational, cultural, and others) that does not distribute enough chairs.

A more sophisticated understanding of root causes challenges us to be more innovative, creating communities that are better in the long term for everyone. When our goal is to aim for change by addressing the root causes of social problems, we begin asking challenging questions:

Examining Social Change

- How did the situation come to be this way?
- How do our economic, political, and social systems and cultural values enable the problem to continue?
- What local, state, and national policies contribute to the problem?
- Why does the general public accept the ongoing existence of this problem?

The answers to these questions may result in initiatives that look different from traditional community service or charity. Social change might involve public awareness-raising campaigns, lobbying elected officials, or collecting data to research the issue. Systems thinking will also indicate the need to build relationships and work collaboratively.

Social Change Is Collaborative

Superheroes arrive on the scene, fix all the problems, and disappear, leaving behind a community who wave good-bye in admiration and wonder. Unfortunately, some people approach community service projects the same way. These individuals do service *to* others rather than *with* them. Social change, in sharp contrast to the superhero approach, requires building relationships with others and taking action together. Social change agents do not see themselves as outsiders who help or fix others but as fellow members of a community working to make it better. This suggests collaboration, particularly *equitable collaboration* so that those who are most affected by the change will have a strong and sustained voice in what the change will be and how it will be implemented.

Social change cannot be done alone. Paul Loeb (2010) asserts, "Our most serious problems—both the public ones and those that seem most personal—are in the large part common problems, which can be solved only through common efforts" (p. 9). People who intend to make a lasting difference in communities realize they need to bring as many people to the table as possible. Casting such a wide net involves asking themselves these questions:

- Who else is affected by this issue?
- Who else has a stake in the outcome? How can we partner with multiple stakeholders?
- Who has access to resources we need?

- Who has influence on the rules (e.g., policies, legal requirements, enforcement of existing law)?
- Who knows the members of the public we are trying to educate?

One can quickly see why social capital (a concept discussed in Chapter 9) plays such an important role in leadership for social change.

Historically, mainstream United States culture has valued individualism, each person's freedom to live how he or she chooses. We admire self-reliance and the ability to take care of one's own problems without burdening others. For some, the biggest challenge of coming to be a leader for social change is overcoming a deeply felt belief that our strength is demonstrated by our independence and the evidence of successful leadership is something we can take sole credit for. We need new beliefs about what strength is and what excellent leadership looks like.

Perhaps California redwood trees can inspire this shift in beliefs. They are the tallest living things in the world, reaching as high as 300 feet. However, they have astonishingly shallow root systems. Redwoods are able to survive strong winds and storms without toppling over because they always grow together in groves with their roots intertwining together in a way that supports each tree. How can social change leaders collaborate across diversity to create communities that resemble the intertwined supportive roots of the California redwoods? It isn't simple.

Social Change Is Not Simple

Engaging in work for the benefit of others is a concept with broad appeal. Many civic leaders and educators make a point of encouraging everyone to participate in volunteerism. It is true that everyone has the potential to make a positive contribution. However, sometimes in their zeal to encourage all people to engage in their communities, they oversimplify the work itself, as if solving social problems is easy and uncomplicated. *Just serve. Anyone can do it.* These simplistic calls to action imply that the right action to take will be clear, and as long as people have good intentions the community will experience good results.

The social problems in our communities are rarely so straightforwardly right or wrong. Gaining consensus across the community means navigating strongly felt differences of opinion on issues, such as whether a problem is a problem (some may believe there is nothing wrong with what is happening), whether it is the most important problem facing the community right now, or whether the problem is worth the attention if it only affects a few people. Consider again the parable of saving babies from the river. What if another group arrived saying the babies should stay in the water because they have heard that the people upstream subscribe to a tradition that teaches swimming in infancy? While someone goes upstream to determine if this is true, should the group keep trying to save babies in the meantime or should they not? What criteria dictate when the traditions of other communities should not be respected and upheld by others? These are questions of personal ethics that require groups to practice Controversy With Civility while individuals maintain their own Congruence. Although this example may seem extreme to some, it is difficult to identify many acts of beneficence that do not represent a belief or value that is personal and not necessarily held by others. To say "everyone should serve" is overly simplistic if it doesn't also include an admonishment that everyone should first have Consciousness of Self about their values and be capable of thinking critically about the impact of their behavior on people who hold different beliefs.

Even when communities agree that a problem exists and is a priority to address, there is disagreement about the best approaches. Charles Strain, a professor at DePaul University, illustrated the complexity of social change by examining the well-known proverb "Give a man a fish and you feed him for a day. Teach a man to fish and you feed him for a lifetime." This maxim makes a nice point about the importance of building capacity rather than creating dependence. However, in real situations, problem solving is more complex. As Strain (2006) points out, if people are starving, they will need to have something to eat while they try to learn to fish. Going even further, he argues that "teaching someone to fish presumes that the person a) has access to a lake, b) that a corporate conglomerate has not fished out that lake, and c) that our industrial waste has not poisoned all of the fish" (p. 6). One could continue Strain's critiques, identifying many other complicating realities of doing service work in communities.

- What will be the criteria to determine which person to teach among the many demonstrating need?
- If we can't afford to provide fishing poles, is there any point in continuing the lessons?
- How will we foster collaboration when others in our group insist we should be teaching gardening instead?

- Do we have a responsibility to those who were already using this lake and now have to share the available fish with the new fishers that we trained?

Even the simplest of goals can become complicated when enacted in real communities, where the history of the issue, local politics, and lack of resources mean that "the right thing to do" is much less clear.

During my time at Santa Clara University I worked in several capacities with women, both globally and locally. I studied abroad in El Salvador, learning about women studying, working, and raising families there. Through the Global Social Benefit Fellowship, I observed women's tailoring training centers in Kolkata, India, and developed computer curriculum for them. I taught ESL classes to women at Washington Elementary School and led small groups for women in the Core Christian Fellowship on campus. I also explored Martha Nussbaum's capabilities approach, a theory that has inspired and advanced the United Nation's Human Development Index, and used this approach in my honor's thesis. I listened to the stories of the many women I met, which expanded my own perspective and inspired me to keep working for a more just and humane world.

—Monet Gonnerman is a recent graduate from Santa Clara University and is currently a community coordinator with the Casa de la Solidaridad study-abroad program in El Salvador.

CHALLENGES IN LEADERSHIP FOR SOCIAL CHANGE

These attributes introduce complicated challenges for leadership for social change. The work is important and rewarding but not for the faint of heart. Social change leaders facilitate collective decision making in ambiguous circumstances and problem solving when it is not possible to know everything. Social change leaders also do work that is scrutinized and occasionally criticized by others for not being good enough: those who do advocacy work are criticized for not responding to immediate needs; those who engage others in volunteerism are criticized for not advocating for change. The public's social change heroes are larger than life and intimidating to emulate. In reality, everyone is flawed, makes mistakes, and has more to learn.

Handling these challenges requires top-level leadership skills—but skills that are continually improved as they are practiced when we are open to learning as we go. Morton (1999) cautions against the oversimplification of service while also offering encouragement to be involved in creating solutions. "Don't go charging out to help. Talk, listen, build relationships, know your self, your environment; work with others where they and the situation itself can teach you how to act with more and more knowledge and effectiveness" (p. 23).

What About People's Immediate Needs?

Certainly there are people in our communities with immediate needs who cannot wait for our systemic solutions to take effect. Do the values of social change mean we ignore those needs in order to focus on root causes? No, in fact, social change values will also improve our approach to providing direct services. Keith Morton's (1995) classic work, "The Irony of Service," described three forms of service:

- Charity: work that addresses immediate needs
- Projects: work that builds the capacity or efficiency of groups who attend to immediate needs
- Social change: work aimed at changing the systems that cause the needs

Morton described each of these forms as varying in "integrity and depth." Thin forms of service, at any of the three levels, are "disempowering and hollow" (p. 24). Thick forms of service are "sustainable and possibly revolutionary" (p. 24). What makes the difference between thin and thick service? According to Morton: (1) building relationships in the communities we serve and (2) having an awareness of the systemic causes at the root of the problem. The values of the Social Change Model address both of these elements, meaning that whether our aim is to create social change or address immediate needs, we will do that work with more integrity if we are concerned with social change values. People with relationships in the community and an understanding of how flawed systems in the environment contribute to the problem will provide direct service in a way that is empowering and restores dignity. They will listen and respect the perspectives of the people they intend to serve.

Social Change and Volunteerism

The values of social change suggest many ways that typical community service can and should be done differently. One's involvement in occasional volunteerism can provide temporary relief, but it rarely produces a cure. The argument of this chapter is not that volunteer projects are bad. The point is that congruence with our value for change means volunteerism should be considered a first step toward more, not the goal itself.

Simpler social good projects, such as canned food drives or painting playground equipment, have the benefit of feeling rewarding for those who serve. The impact is immediate and measurable, and it is easy to attribute credit for the work. By contrast, leadership for social change means being invested in changing larger systems, which is time consuming and involves input from more stakeholders. It is easy to see the appeal of more direct volunteer work, but social change leaders find ways to derive satisfaction from being part of the ongoing progress of a larger movement.

Stephen Black, the president and founder of Impact America works for social change in a way that recognizes the place of volunteerism:

> I'm always trying to encourage more and more students to volunteer—not because volunteering solves our social problems, but because we need more people who have direct personal experiences that help them understand the social problems so they can do something about it. Trying to make change at the policy level takes commitment and stamina. People don't stick to it if they don't have a personal connection to the problem. For many people it is volunteerism that gave them that connection. So, yes of course volunteerism is good, but it is good as a first step that inspires a person to work for real solutions. Volunteerism that results in learning and motivation to act is what we need. What is concerning about volunteerism is how often it results instead in people walking away from the problem, feeling satisfied that they have done their part. (S. Black, personal communication, April 2016)

How do we change volunteer projects to make them a first step rather than an end to people's efforts? Thinking about volunteer service projects from the perspectives of organic change described in Chapter 10 can help us know what small shifts in volunteer project design would create more long-term impact.

- How can this service project be connected to the other multipart solutions being enacted in other parts of the system?
- How can the process of creating and implementing this project build relationships among people and groups in the community who address this issue?

- How can the project be designed to give volunteers an experience that creates a personal connection to this issue and educates them about the current policies and the systemic complexity involved in changing the upstream causes of the problem?
- How might reflective discussions among volunteers and other stakeholders shed light on the individually and collectively held mental models about the issue?
- How might social media be leveraged so that the volunteer experience is not an end for participants but the intentionally designed initial conditions for exponential growth?

But I'm Not a Hero, I'm Just a Regular Person

Discussions about the complexities of social change often lead to celebrated examples of well-known historical figures, such as Harriet Tubman, Abraham Lincoln, Susan B. Anthony, and Martin Luther King Jr. Some might conclude that the kind of people who get involved to make a difference must be fundamentally different from "regular" people—more clever, charismatic, and committed than the rest of us. But attributing historic successes to the imagined heroic attributes of the leaders at the time ignores the reality that these successes are the result of a collective effort. It also ignores that our heroes are imperfect people, whose lives represent a long journey of intentions, mistakes, and ongoing learning—just like ours. When we imagine the people who make a difference in the world are somehow not like us, we are missing the lessons to be learned from these heroes. In his years of working with civically engaged community members, Paul Loeb (2010) observed the following:

> The main distinction between those who participate fully in their communities and those who withdraw in private life doesn't rest in the active citizens' grasp of complex issues, or their innate moral strength.... They have learned specific lessons about approaching social change: that they don't need to wait for the perfect circumstances, the perfect cause, or the perfect level of knowledge to take a stand; that they can proceed step by step, so that they don't get overwhelmed before they start. They savor the journey of engagement and draw strength from its challenges. Taking the long view, they come to trust that the fruits of their efforts will ripple outward, in ways they can rarely anticipate. (pp. 8–9)

History is full of examples of tentative first steps leading to lives of commitment. The people we now see as heroes were once just getting started, learning as they went, just like everyone else does.

- While she was still in college, Marion Wright Edelman joined her professor Howard Zinn and other Black students to challenge segregation by sitting in the "Whites only" section of the state legislature. This and other early experiences through which she observed how the legal and political systems favored Whites motivated her to become a civil rights attorney (the first Black woman admitted to the Mississippi bar). She eventually became a critical figure in the Civil Rights Movement and later went on to form the Children's Defense Fund (Edelman, 1999).

- Eleanor Roosevelt's family hoped only for her to marry well. However, she did not find meaning in the lifestyle of the wealthy socialite and instead decided to join a group of women who were activists for women's equality and rights for the working poor (Gerber, 2002). Despite her concerns about having no experience or qualifications for this kind of work, she decided to accept a position on the board of directors of the New York League of Women Voters. She would later call this period "the intensive education of Eleanor Roosevelt" (Roosevelt as cited in Gerber, 2002, p. 87).

- César Chávez also began his journey with simple small steps. He accepted a job with a Latino civil rights group in which he traveled across California, encouraging Mexican Americans to register and vote (Ross, 1989). For Chávez, just like for anyone else, the courage to get out there and try opened the doors to the opportunities that followed.

The lesson from these stories is that one does not become an expert on social issues before getting involved; one becomes an expert through involvement and learning from experience. Social change agents must be willing to learn as they go, listening to those around them and those most directly affected, and be open to learning where they were wrong. "Each step, no matter how awkward or hesitant, prepares us for the next" (Loeb, 2010, p. 62).

When people begin to feel that the world's problems are too big for them as individuals to make a difference, Beverly Tatum (1997), former president of Spelman College, responds this way: "While many people experience themselves as powerless, everyone has some sphere of influence in which they can work for change, even if it is just in their own personal network of family and friends" (p. 204). The more a person gets involved in the ways that they can, the more experience they will gain and the more influential relationships they will form. One's sphere of influence grows as one uses it.

In 2004, Eli Winkelman was a student at Scripps College with a popular recipe for challah bread. Her friends could not get enough of it and even asked her to teach them how to make it for themselves. She recognized the demand for a product and how much people enjoyed the activity of making it. Meanwhile, her friend Melinda Koster at nearby Pomona College was deeply concerned about the genocide in the Darfur region of Sudan. Although unsure of what she could do from her residence hall in Claremont, California, she was determined to get involved somehow. One day, Melinda's concern met Eli's fund-raising idea and they decided to give it a try. With some initial success, Eli began asking questions of people within her sphere of influence. Would other students help her with the baking to have more to sell? Yes. Would the college dining hall let them use the kitchen equipment after hours in order to produce even more? Yes. Would the on-campus café sell them in the shop for her? No, but she kept asking questions. Could they set up a sales table every week in the café instead? Yes. Eli later said that the rejection from the campus café initially seemed like a setback. However, staffing their own sales table turned out to be important to their success.

> We could interact with people at our table, engage them in our activism, and it provided another opportunity for us to get our volunteers deeper into their own activism. That was so much more powerful than simply putting our bread in the pastry case with the rest of the cookies and bagels. (E. Winkleman, personal communication, April 29, 2016)

Winkleman's tentative first steps resulted in what is today a thriving nonprofit organization with thousands of Jewish students involved in 78 campus chapters across the country. In 2013, Eli stepped down as the CEO and now sits on its board of directors.

After several failed attempts at running for student council officer positions in high school, I eventually assumed that I was not fit to be a leader. However my perception of leadership changed my junior year of high school, when my family took a service trip to the Bahia

Honda community in Bocas del Toro, Panama. Before we went, we learned from the program coordinator that the community needed reading glasses. I decided to organize a reading glasses drive at my high school. I only knew a fraction of the students and teachers at my large city school and was not very popular (probably my problem when I kept running for student council). However, I eventually found several ways to raise awareness for my glasses drive, including making a commercial wearing ridiculous glasses that aired during school-wide afternoon announcements. I also convinced several key teachers to keep glasses collection boxes in their classrooms. With the help of the Springfield High students and staff, I collected 250 pairs of glasses to bring with me to Panama. After that experience, I realized that good leadership resulted from focusing on what I wanted to do, not what I wanted to become.

—Nadia Syed is a junior at The George Washington University, where she majors in human services and social justice.

ENACTING SOCIALLY RESPONSIBLE LEADERSHIP

The Social Change Model of Leadership Development was created for people learning to work effectively with others for positive social change. Some readers might be thinking, "But my group's purposes are not social change goals, so how does the Social Change Model apply to us?" The values of the model are useful for all leadership efforts. It is an approach to leadership that has the following traits:

- Collaborative rather than coercive
- Civil and respectful rather than defensive
- Open to different perspectives rather than controlling and single-minded
- Clear and consistent about values rather than hypocritical

Although the primary mission of a group may not relate to social change, leaders in a wide variety of contexts, such as business, sports, or theater groups, can benefit from this socially responsible approach to leadership.

Socially responsible leadership refers to leadership that maintains a sense of responsibility for the welfare of others. Socially responsible leaders are concerned about group members' well-being and sense of belonging. They operate with an awareness of how the group's decisions and actions affect others. They are aware of opportunities to create more fairness and equity within their spheres of influence. They pay attention to individuals and groups that have been marginalized and work to build a sense of belonging so everyone feels valued. They continually challenge themselves and others with questions that push for equity: who is here and who isn't and why? Who is listened to and who is ignored? A socially responsible approach to leadership will influence any group's purposes and decision making, and how members work together.

The recreational sports unit of the Office of Student Life at The Ohio State University bases the leadership development program for student employees and program leaders on the Social Change Model. The students report that they are able to apply many aspects of the model in their recreational sports roles as well as other leadership roles they hold on campus. These student leaders have learned to be inclusive of others' ideas, have become comfortable with controversy, and have a greater awareness of how their work in the recreational sports unit intersects with the work of other offices and student groups to create a campus in which everyone has a place to belong (A. Kwasnieski, personal communication, April 26, 2016).

POSSIBLE PITFALLS IN SOCIAL CHANGE AND SOCIALLY RESPONSIBLE LEADERSHIP

Even with the best intentions and the desire to benefit others, it is possible to unintentionally act in ways that are hurtful and insulting, or do others more harm than good. What follows is a short list of pitfalls to avoid when working for social change or socially responsible leadership. As you will see, many pitfalls are connected, and tripping into one can rapidly lead to falling into another.

Assimilation

Assimilation is the pitfall that occurs when we assume that the way our own community or culture addresses a social problem is the best way. Assimilation means that efforts intended to "help" are actually attempts to make *their* community become more like *ours*. Resulting from a lack of awareness of self and others, assimilation ignores the differences among communities and the expertise that exists outside of our own. In groups, assimilation may involve subtle messages that suggest that in order for group members to be fully accepted and appreciated, they need to conform to the rest of the group.

Paternalism

Paternalism is an underlying cause of many problems in community service. The root of the word hints at the implication: father knows best. Paternalism reduces recipients of service to a childlike status, assuming the ones doing the service know better than those receiving it what action should be taken, even when that "help" is coming from outsiders to the community's context. Paternalism maintains inequality between "the helpers" and "the helped." Helpers keep decision-making power to themselves rather than empowering people to be involved in creating the solutions.

As a feminist and Muslim woman at George Washington University, Amira Bakir occasionally finds herself on the receiving end of assimilation and paternalism by mainstream feminists who believe they are helping her work. She believes they mean well, but many such students make assumptions about the kinds of "help" Muslim feminists want. For example, it is typical for students to suggest working together to change things like Saudi dress codes:

> They think, "this poor thing can't express herself." But the truth is, they are more bothered by her being covered than she is.... What we want to focus on are issues like the right to vote and equal pay, not how we dress.... There is little recognition of the work already under way. The Egyptian feminist movement pre-dates Susan B. Anthony. You aren't bringing this to us. I want to collaborate, because we are stronger together, but don't treat us like we're just helpless girls waiting for the Western world to come save us. (A. Bakir, personal communication, April 22, 2016)

Ignoring the Historical and Political Contexts

Imagine a town in which members of Group A came to have political power and used it to shuffle resources from Group B to benefit Group A. They separated the schools and then gave Group A schools more funding. They secured more jobs for group A. They allowed group B to only live in certain areas of town. Now imagine that generations later, well-intended individuals from Group A go out to Group B with service projects aimed at teaching Group B how to be more successful. If you were in Group B, how would you feel about being on the receiving end of this service from Group A?

All communities have histories. Given the Social Change Model's emphasis on collaboration and relationships, it is important to have awareness that those relationships exist in a political, historical context. Social change efforts nearly always occur in a historical context in which one community benefitted at the cost of another. Often even the current climate is such that one community has more political power and resources than another. Although we enter into individual relationships with values of equity and a desire to be inclusive, we should not pretend that the general social context treats or has treated everyone equally. The historic and political realities affect our preconceived ideas about each other as well as the ongoing work of building trust. If we ignore the history of one group dominating another or ignore the current unequal political power, we enter into relationships across those groups in a way that runs the risk of actually re-creating or reinforcing that inequality.

As a student coordinator for the Making Our Society an Inclusive Community (MOSAIC) program, I have organized many events aimed at informing others about important issues in our local community and engaging students in volunteer service. For example, this semester, a team of MOSAIC coordinators held a series of campus events-related current problems in the U.S. criminal justice system. We screened the film *Broken on All Sides* followed by a panel discussion. A lunch discussion was held among students and local criminal justice officials. We also held an art exhibition of the works of female inmates, expressing their experiences in the criminal justice system. All of these events have sparked student thinking about how we can influence change on this issue. It has been an empowering experience to see that I can be the person who starts these important discussions. I can be the person who works in the community to understand how student volunteers can be of best use.

—Deniz Bengi, junior, Lafayette College, Easton, Pennsylvania.

A Deficit-Based Perspective of Others

A deficit-based perspective sees only the problems in communities and people: buildings that need repair, underperforming schools, and loitering teenagers. Although it can be useful to inform our actions by doing a needs assessment, it is just as important to identify the assets in the community. Looking for these assets and the strengths of individuals encourages engagement and builds social capital.

The recent trend of creating senior villages for senior citizens in cities such as Boston and Washington, DC, illustrates the difference an asset-based perspective can make. It is typical for government agencies or nonprofits to focus on all the things seniors can no longer do for themselves and create programs *for* the seniors. Senior villages are grassroots neighborhood associations run *by* seniors themselves, along with some administrative and financial support from local government agencies (DC Office on Aging, n.d.). Given their years in the community, many seniors have a large network of friends and contacts to draw from—an often overlooked asset of this population. With the right support, seniors can work together to schedule interesting speakers, classes, or workshops for their senior village.

John McKnight (2013) is a long-time advocate of asset-based community development. To start, he recommends (1) identifying all the resources the community has to build on to make it stronger and then (2) thinking creatively about how these assets can be applied in new ways. He suggests asking community stakeholders four questions:

- What do you know (e.g., accounting, neighborhood history)?
- What skills do you have (e.g., cooking, carpentry, how to play an instrument)?
- What are you committed to, willing to work tirelessly on (e.g., children, the environment, veterans)?
- Who are you connected to (e.g., associations, groups, communities)?

The answers to these questions lead to an asset map of the community, helping organizers connect people to each other. Citizens are empowered to get involved when they become aware of where their talent and skills would be useful. McKnight (2013) described many signs that community development projects are on the right track, such as when: people feel valuable rather than needy, there is creativity and invention, and initiatives grow organically through personal connections rather than structures and reporting lines.

For groups practicing socially responsible leadership rather than social change, an asset-based practice means that members will be able to leverage the strengths and skills of everyone in the group. For example, first-year students bring a lot of past experience and fresh perspectives and should not be dismissed by seniors as not having "earned" the right to fully participate.

Ignoring Cultural Differences

When Malcolm X was a child, soon after his father died, a neighbor provided a butchered pig to his family so they would not go hungry. Because of religious-based diet restrictions, his mother would not serve it to the children. (If it is hard to imagine choosing hunger over a cultural or religious dietary restriction, imagine an American food bank serving dog meat to the poor.) His mother's decision was among a chain of events that led to the state taking the children out of her custody, claiming she was not taking proper care of them (Haley & Malcolm X, 1964). Assuming our own cultural norms are universal is called *ethnocentrism*. It is not possible to understand how to benefit the common good while simultaneously judging other community members because their views differ from our own ethnocentric perspective.

Cultural differences arise within groups as well, calling for socially responsible leadership. For example, in many student groups, there are some members who like to gather and visit first before starting the meeting; forming friendships and personal support is important to them. Other members like to start and end meetings on time and consider those who are late or who do not get right down to business to be disrespectful of others' time. Those two cultural contrasts can be accommodated in a single group when the group works toward its processes in ways that reflect mutual respect for all members' values.

Confusing Social Change with Public Relations

There is nothing inherently wrong with drawing more public attention to our work. Using the news or social media to build awareness of our accomplishments and continuing goals is good strategy for change. However, it can be easy to lose our way and confuse the strategy with the goal itself. Being featured in the news is not the goal. The goal is to make a real, lasting change. We make different decisions when our goal is to attract attention rather than to make a difference. Do we attend long town-hall meetings about affordable housing and lobby elected officials? Or do we make 500 peanut butter sandwiches for people who are homeless? Option 2 is easier to post to Twitter or Instagram, and it is more likely to attract attention from local media. If public relations is the goal, the smarter choice is to make the sandwiches. But does that create social change?

Despite this simplistic example, it must be made clear: there is nothing simple about this pitfall. Social change leaders have a difficult balance to tread here. Needing public support (including the funding that can arise from high-profile projects) to keep our efforts afloat is a reality. We do need to communicate the importance of our work to the public in order to generate broader support. Long-term social change goals are not always conducive to short-term evidence that our efforts are working, let alone fodder for headlines, photos, and viral tweets. We need to be intentional about using the media to leverage support; however, our desire for media coverage should not drive our actions or change the direction of our social change goals.

AVOIDING THE POTENTIAL PITFALLS

One of the risks of pointing out these pitfalls is intimidation to the point of inaction. Fear of making a misstep can lead to not taking any steps at all. Perfection is neither an expectation nor a goal. We all trip sometimes. To lead for social change in the context of real communities is to embrace a certain degree of uncertainty. The purpose of identifying the pitfalls in this way is to offer a framework for ongoing reflection and learning.

Leaders who act from no more than naive hope do not create a lasting impact. Our communities need leaders who are able to think critically about the historical, political, and cultural contexts and start challenging well-intended ideas with hard questions. We need leaders who are ready to accept critique and feedback because they want to do better. Two frames of mind can help social change leaders to avoid the potential pitfalls and bounce back with resilience when they do misstep: an awareness of interdependence and a growth mind-set to experience.

Awareness of Interdependence: They Are Us

One key to avoiding many of these pitfalls is to replace the "us and them" mind-set with a sense of "being in community" with others. The underlying assumption that "we are here to help them" must be replaced by a deeply felt sense that "we and they are us." Leaders play a role in creating that sentiment by modeling it themselves and by creating inclusive groups that invite the participation of a broad range of stakeholders. Leaders set the tone for inclusion by empowering others to contribute to the co-creation of solution, rather than creating programs *for* other people.

The very act of distinguishing between the help giver and the help recipient can lead to many of the noted pitfalls. Building relationships in the community and collaborating with others is the key to avoiding the imposition of one person's point of view onto others. Working *with* others and not *unto* others ensures that those most affected by the change have a say in what the change should be. Collaboration means the people in a community decide on a vision for change together and then work together to devise the means to achieve it.

Shifting our frame of reference from "I help them" to "we work together as an us" may require a real paradigm change for some. Juana Bordas (2012) observes that

> I and We are not a dichotomy. The I is intrinsic to the We orientation—individuals must be strong for the collective to thrive. We do not have to choose one or the other.... The challenge is to balance communal good with individual gain—to reach the higher ground of interdependence, where personal gain is not achieved at the expense of the common good. (p. 55)

Rather than being competing opposites, the individual and the community reinforce each other. Each person's ability to be a self-reliant individual is bolstered by having a strong, supportive community. Likewise, communities are strong when the individuals in them are free to think for themselves and act on their consciences.

McKnight (1989) describes a historical example of what communities look like when *they are us*. In the early 1700s to 1900s, in the island community of Martha's Vineyard in Massachusetts, about 10% of the population was deaf (Groce, 1985). A researcher studying this community noticed that students graduated from high school at similar rates regardless of whether they were deaf or hearing. The two groups also had similar income levels and a similar variety of job options. Meanwhile in Massachusetts generally, 50% of students who were deaf graduated from high school, compared to 75% of students with typical hearing. People who were deaf had one-third less income than the rest of the state population. This was particularly surprising news because the state of Massachusetts was actually known at that time for having among the best services in the country for people who are deaf. The island community had no services available at all. The key difference: everyone living in the island community had learned sign language. One "they are us" adjustment made by the community and there is no longer a need for a certain population to "need services."

A Growth Mind-Set: Awareness of the Need to Keep Learning

A second key to avoiding the pitfalls is to assume we have a lot to learn rather than being headstrong in our own rightness and righteousness. It is critically important to enter relationships and coalitions with an assumption that you have much to learn from each other. Even the most successful social change agents have moments when they realize they have more to learn. Martin Eakes is the founder and CEO of Self-Help, an organization identified as one of the most effective nonprofit organizations in the United States (Crutchfield & Grant, 2012). For Eakes, being open to learning and improving is an important part of his success: "I need to have impact more than I need to be right" (Crutchfield & Grant, 2012, p. 41).

For social change leaders to persist through challenges and learn from missteps, they need to approach challenge with an expectation to learn and grow. These leaders assume that experience will result in enhanced skills and a more complex understanding of the problem so they can handle it better next time. Carol Dweck, a leading researcher of motivation, calls this attitude a *growth mindset* (2006). Dweck's research has shown that developing a growth mindset is a learned skill and relies primarily on mindfulness. The practice involves first becoming aware of when we are not operating from a growth mindset, then making a mental shift and reframing the situation to identify how it can result in learning from the experience and from others. A growth mindset is highly correlated with developing resilience—the ability to bounce back from failures, finding a way to make the experience meaningful as a moment of learning and growth. It is also connected to being comfortable with critique and feedback, a key path out of the pitfalls previously described.

SOCIAL CHANGE AND LEADERSHIP DEVELOPMENT

Juana Bordas, an expert in multicultural leadership, describes the day she was sitting outside her residence hall in 1963 when she saw her political science professor leading a large group of people toward the administration building. When she asked what was happening, she was invited to join them on a protest march to racially integrate the University of Florida. Juana says, "I stood up and said, 'Yes I'll go.'

On that day, I became a leader" (J. Bordas, personal communication, July 27, 2008). It is in this spirit that the Social Change Model intersects leadership development and social change. It is through working with others for common benefit that people learn just how much they are capable of and how they can continue to improve. Put another way, Julie Owen, leadership studies professor at George Mason University, often asks an important question: "Do leaders create social movements or do the social movements create leaders?" (J. Owen, personal communication, April 10, 2016).

Findings from the Multi-Institutional Study of Leadership are in alignment with the assertion that collaborative work for social change can foster leadership development, but only when implemented with intention.

> Involvement in community service experiences consistently emerge as strong predictors of leadership capacity. However, it isn't the act of simply doing service that matters. Educators must create opportunities that reflect the values of the leadership constructs being taught. The quality with which the experience is processed is of equal importance. Community service experiences are particularly powerful because they have the potential to: develop critical group-related skills; deepen personal commitments to specific issues; build resilience for working in complex systems to create change; and disrupt assumptions about social systems and how they operate. (Dugan, Kodama, Correia, & Associates, 2013, p. 15)

The Social Change Model provides a framework to guide individuals, groups, and communities through the learning opportunities that emerge from social change initiatives. The model was created by a group of leadership educators who believed that working collaboratively toward Common Purposes is a powerful way for individuals, groups, and community to learn to engage in leadership processes. The model helps identify areas of strength that can be leveraged more intentionally. It can diagnose problems and areas where more learning and growth is needed. By taking on challenging new experiences and reflecting on the learning along the way, individuals, groups, and communities can experience an ongoing sense of improvement. In social change leadership, a successful outcome not only makes positive change but also boosts the confidence of groups and communities, making them even stronger when they take on their next challenge together.

CONCLUSION

Working for social change means working to make a positive difference for the common good in ways that are collaborative and use systems thinking to address the root causes of problems. Leaders who are grounded in the values of the Social Change Model, while valuing Collaboration and being open to learning, will find that every experience builds their leadership competence and their capacity to influence positive change.

 ## DISCUSSION QUESTIONS

1. How are the intersections between the concepts in this chapter and the conceptualization of change as *organic* from Chapter 10?
2. Can you think of an example of an organization (that you have been involved with or not) that did a particularly good job of collaborating with others and addressing the root causes of problems? What did that look like?
3. Think of a group you belong to that is not defined by its goal to do social change, such as a residence hall community, sports team, or academic club. How does that organization affect its members? How does it affect others in its community? How could that organization practice socially responsible leadership?
4. Do you think leaders create social movements or do social movements create leaders? How have your experiences with leadership shaped your motivation to work for the common good? How have your experiences trying to make a difference for the common good affected how you approach leadership?

 ## ACTION AND REFLECTION

1. Identify an existing volunteer project on your campus or community. Learn more about how the stakeholders involved are addressing some of the concerns described here. Consider how you or a group you belong to could support the project in ways that would advance social change.
2. At an upcoming meeting of a student group you are part of, pay particular attention to opportunities for the group to engage in socially responsible leadership.

Irrespective of the group's mission and purpose, how can your group contribute to social equity and inclusiveness through its leadership processes alone?

3. Think of a time when you were involved in a community engagement effort that experienced one of the pitfalls described here. What did you learn from that experience? What realistic changes could be made to continue the project with social change values to avoid the pitfall(s)?

4. Who is in your sphere of influence? In what arenas do you have the power to have a positive influence? How could you use your current sphere of influence to create change on an issue that matters to you?

5. Describe someone you would consider a hero in terms of his or her commitment to making a positive difference for others. In what ways can you see yourself being like him or her? In what ways does his or her achievement intimidate you? How might you learn more about this person, particularly his or her learning journey?

REFERENCES

Bordas, J. (2012). *Salsa, soul, and spirit: Leadership for a multicultural age* (2nd ed.). San Francisco, CA: Berrett-Koehler.

Crutchfield, L. R., & Grant, H. M. (2012). *Forces for good: The six practices of high-impact nonprofits*. San Francisco, CA: Jossey-Bass.

DC Office on Aging. (n.d.). Home page. Retrieved from http://dcoa.dc.gov/service/senior-villages

Dugan, J. P., Kodama, C., Correia, B., & Associates. (2013). *Multi-Institutional Study of Leadership insight report: Leadership program delivery*. College Park, MD: National Clearinghouse for Leadership Programs.

Dweck, C. (2006). *Mindset: The new psychology of success*. New York, NY: Random House.

Edelman, M. W. (1999). *Lanterns: A memoir of mentors*. Boston, MA: Beacon Press.

Egger, R. (2010). *Begging for change: The dollars and sense of making nonprofits responsive, efficient, and rewarding for all*. New York, NY: HarperCollins.

Gerber, R. (2002). *Leadership the Eleanor Roosevelt way: Timeless strategies from the first lady of courage*. New York, NY: Penguin.

Groce, N. W. (1985). *Everyone here spoke sign language: Hereditary deafness on Martha's Vineyard*. Boston, MA: Harvard University Press.

Haley, A., & Malcolm X. (1964). *The autobiography of Malcolm X*. New York, NY: Ballantine.

Hartman, E. (2016). Decentering self in leadership: Putting community at the center in leadership studies. In W. Wagner & J. M. Pigza, *Leadership development through service-learning* (New Directions for Student Leadership, no. 150, pp. 73–83). San Francisco, CA: Jossey Bass.

Higher Education Research Institute (HERI). (1996). *A social change model of leadership development* (Version III). Los Angeles, CA: University of California, Los Angeles, Higher Education Research Institute.

Impact America. (n.d.). SaveFirst. Retrieved from http://impactamerica.com/savefirst/

Loeb, P. R. (2010). *Soul of a citizen: Living with conviction in a cynical time* (2nd ed.). New York, NY: St. Martin's.

McKnight, J. (1989). Why "servanthood" is bad. *The Other Side*, pp. 38–44.

McKnight, J. (2013). *A basic guide to ABCD community organizing*. Detroit, MI: Asset-Based Community Development Institute.

Mitchell, T. D. (2008). Traditional vs. critical service-learning: Engaging the literature to differentiate two models. *Michigan Journal of Community Service Learning, 14*(2), 50–65.

Moore, A. J. (2014). *The food fighters: DC Central Kitchen's first twenty-five years on the front lines of hunger and poverty*. Bloomington, IN: iUniverse.

Morton, K. (1995). The irony of service: Charity, project and social change in service-learning. *Michigan Journal of Community Service Learning, 2*(1), 19–32.

Morton, K. (1999). Starfish hurling and community service. In *Campus Compact Reader* (May 2000), p. 23. Retrieved from http://www.compact.org/reader/archives/Reader-V1-I1.pdf

Piedmont/Tidewater Rain Garden. (n.d.). Home page. Retrieved from http://green.gmu.edu/pgf/raingarden.cfm

Rank, M. R. (2011). Rethinking American poverty. *Contexts, 10*(2), 16–21.

Ross, F. (1989). *Conquering Goliath: César Chávez at the beginning*. Keene, CA: United Farm Workers.

Strain, C. R. (2006). Moving like a starfish: Beyond a unilinear model of student transformation in service learning classes. *Journal of College & Character, VIII*, 1–12. Retrieved September 5, 2008, from www.collegevalues.org/pdfs/moving.pdf

Tatum, B. D. (1997). *"Why are all the black kids sitting together in the cafeteria?" and other conversations about race*. New York, NY: Basic Books.

Thoreau, H. D. (1908). *Walden, or, life in the woods*. London, UK: J. M. Dent.

12

Applying the Social Change Model

Marguerite Bonous-Hammarth

> ... and the means we use must be as pure as the ends we seek.
> —MARTIN LUTHER KING JR.

It is a humbling experience for me to be asked to share thoughts about applying the Social Change Model of Leadership Development (Higher Education Research Institute [HERI], 1996). I was a graduate student at the time when legendary thinkers convened first at the University of California, Los Angeles, and later with larger groups of innovators at several national conferences to critically examine, refine, and then support practical strategies to nurture college student leadership, which became the Social Change Model of Leadership Development. The experience not only broadened my understanding about the vastness of the national and international networks ready to put relational leadership strategies to work but also it focused my attention on the process and relationships among change agents that were needed for these leadership collaborations to bear fruit.

You now bring your own enthusiasm and skills into leadership networks that will take the Social Change Model further still. Your role modeling of socially responsible leadership will broaden this circle of agency. Your involvement with the SCM will also have reciprocal benefits—for you as you directly enhance leadership expertise, for me and the original ensemble members as you extend the literature with your narratives, and for society as your efforts indelibly influence justice outcomes and the ways in which they are achieved.

CHAPTER OVERVIEW

The authors of the preceding chapters of this book have examined the SCM concepts using contemporary lenses to define with greater precision the fundamental competencies needed for leadership in an increasingly complex world. This chapter will build on their insights and shift from conceptualizing the model to applying it—when leading social change and when using socially responsibly leadership in any context. Although there are many ways to positively influence change in society today, this model provides a compass for a lifelong journey of continual learning about leadership and social change. Although the model and the Cs are easy to grasp and remember, they represent concepts that grow in complexity as we gain experience and engage in critical reflection about approaches to collective action that work. This chapter will first situate the model in the context of social justice goals. From there, I will present a four-part set of questions to help guide your application of the model. Finally, the chapter will address how to tackle some of the persistent issues in group process that arise from applying the model.

BRINGING JUSTICE TO THE CENTER OF YOUR PRACTICE

Social justice is a term that may have varied applications depending on the purpose for its use, but it typically refers to either one or all aspects of societal principles of fairness, fair decision-making processes and policies, and social inclusion or the ways that members of different social groups treat one another (Jost & Kay, 2010). Whether using the Social Change Model to address a social change issue in your community or to lead any group in a socially responsible way, it is helpful to define what your initiative will and will not entail. How will your group be inclusive of people and perspectives that are marginalized by our larger society? How will the social change your group is pursuing contribute to creating a more equitable community?

Current views about what it takes to promote social justice are equally varied but underscore some of the dynamic ways in which individual beliefs create welcoming inclusive environments and how inclusive environments influence individual beliefs. Consider the research on college campuses in which students who participate in organized clubs reported higher social justice beliefs, as well as higher perceptions of belonging to their campus communities—even after controlling for initial intentions to engage on campus (McAuliff, Williams, & Ferrari, 2013). This specific example underscores the recipe for reciprocal benefits in student retention and higher equity norms that may stem from campus initiatives to support engagement opportunities. By carefully defining the justice outcomes that you seek as change agents, you can chart manageable plans with community members to support the most pressing needs while remaining cognizant of contextual factors that also will bear on your initiative.

FOUR QUESTIONS AND INDICATORS TO MOVE IDEAS TO AGENCY

The ensemble authors originally described the Social Change Model as a simple yet robust tool to develop leadership through an intersection of personal and group reflections on service and other activities (Astin, 1996). Although the work of change agents may be through positional or nonpositional roles, individuals coming together to make a positive difference continually highlight the importance of Common Purpose and Commitment. Most important, justice orientations, such as those discussed here, require continued focus on the process and means by which change is envisioned to occur: knowledge of issues, self-values, relationships among change agents, as well as the factual outcomes of the change efforts. In this section, four overarching questions summarize the important considerations in applying the Social Change Model—from generating ideas to taking action. These questions encourage reflection among those invested in change efforts to set important benchmarks and means to assess impacts and progress along the way. The process of applying the model may consistently guide the motivated throughout the change process, and they may remind those facing stalls in their change initiatives about the need to conduct honest evaluation and skill building to enhance interactions for change. Table 12.1 provides an overview of these questions.

What Do We Know?

In Chapter 1, ensemble member Dennis C. Roberts invited you to join us in embracing and modeling a collaborative approach to leadership. I encourage you to be fearless in dreaming big about the social changes that you long to see in this world.

TABLE 12.1 Applying the SCM: Four Questions

What do we know?	• Knowledge about the social issues of concern • Awareness of knowledge gaps and how to research the issue further • Knowledge about individual strengths and commitments • Knowledge about our group purposes and processes • Knowledge about the community, the history of this issue in it, other leaders and groups concerned with this issue
What are our values?	• Individual values • Group shared values and common purposes • Community values
What actions will we take?	• Identification of tasks • Division of labor • Agreed modes of communication and skill building needed • Quality of processes and dedicated reflection about relationships • Coalition building with other individuals and among groups
How are we measuring our change and success?	• Clearly articulated envisioned outcomes • Evidence of change • Identification of intended and unintended outcomes • Conversations across coalition about continued action and next steps • Sense of community and belonging among individuals in the group • Growth in the group's ability to be collaborative and embrace Controversy With Civility

I also encourage you to use your talents and energies in the most efficient ways possible by understanding how your clearly defined change initiative will realize desired results. An important step in this part of your process would include doing some background research on the change you want to make and the community you will be making it in. Gather and review as much information as possible—including local knowledge from community members and general knowledge from scholarly experts—to ensure that your plans are relevant.

For example, you and your members may be very interested in issues related to food security or, specifically asking, does everyone in my community have access to "sufficient, safe, and nutritious food?" (United Nations, 1996). In order to understand where your group can best contribute, you may want to start by understanding food security among college students and among members on your campus and in your community. Where do families in the local community obtain their food? Are there healthy options? Can they afford them? These actions, as well as information from scholars in and around your community, may inform you, as it did on my campus, about approaches to be effective through campus-community partnerships and student interest to volunteer for and use food pantries, among other ideas. By understanding what the problem is, what is currently done, and what additional actions could be effective, you narrow the gap in knowledge about awareness about issues and leadership actions to take to resolve the issues.

What Are Our Values and Reasons for Involvement?

The real impact from social justice in action is to witness that its impetus comes from and can touch many sources. Like-minded souls will typically explore their justice ideas together. For example, the research suggests that students with justice beliefs tended to engage civically more than peers without these beliefs (Torres-Harding, Steele, Schulz, Taha, & Pico, 2014). However, in order for group members to represent the broadest possible sets of talents and enhance a team's capacities for creativity and innovation, group processes must support a culture of trust and appreciation for each person's unique expertise (Mannix & Neale, 2005). It is important to provide opportunities to recognize how the distinct and common values expressed by members of your change initiative can translate into unique contributions toward your Common Purpose.

One important way to maximize understanding about individual values is first to build skills in one's own Consciousness of Self and to share as members how these values result in Congruence between values and behaviors and in Commitment to justice causes. These reflections will enable group members to identify threads of Common Purpose and preferences to navigate Collaboration and Controversy With Civility related to social justice initiatives. As social justice work is focused equally on purpose and process, groups will continually develop essential group skills throughout their interactions together, particularly when the group members can identify how the expectations for core elements of the Social Change Model should be modeled.

What Actions Will We Take?

When our goal is to make a real difference our action steps need to be purposeful and well considered. How do we know our project will result in the change we intend it to? This aspect of applying the Social Change Model benefits from an organized planning process, particularly one that is inclusive of multiple perspectives and facilitates decision making. As you consider the relationships and division of responsibilities among your group members and the goals shared for social change, you may benefit from the scholarship related to theory of change and its focus on planning and a collaborative decision-making process to meet social needs and this level of collective agency.

As summarized by Taplin and Clark (2012), a theory of change process may begin simply by identifying long-term goals for the social change concern and then visually mapping, in reverse, all the preconditions or situations needed to make the long-term outcomes possible (p. 3). During a facilitated dialogue, the group is challenged to identify all of the assumptions they might be making at each connection on the map. Only after the framework is developed should members identify the specific actions that the group will take to intervene and attain the long-term goal, with related ways to measure successful completion and the time lines for group activities (p. 5). As a final self-check, group members should step back and question: are arguments and outcomes appropriately connected and *plausible*, are planned activities achievable and *feasible*, and are planned activities measurable and *testable*? (p. 8). Finally, writing an overarching summary of this process and the resulting plans provides the written steps and clear communications about process and initiative goals to navigate social change.

Once the group is clear about the logic and feasibility of its strategic plan, it can begin the work of implementation. This stage includes leveraging impact by forming coalitions with other groups who have a stake in the project's outcomes, recruiting other individuals to join the effort, establishing group roles, identifying tasks to be completed, agreeing on the division of labor and delegating the work, and establishing plans for ongoing communication and reporting.

How Are We Measuring Our Change and Success?

Transformation through collective agency is a central focus of social action work (Chung, Bemak, & Graboski, 2011; Gunewardena, 2009). Therefore, a last and important consideration of social change in action should be to examine the initiative's impact and examine its process. A group's process should not only foster greater capacities from division of labor to accomplish specific aims but also it should nurture greater learning from transformative knowledge gained through Collaborations not easily possible through solo efforts.

The experiences of group work and interactions may enable entire teams to improve the ways that members "connect, consume, create and contribute knowledge" across broad social networks (Littlejohn, Milligan, & Margaryan, 2011). Using the opportunities available through group dialogues and tasks, the collective (compared to an individual member) gain more and effective justice skills that have domino effects for inclusive practice across more social networks.

As the opening quote for this chapter suggests, the way that social agendas are accomplished is extremely important. Moreover, our aims to model SCM while implementing social change should ensure that actions are Congruent with guiding SCM philosophy and addressing relevant social concerns. How do we know that our actions have impact? We must focus on assessing our work efforts and the quality of the partnerships that we make to achieve justice aims.

Assessment may appear complicated or time-consuming, but it is an essential part of creating and sustaining any initiative or intervention. Many people at some point have wondered whether the time and energy spent in assessing a program would have been better spent on implementing another program. But our actions and next steps must come from an informed place and an attitude of being open to learning means learning how our program did and did not have an impact.

When using a SCM as a guide, the assessment considerations are even more important to avoid the trap of changing for the sake of change without having systemic impact. Too often, a group of dedicated individuals will identify Common Purpose and effective means to Collaborate and observe Controversy With Civility without having a clear sense of the big or little impacts they have had in the seventh C of Community. Effective assessment of leadership development and its application process are important antidotes to expending tons of energy but seeing no visible change or expected results.

Given the values of the SCM, a successful initiative is measured by the extent to which the outcomes influenced positive change and the extent to which the leadership processes fostered individual growth and increased the group's capacity to work collaboratively. Individuals and groups should learn and improve the ability to do collaborative leadership with each project they take on. Assessment should examine the processes as well as the impact. Whether group members engage in formal workshops or have informal experiences, there should be a process in place through which individuals and the group take time to assess the ways leadership is being enacted. For example, self-inquiry and interviews with peers and those receiving benefits from social change initiatives would give multiple perspectives. Some groups engage in a 360-degree review, which means feedback is obtained from perspectives all around them: people in authority "above" them such as administrators, people who report to them, stakeholders who work alongside them, and people who are recipients of the outcomes they produce (Rosch & Schwartz, 2009). This collective information offers a balanced perspective on the collaboration by including multiple perspectives.

PUTTING IT ALL TOGETHER

There will be moments throughout your interactions with other change agents that are transformative. As individual members of a group or initiative, you will bring unique talents, perspectives, and skills to bear on social issues of concern. An important next step in your application of SCM would be to use these diverse talents in ways that identify manageable and measurable solutions.

For example, I aimed to apply the SCM to work with transfer students as they planned for effective transitions from community college to a four-year institution of higher education. The resulting seminar, an Alliance for Coordinated Transfer for Leadership (ACT for Leadership), used a workshop setting for students to practice self-reflection and collective knowledge sharing. ACT for Leadership involved 50 undergraduates from community colleges in Southern California, and during the experiential workshop, students participated in activities to clarify values (Consciousness of Self), to network with transfer students for Collaboration, and to examine Controversy With Civility about their concerns related to college transfer and to broader social issues in their communities.

Although the mode of our interactions and the topical research about identity development, conflict resolution, and academic success factors were provided to students, the social issues of concerns and tasks to reach these goals emerged through research, journal narratives, dialogues, and proposals for social change projects developed by the students. Within our brief time together, students negotiated tasks from their strengths and interests—sorting through divisions of labor to develop cohesive proposals directly connected to major objectives for transfer and community engagement. The journals and individual transfer road maps that they developed became subtle ways to reflect on leadership growth as part of group processes and to identify future individual indicators of success in plans for civic engagement at four-year campuses. Follow-up evaluation with the students suggested that their ACT for Leadership experiences not only provided multiple sources of information to reduce transfer shock but also enlightened students about their capacity to address social issues of concern (Bonous-Hammarth, 2010).

Having read the preceding chapters about specific SCM skills, you and your group members would have a solid background about how your change initiative will support your individual and collective leadership development. I now suggest that you and your team apply several of the practical steps that theory of change leaders used to accomplish community action.

TACKLING PERSISTENT GROUP DYNAMICS ISSUES

Although the four-question approach to applying the SCM provides very practical ways to forge collaborations for community initiatives, there is no panacea to address most of the persistent issues related to group work and the ways that groups collaborate in the modern age. Perhaps one of the most vexing issues surrounding social justice initiatives is that change is inevitable and the opportunities to use selected approaches to enact change may shift. The specific task or justice concern may deepen or change to create different needs that were previously unconsidered but are equally complex. These two ideas related to the constantly changing nature of opportunities and issues in group work suggest that change agents need to be mindful about not only what is accomplished but also how their interactions and work with others will build inclusive models of practice.

Examine Your Process

The beauty of the SCM for me was always in its intent to address social issues of concern through the talents of those participating in leadership journeys. As a continual learner in the leadership process who often worked with more learned colleagues, I found an easy point of entry into SCM because ensemble conversations met me where I was as an enthusiastic participant and shaped my understanding about our interdependence in the leadership process.

I recall that there often were times during ensemble research and discussions when our process reflected the values of the very model we were creating. During one discussion to wordsmith between *conflict* and *controversy*, an ensemble member commented that our model seemed too neat and tidy. Rather than citing tomes of research about conflict resolution, our group member led us through a brief activity in which we were assigned to focus on specific group perspectives during conversations about one common social concern. Our role-playing gave us all insights about how different perspectives would shape Collaboration and enabled us to avoid getting stuck in debates over who was right and who was wrong (as often happens in conflict). Rather, we were able to reflect on the Common Purpose that we desired to enact while valuing all the differences still present (something that is still possible amid controversy).

As Dennis C. Roberts did in Chapter 1, I share these reflections about my involvement in a SCM process to encourage your own reflections as leaders concerned with change. As the opening quote by Martin Luther King Jr. (1963) suggests, social justice may best be realized when we model in practice the intents and expectations desired. Urging leaders to *practice what they preach* oversimplifies the complex process involved to apply social justice tenets. Yet, connecting the dots between ideology and actions enhances the odds that all participants who lead actions for change will take practical steps to discern how context—the situations unique to their groups and group dynamics—will influence Collaboration and the potential impacts of change initiatives. The SCM provides a blueprint to guide such efforts for positive outcomes.

Speak Truth to Leadership in a Group Process

Leadership interactions for social change also face persistent challenge from how individuals handle group exchanges and difference that may emerge. Specifically, I believe that it may be beneficial to understand that controversy is not only likely during a group process but also that it may be motivating.

In fact, the opening quote used in this chapter was Reverend King's direct response to criticisms from his fellow clergy. King uses his letter to remind readers that the tension created by nonviolent means is exactly what raises public awareness until unjust actions can no longer be ignored. Leaders will be most successful when they use tension and controversy from this tension to disrupt ineffective systems creatively (Kouzes & Posner, 2011) and to engage others involved in the controversy to understand what power dynamics and other justice issues may prevent or block change momentum (Deutsch & Coleman, 2000).

Maximize Individual and Group Growth

Continuing to reflect on the opening quote of this chapter reminds us about the needs to create formal and informal spaces to become more Conscious of Self and more aware of assumptions that are driving interests and actions. How can we build coalitions of care through Collaboration? In the end, the most effective ways to enact social change initiatives may be to refocus on ways to enhance individual leadership growth and the interactions across positional and nonpositional leaders. Reflecting on more than 50 years of involvement with college students and their development, Astin and Astin (2015) echoed these thoughts by acknowledging the strong influence of student-level leadership to spark self-resiliency and purpose, as well as to guide broader civic practices and caring values among students. The idea that the actions taken to implement any initiative hinge on not only the effectiveness of the outcomes but also shaping the integrity of the group's process are realities about the challenges to act as leaders found in research and in practice (Kouzes & Posner, 2011).

Leverage Technology

An increasingly global society demands that individuals find multiple ways to span geographic and ideological distances to foster awareness about social needs and movements, as well as to enhance leadership training and the means to achieve social agendas. Emerging evidence about technology use shows that leaders and emerging leaders with high online connectivity are perceived as effective and proactive leaders and, more important, enhance their face-to-face leadership through online applications (Kolb, Prussia, & Francoeur, 2009).

Groups may use technology for political and other social issue collaborations that raise antennae further about new ways to apply and assess change efforts (Pew Research Center, 2015). Whether organized predominantly by faculty and staff members or emerging as initiatives and actions by students themselves, the conscious focus on individual self-examination of values, common purposes, and clear definition of the change task, research and potential redefinition of tasks, and shared accountability combine to create potent synergy that now may require greater attention about how to bring to scale and assess impact across technological divides.

CONCLUSION

It is important to begin any justice intervention using the original SCM implementation features to identify the problem or justice issue, help members to clarify values, research important knowledge and knowledge gaps related to issues of interest, and enact accountability. In a nutshell, the four questions identified here encourage reflection among those invested in change efforts, setting important benchmarks and means to assess impacts and progress along the way. To describe a leadership initiative as "successful" requires not only a well-implemented idea that creates positive change but also a process that fosters growth and development for the group and the individuals in it. The SCM is a very useful framework for addressing several persistent issues related to how groups collaborate and share collective knowledge.

DISCUSSION QUESTIONS

1. How, as individuals, do we enter and interact with others for change initiatives?
2. What are the strategies that we use to clarify social issues?
3. How do we verbalize or demonstrate our opinions and beliefs about social issues? How do we invite and recognize the Common Purpose and unique values represented by members working with us on social justice issues?
4. Under what circumstances do we encourage accountability in ourselves and among others for the change process and, ultimately, the social change objectives?
5. What tools or data gathering strategies might be used to guide the assessment of an initiative's progress and the quality of the change process?

ACTION AND REFLECTION

1. At an upcoming group meeting, use the four questions for applying the SCM to facilitate a conversation about your group's goals, what you know and need to find

out, what your individual and collective values are related to a good outcome and a good process, what actions you should take next, and how you will measure the outcome and process.

2. In advance of planning your next change initiative, make a time line that indicates the specific points in the process that you will check the facts for evidence of whether your actions steps are going as planned. Make this practice routine and build trust with one another so these check-ins will be authentic sharing about what is and is not working.

3. As your initiative progresses, set aside 5 minutes at the close of planning and implementation meetings to discuss how the group is feeling at this particular moment about their process. Is this where they want to be or where they imagined they would be? What can they do individually and as group members to enhance momentum and interactions?

4. Journal either individually or collectively about completed activities and the quality of interactions shared by group members.

5. How receptive do you think your group will be to these four action items? How might you go about introducing these approaches to encourage others to try them?

REFERENCES

Astin, A. W., & Astin, H. A. (2015). Achieving equity in higher education: The unfinished agenda. *Journal of College & Character, 16*(2), 65–74. doi:10.1080/2194587X.2015.1024799

Astin, H. A. (1996). Leadership for social change. *About Campus, 1*(3), 4–10. doi:10.1002/abc.6190010302

Bonous-Hammarth, M. (2010). *A research report examining leadership, community service, and potentials for transfer among community college students.* Irvine, CA: Center for Educational Partnerships.

Chung, R. C., Bemak, F., & Grabosky, T. K. (2011). Multicultural-social justice leadership strategies: Counseling and advocacy with immigrants. *Journal for Social Action in Counseling and Psychology, 3,* 86–102. Retrieved from http://www.psysr.org/jsacp/chung-v3n1-11_86-102.pdf

Deutsch, M., & Coleman, P. T. (Eds.). (2000). *The handbook of conflict resolution: Theory and practice.* San Francisco, CA: Jossey-Bass.

Gunewardena, N. (2009). Pathologizing poverty: Structural forces versus personal deficit theories in the feminization of poverty. *Journal of Educational Controversy, Article 5*(4), 1–11. Retrieved from http://cedar.wwu.edu/jec/vol4/iss1/5

Higher Education Research Institute (HERI). (1996). *A social change model of leadership development* (Version III). Los Angeles, CA: University of California, Los Angeles, Higher Education Research Institute.

Jost, J. T., & Kay, A. C. (2010). Social justice: History, theory, and research. *Handbook of Social Psychology, 30*, 1122–1165. doi:10.1002/9780470561119.socpsy002030

King, M. L., Jr. (1963). *Letter from a Birmingham city jail*. Philadelphia, PA: American Friends Service Committee.

Kolb, D. G., Prussia, G., & Francoeur, J. (2009). Connectivity and leadership: The influence of online activity on closeness and effectiveness. *Journal of Leadership & Organizational Studies, 15*, 342–352. doi:10.1177/1548051809331503

Kouzes, J. M., & Posner, B. Z. (2011). Practicing the 10 truths about leadership. *Lifelong Faith, 5*(1), 3–9. Retrieved from: http://www.lifelongfaith.com/journal.html

Littlejohn, A., Milligan, C., & Margaryan, A. (2011). Collective learning in the workplace: Important knowledge sharing behaviours. *International Journal of Advanced Corporate Learning, 4*(4), 26–31. Retrieved from http://online-journals.org/i-jac/article/view/1801

Mannix, E., & Neale, M. A. (2005). What differences make a difference? The promises and realities of diverse teams in organizations. *Psychological Science in the Public Interest, 6*(2), 31–55. doi:10.1111/j.1529–1006.2005.00022.x

McAuliff, K. E., Williams, S. M., & Ferrari, J. R. (2013). Social justice and the university community: Does campus involvement make a difference? *Journal of Prevention & Intervention in the Community, 41*(4), 244–254. doi: 10.1080/10852352.2013.818486

Pew Research Center. (2015). Social networking fact sheet. Online Advisory. Retrieved from http://www.pewinternet.org/fact-sheets/social-networking-fact-sheet/

Rosch, D. M., & Schwartz, L. M. (2009). Potential issues and pitfalls in outcomes assessment in leadership education. *Journal of Leadership Education, 8*(1), 177–193. Retrieved from http://www.journalofleadershiped.org/

Taplin, D. H., & Clark, H. C. (2012). *Theory of change basics: A primer on theory of change*. New York, NY: ActKnowledge. Retrieved from http://www.theoryofchange.org/wp-content/uploads/toco_library/pdf/ToCBasics.pdf

Torres-Harding, S. R., Steele, C., Schulz, E., Taha, F., & Pico, C. (2014). Student perceptions of social justice and social justice activities. *Education, Citizenship & Social Justice, 9*(1), 55–66. doi: 10.1177/1746197914520655

United Nations. (1996). *World food summit newsletter*. Rome, Italy: Food and Agricultural Organization of the United Nations. Retrieved from http://www.fao.org/wfs/

Epilogue

Susan R. Komives and Wendy Wagner

> This process of the good life is not, I am convinced, a life for the faint-hearted. It involves the stretching and growing of becoming more and more of one's potentialities. It involves the courage to be. It means launching oneself fully into the stream of life.
> —CARL ROGERS

Convinced that college students want their lives to make a difference in the world, the Social Change Model of Leadership Development provides a framework for engaging in life in ways that matter. Ensemble member and coprincipal investigator of the project, the late Helen Astin (1996), shared a reflection from a group of University of California, Irvine, students who implemented a social change project using the Seven Cs of this model. She reported:

> Among their many observations about the model and its underlying values, one is of particular interest. They decided to add one more C to the list: *courage*. Their reasoning was, as one student stated, "You can see the need to change something but it takes courage to do it." They also felt that the power of the group inspired courage among them and helped them persist in achieving their common purpose. (p. 10)

She went on to reflect, "Too often, courage is characterized as a trait exclusive to heroes—people who are glamorized for their individual and essentially solitary efforts to rise above common achievements or to rescue the rest of us." She encourages students to "embrace another view of courage, a view that honors the power of individuals coming together to work for change, and yes, the bravery required to do this collaborative work" (p. 10).

The ensemble members, editors, and authors of this book applaud that you not only have the courage to make a difference with your life but also that above it all you are the difference. In implementing the values of the Social Change Model of Leadership Development, you live the commitments of this model through your very being and you hold others in your groups and communities to higher expectations.

REFERENCE

Astin, H. S. (1996). Leadership for social change. *About Campus, 1*(3), 4–10. doi:10.1002/abc.6190010302

Additional Resources

SOCIAL CHANGE MODEL OF LEADERSHIP DEVELOPMENT

Astin, A. W., & Astin, H. S. (2000). *Leadership reconsidered: Engaging higher education in social change.* Battle Creek, MI: W. K. Kellogg Foundation.

Astin, H. S. (1996). Leadership for social change. *About Campus, 1*(3), 4–10. doi:10.1002/abc.6190010302

Bonous-Hammarth, M. (1996). Developing social change agents: Leadership development for the '90s and beyond. *Concepts & Connections, 4*(2), 1, 3–4.

Dugan, J. P., Gehrke, S. J., Komives, S. R., & Martinez, M. (2007). Student programmers and leadership development: Select findings from the Multi-Institutional Study of Leadership. *Campus Activities Programming, 40*(1), 46–49.

Dugan, J., & Komives, S. R. (2011). Leadership theory. In S. R. Komives, J. P. Dugan, J. E. Owen, W. Wagner, C. Slack, & Associates, *The handbook for student leadership development* (pp. 35–58). San Francisco, CA: Jossey-Bass.

Dugan, J. P., & Velázquez, D. (2015). Teaching contemporary leadership: Advancing students' capacities to engage about and across difference. In S. Watt (Ed.), *Transformative multicultural initiatives: Theoretical foundations, practical applications, and facilitator considerations.* Sterling, VA: Stylus.

Guthrie, K., Osteen, L., & Associates. (2012). *Developing students' leadership capacity* (New Directions for Student Service, no. 140). San Francisco, CA: Jossey-Bass.

Higher Education Research Institute (HERI). (1996). *A social change model of leadership development* (Version III). Los Angeles, CA: University of California, Los Angeles, Higher Education Research Institute.

Kezar, A. J., Carducci, R., & Contreras-McGavin, M. (2006). Rethinking the "L" word in higher education: The revolution in research on leadership. *ASHE Higher Education Report, 31*(6). San Francisco, CA: Jossey-Bass.

Komives, S. R. (2011). *The social change model of leadership development with Susan R. Komives.* YouTube video. College Park, MD: International Leadership Association. Retrieved from https://www.youtube.com/watch?v=PpjGCP5ee-k

Komives, S. R. (2016). 20 years of impact: The social change model of leadership development. *NASPA Leadership Exchange, 14,* 36, 38–39.

Komives, S. R., & Dugan, J. P. (2010). Contemporary leadership theories. In R. A. Couto (Ed.), *Political and civic leadership: A reference handbook* (pp. 109–125). Thousand Oaks, CA: Sage.

Komives, S. R., & Dugan, J. P. (2014). Student leadership development: Theory, research, and practice. In D. Day (Ed.), *The Oxford handbook of leadership and organizations* (pp. 805–831). New York, NY: Oxford University Press.

Komives, S. R., Dugan, J., Owen, J. E., Slack, C., & Wagner, W., and Associates. (2011). *The handbook for student leadership development* (2nd ed.). San Francisco, CA: Jossey-Bass.

Komives, S. R., Lucas, N., & McMahon, T. (2013). *Exploring leadership: For college students who want to make a difference* (3rd ed.). San Francisco, CA: Jossey Bass.

Outcault, C. L., Faris, S. K., & McMahon, K. N. (Eds.). (2001). *Developing non-hierarchical leadership on campus: Case studies and best practices in higher education.* Westport, CT: Greenwood.

Outcalt, C. L., Faris, S. K., McMahon, K. N., Tahtakran, P. M., & Noll, C. B. (2001). A leadership approach for the new millennium: A case study of UCLA's Bruin Leaders Project. *NASPA Journal, 38*(2), 178–188.

Owen, J. E. (Ed.). (2015). *Innovative learning for leadership development* (New Directions for Student Leadership, no. 145). San Francisco, CA: Jossey-Bass.

Roberts, D. R. (2007). *Deeper learning in leadership: Helping college students find the potential within.* San Francisco, CA: Jossey-Bass.

Seemiller, C. (2006). Impacting social change through service learning in an introductory course. *Journal of Leadership Education, 5*(2), 41–49.

Skendell, K. C., Ostick, D., Wagner, W., Komives, S. R., & Associates. (2017). *The social change model: Facilitating leadership development.* San Francisco, CA: Jossey-Bass.

Stenta, D., & McFadden, C. (Ed.). (2015). *Developing leadership through recreation and athletics* (New Directions for Student Leadership, no. 147). San Francisco, CA: Jossey-Bass.

St. Norbert College. (1996). *Citizens of change: The application guidebook.* College Park, MD: National Clearinghouse for Leadership Programs.

Wagner, W. (2006). The social change model of leadership: A brief overview. *Concepts & Connections, 15*(1), 9.

Wagner, W., Ostick, D. T., Komives, S. R., & Associates. (2010). *Leadership for a better world: Instructor manual.* National Clearinghouse for Leadership Programs. San Francisco, CA: Jossey-Bass.

Wagner, W., & Pigza, J. (Ed.). (2016). *Leadership development through service-learning* (New Directions for Student Leadership, no. 150). San Francisco, CA: Jossey-Bass.

SELECTED RESEARCH ON THE SOCIAL CHANGE MODEL OF LEADERSHIP DEVELOPMENT

Buschlen, E., & Dvorak, R. (2011). The social change model as pedagogy: Examining undergraduate leadership growth. *Journal of Leadership Education, 10*(2), 38–56.

Campbell, C. M., Smith, M., Dugan, J. P., & Komives, S. R. (2012). Mentors and college student leadership outcomes: The importance of position and process. *Review of Higher Education, 35,* 595–625.

Dugan, J. P. (2006a). Explorations using the social change model: Leadership development among college men and women. *Journal of College Student Development, 47,* 217–225.

Dugan, J. P. (2006b). Involvement and leadership: A descriptive analysis of socially responsible leadership. *Journal of College Student Development, 47,* 335–343.

Dugan, J. P. (2008). Exploring relationships between fraternity and sorority membership and socially responsible leadership. *Oracle: The Research Journal of the Association of Fraternity/Sorority Advisors, 3*(2).

Dugan, J. P., Bohle, C. W., Gebhardt, M., Hofert, M., Wilk, E., & Cooney, M. A. (2011). Influences of leadership program participation on students' capacities for socially responsible leadership. *Journal of Student Affairs Research and Practice, 48,* 65–84.

Dugan, J. P., Bohle, C. W., Woelker, L. R., & Cooney, M. A. (2014). The role of social perspective-taking in developing students' leadership capacities. *Journal of Student Affairs Research and Practice, 51,* 1–15.

Dugan, J. P., Fath, K. Q., Howes, S. D., Lavelle, K. R., & Polanin, J. R. (2013). Developing the leadership capacity and leader efficacy of college women in science, technology, engineering, and math fields. *Journal of Leadership Studies, 7*(3), 6–23.

Dugan, J. P., Garland, J., Jacoby, B., & Gasiorski, A. (2008). Understanding commuter student self-efficacy for leadership: A within-group analysis. *NASPA Journal, 45,* 282–310.

Dugan, J. P., Kodama, C., Correia, B., & Associates. (2013). *Multi-Institutional Study of Leadership insight report: Leadership program delivery.* College Park, MD: National Clearinghouse for Leadership Programs.

Dugan, J. P., Kodama, C. M., & Gebhardt, M. C. (2012). Race and leadership development among college students: The additive value of collective racial esteem. *Journal of Diversity in Higher Education, 5*(3), 174–189.

Dugan, J. P., & Komives, S. R. (2007). *Developing leadership capacity in college students: Findings from a national study.* College Park, MD: National Clearinghouse for Leadership Programs.

Dugan, J. P., & Komives, S. R. (2010). Influences on college students' capacities for socially responsible leadership. *Journal of College Student Development, 51,* 525–549.

Dugan, J. P., Komives, S. R., & Segar, T. (2008). College student capacity for socially responsible leadership: Understanding norms and influences of race, gender, and sexual orientation. *NASPA Journal, 45,* 475–500.

Dugan, J. P., Kusel, M. L., & Simounet, D. M. (2012). Transgender college students: An exploratory study of perceptions, engagement, and educational outcomes. *Journal of College Student Development, 53,* 719–736.

Dugan, J. P., Rosseti Morosini, A. M., & Beazley, M. R. (2011). Cultural transferability of socially responsible leadership: Findings from the United States and Mexico. *Journal of College Student Development, 52,* 456–474.

Dugan, J. P., Torrez, M. A., & Turman, N. T. (2014). *Leadership in intramural sports and club sports: Examining influences to enhance educational impact.* Corvallis, OR: NIRSA.

Dugan, J. P., & Yurman, L. (2011). Commonalities and differences among lesbian, gay, and bisexual college students: Considerations for research and practice. *Journal of College Student Development, 52,* 201–216.

Gehrke, S. J. (2008). Leadership through meaning-making: An empirical exploration of spirituality and leadership in college students. *Journal of College Student Development, 49,* 351–359.

Haber, P., & Komives, S. R. (2009). Predicting the individual values of the social change model of leadership development: The role of college students' leadership and involvement experiences. *Journal of Leadership Educators, 7*(3), 133–166.

Hevel, M. S., Martin, G. L., & Pascarella, E. T. (2014). Do fraternities and sororities still enhance socially responsible leadership? Evidence from the fourth year of college. *Journal of Student Affairs Research and Practice, 51,* 233–245.

Kodama, C. M., & Dugan, J. P. (2013). Leveraging leadership efficacy for college students: Disaggregating data to examine unique predictors by race. *Equity & Excellence in Education, 46*(2), 184–201.

Maia, A. (2016). *Research findings on the social change model of leadership development.* College Park, MD: National Clearinghouse for Leadership Programs.

Martin, G. L. (2013). The impact of interaction with student affairs professionals on socially responsible leadership development in the first year of college. *Journal of College and Character, 14,* 289–299.

Owen, J. E. (2012). *Findings from the Multi-Institutional Study of Leadership Institutional Survey (MSL-IS): A national report.* Washington, DC: National Clearinghouse for Leadership Programs. Retrieved from http://leadershipstudy.net/wp-content/uploads/2012/07/msl-is-publication-final.pdf

Ricketts, K. G., Bruce, J. A., & Ewing, J. C. (2008). How today's undergraduate students see themselves social responsible leaders. *Journal of Leadership Education, 7,* 24–42.

Rosch, D. M., & Coers, N. (2013). How are we educating agricultural students? A national profile of leadership capacities and involvement in college compared to non-agricultural peers. *Journal of Agricultural Education, 54,* 83–96.

Rosch, D. M., Collier, D., & Thompson, S. E. (2015). An exploration of students' motivation to lead: An analysis by race, gender, and student leadership behaviors. *Journal of College Student Development, 56,* 286–291.

Shalka, T. R., & Jones, S. R. (2010). Differences in self-awareness related measures among culturally based fraternity, social fraternity, and non-affiliated college men. *Oracle: The Research Journal of the Association of Fraternity/Sorority Advisors, 5,* 1–11.

Tyree, T. M. (1998). Designing an instrument to measure the socially responsible leadership using the social change model of leadership development. *Dissertation Abstracts International, 59* (06), 1945. (AAT 9836493)

Wolniak, G. C., Mayhew, M. J., & Engberg, M. E. (2012). Learning's weak link to persistence. *Journal of Higher Education, 83,* 795–823.

Concepts & Connections (a publication of the National Clearinghouse for Leadership Programs; available at www.nclp.umd.edu) featured the Multi-Institutional Study of Leadership (MSL) in its 2006–2007 volume.

- Vol. 15 (1): MSL methods, MSL descriptive findings, the Social Change Model
- Vol. 15 (2): Identity-based MSL findings (e.g., gender, sexual orientation, race)
- Vol. 15 (3): Training and curricular findings
- Vol. 15 (4): Cocurricular findings (e.g., service, mentoring, involvement, discussions of sociopolitical issues)

Index

A

Abes, E., 119
Accountability, 125
ACPA (American College Personnel Association), 31
ACT for Leadership (Alliance for Coordinated Transfer for Leadership), 258
Action: applying SCM principles in, 268–269; choosing responsible, 2; questions generating SCM, 263–268; supporting Citizenship, 181–184
Active listening, 139–140
Adaptive change: balancing stability and disequilibrium in, 226–227; community-level, 222–223; group-level, 221–222; individual-level, 219–221; technical vs., 217–219, 223–224
Additional resources, 277–281
Adjourning stage, 135
Allen, K. E., 8, 10, 17, 105, 203, 205, 208, 224
Alliance for Coordinated Transfer for Leadership (ACT for Leadership) 268
Allison, E., 98–99
Alvarez, Cecilio, 149–173
American College Personnel Association (ACPA), 31
American Society of Mechanical Engineers, 26
Annan, Kofi, 70
Applewhite, A., 101
Applying SCM: generating social action, 263–268; measuring success, 266–268; overview, 262, 272; promoting social justice, 262–263; steps for, 268–269; tackling group dynamics, 269–272
Archimedes, 201, 229
Ashford, S.J., 57
Asking the Right Questions (Browne & Keeley), 159

Assessments, 37, 57
Assimilation of leaders, 249–250
Associated living, 177
Association for Conflict Resolution, 162
Astin, Alexander, xvi, xvii, 2, 10–11, 18, 88 92, 185–186, 198, 271
Astin, Helen, 2, 10–11, 18, 88, 89, 92, 93, 185–186, 198, 263, 271, 275
Authenticity, 77–79, 90–91
Avolio, B. J., 45, 77, 78
Awareness. See Self-awareness

B

Baby boomers, 49
Bakir, A., 250
Bandura, Albert, 54
Bank, J. A., 184
Barber, P., 190
Barksdale, Vanessa, 96
Baruch, Heather S., 168
Baxter Magolda, Marcia, 71
Be a Good Neighbor Program, 179
Begging for Change (Egger), 236
Bemak, F., 266
Bengi, Deniz, 251
Bennis, W. G., xviii
Bettez, S. C., 184
Biggs, Danielle M., 69–70
Black Lives Matter, 109–110
Black, Stephen, 244
Boaty McBoatface, 216
Boggs, Grace Lee, 175

283

Bohle, C. W., 20, 187
Bohm, D., 163
Bolman, L. G., 130, 131, 136
Bonding, 183
Bonnet, Jennifer, 175–196
Bonous-Hammarth, Marguerite, xvi, 10, 39, 261–274
Bordas, J., 17, 48, 91–92, 178, 255, 256–257
Boycotting, 190, 213–214
Boyd, R., 154
Boyle, Christopher R., 168
Brewer, Jake, 13
Bridging, 183
Brinkworth, M., 158
Broken windows theory, 215
Brookfield, S. D., 59
Brown, B., 116, 120, 203
Brown, Juanita, 141
Browne, M. N., 159
Buechner, Frederick, 93
Building trust, 116, 117–118, 125
Burke, Edmund, 172
Burnout, 97
Burns, J. M., 2, 7, 18
Buycotting, 190

C

Campus communities. *See* Communities
Carducci, R., 5, 18
Care-based thinking, 76
C.A.S.E., 187
Cat's Cradle (Vonnegut), 13
Celebrating success, 117
Challenges, 53–54, 242–248
Change: adapting to, 217; civility in social, 154–155; commitment as focus for, 87–88; constancy of, 2; courage required, 275; cultivating social, 13; exponential, 212–215; individual, group, and community levels of, 203–204; influencing, 215–216; knowing-begin-doing framework for, 32, 33; leadership roles for, 225–229; measuring initiatives, 266–268; noticing signs of, 214; ongoing, organic, 205–206, 210–215; overview, 198–199, 203, 229–230; questions generating, 263–268; resistance to, 224–225; SCM and, 21, 28–29, 202–203; social media for, 34; systems approach to, 206–209; traditional vs. organic, 205–206; *See also* Adaptive change; Social change

Chávez, César, 27, 246
Cherrey, C., 8, 10, 17, 106, 203, 205, 208, 224
Chrislip, D. D., 114, 116–117, 118, 120, 121
Chung, R.C., 266
Circle K International, 180
Citizenship: about, 28; actions supporting, 181–184; activities exemplifying, 178–179; coalition building for, 187–189; community role in, 179–181; connecting to Seven Cs, 191; consumer activism as, 190; defined, 21, 176; history in U.S., 177–178; knowing-begin-doing framework for, 33; overview, 176, 191–192; rubric for, 192, 193; social media and, 189–190; SPT concept in, 187; *See also* Community
"Civility in America" (Weber Shandwick, Powell Tate, & KRC Research), 162–163
Civility. *See* Controversy With Civility
Clark, H. C., 266
Clicktivism, 190
Clicktivist.org, 190
Cloutier, C., 215
Coalition building, 34–35, 187–189
Coleman, P. T., 271
Collaboration: building, 115–122; Common Purpose and, 36, 44; competition vs., 112–114; compromise vs., 113, 115; connecting to Seven Cs, 122; Consciousness of Self with, 60; cooperation vs., 114–115; defining, 110–111; factors in, 111–112; as group value, 25, 106–111; knowing-begin-doing framework for, 32; leadership as, 18, 19; overview, 111, 122–123; rubric for, 124, 125; as SCM value, 21; social change requiring, 239–240
Collective responsibility. *See* Social responsibility
Colvin, Claudette, 213
Commitment: achieving flow in, 99; burnout of leaders, 97; Citizenship's connection with, 191; Common Purpose and, 44; congruent with values, 90–91; connecting Consciousness of Self with, 60; connection to Seven Cs, 87–88, 99, 100; defined, 21, 24, 87–88; evaluating level of, 89–90; experiences developing, 91–92; external environments supporting, 93; finding one's passion, 91–92, 93, 94; group efforts reflecting, 95–96; knowing-begin-doing framework for, 32; leadership credibility and, 94; meaning of, 88–89; overview, 100–101; resilient leadership, 98–99; spirituality and faith in, 92; sustaining, 96–97

Common Purpose: Citizenship's connection with, 191; Collaboration and, 25, 36, 44; Commitment leading to, 94; communicating, 138–141; connecting to Seven Cs, 144; decision making for, 142–144; defined, 21; developing group's, 120, 127–128, 134–135; groups' understanding of, 129–132; knowing-begin-doing framework for, 32; listening skills to attain, 39–40; overview, 44–45, 128; personal vs. socialized vision of, 132–134; rubric for, 146, 147; sustaining, 137–138; transmitting group culture, 135–137; vision of, 131

Communities: adaptive change by, 222–223; boycotts by, 212–214; building social capital, 181–183; change for, 203–204; civic engagement supporting, 181, 182; civic participation in, 177–178; deficit-based perspectives of, 251–252; defining scope of, 179–181; development of SPT, 187; gaining consensus in, 142, 143, 240–242; groups as, 172–173; providing awareness of history, 183–184; understanding empowerment and privilege of, 184–187; volunteerism within, 243–245

"Comparing Debate, Discussion, and Dialogue", 164

Competition vs. collaboration, 112–114

Compromise, 113, 115

Conchie, B., 50

Conflict: civility vs., 150–151, 168; leading those with conflicting values, 72–77

Congruence: authentic leadership and, 77–79; building, 81; Citizenship's connection with, 191; Commitment and, 90–91; Common Purpose and, 44; concept of, 67; connecting to Seven Cs, 81–82; Consciousness of Self and, 58, 67, 68; Consciousness of Self connecting and, 60; considering dimensions of, 73–74; courage and, 79–80; defined, 21, 23–24; knowing self and, 68–70; knowing-begin-doing framework for, 32; leading others with conflicting values, 72–77; overview, 68, 82; right-versus-right decisions, 74–77; self-authorship, 70–72

Consciousness of Self: aspirations and dreams, 50–51; assessments developing, 57; challenges and experiences, 53–54; Citizenship's connection with, 191; Common Purpose and, 44; Congruence and, 58, 67, 68; connecting with other Cs, 60; defined, 21, 22–23, 44; developmental process in, 52–57; exploring personal style, 49–50; illustrated, 22; knowing-begin-doing framework for, 32; openness to feedback, 56–57; overview, 44, 61; reflecting with Johari Window, 51–52; reflection and, 54–56; research on, 45–47; talents, skills, and specialized knowledge, 50; understanding, 44–45; values, principles, and identity shaping, 47–49

Consensus, 142, 143, 240–242

Consumer activism, 190

Context: for engaging controversy, 162–163; ignoring political, 250–251

Contrera, J., 13

Contreras-McGavin, M., 5, 18

Controversy With Civility: about, 26–27; acknowledging and engaging in, 161–162; awareness of worldview, 157–158; building trust required, 160–161; Citizenship's connection with, 191; Common Purpose and, 44; conflict vs., 150–151, 168; connecting Consciousness of Self with, 60; connecting to Seven Cs, 166; contexts and spaces to engage, 162–163; defined, 21; engaging controversy, 162–163; fostering dialogue, 163–165; goal of, 149–150; group development and, 153–154; knowing-begin-doing framework for, 33; overview, 150, 166; practicing, 155–157; recognizing others' worldview, 158–160; requirement when addressing Commitment, 94–95; rubric for, 167, 168; social change and, 154–155; SPT support of, 152–153; valuing civility, 151–152

Cooney, M. A., 20, 187

Cooperation: collaboration vs., 114–115; Controversy with Civility rubric for, 168

Corey, G., 157

Correia, B., 12, 36

Council of Economic Advisors, 178

Courage, 79–80, 275

Courtesy, 168

Covey, S. R., 114

Critical thinking, 158–159

Crum, T. F., 115, 139

Crutchfield, L. R., 236, 256

Cullors-Brignac, P., 109

Cultivating your karass, 13

Culture: groups practicing Controversy With Civility, 155–157; ignoring differences in, 253; transmitting group, 135–137; values shaping identity, 48

D

Daloz, L. A., 93, 97

Daring Greatly (Brown), 116

DC Office on Aging, 252
de Pree, Max, xiii
de Tocqueville, Alexis, 177, 181
Deal, T. E., 130, 131, 136
Decision making: collaboration and, 113, 121–122; methods of group, 142–144; problem solving with system thinking, 207–208; reaching group consensus, 142, 143, 240–242; right-versus-right, 74–77
Deeper Learning in Leadership (Roberts), 198
Deficit-based perspectives, 251–252
Democracy, 177
Denning, S., 131, 137
DeRue, D. S., 57
Deutsch, M., 271
Dewey, J., xvii, 177
Dialogue: fostering, 163–165; reflective, 141; skills for civility in, 168
Diamond, J., 9
Digital citizenship, 189–190
Disbanding groups, 135
Diversity, 118–120
Domination, 113
Dorfman, P., 73
Dougan, Michael, 160
Drath, W. H., 210
Dugan, J. P., xvii, 8, 12, 20, 36, 37, 46, 53, 54, 56, 74, 90, 122, 152, 153, 157, 165, 187, 257
Dweck, Carol, 256

E

Eakes, Martin, 256
Early, Sherry, xvi, 43–65
Edelman, Marian Wright, 2, 87, 246
Edmunds, J., 17
Egger, R., 236–237
Elliott, Walter, 96
Emery, S., 69
Ends-based thinking, 76
England, Jordan, 109–126
Ensemble: about, xv, 6; acknowledging role of controversy, 150; approach to collaboration, 110–111, 116; change as hub of SCM, 28–29, 202–203; Commitment as defined by, 88; on Consciousness of Self, 44; defining Congruence, 67; developing sense of Common Purpose, 144; exploring collaborative leadership, 106; finding Common Purpose, 128; implications of citizenship, 176, 191; invitation into, 12–13; leadership and change, 234; origins of, 10–11
Ethnocentrism, 253
Evans, T., 101
Exploring Leadership (Komives et al.), 158
Exponential change, 212–215

F

Facebook, 189, 216
Faith, 48, 91
Family, 49
Faris, S. K., 7, 18
Feedback, 56–57, 209
Fincher, Justin, 43–65
Fink, John, 47
Flow, 98
Follett, Mary Parker, 113–114, 118, 121, 228
Forming stage, 134–135
Fostering dialogue, 163–165
Francoeur, J., 271
French, J.R.P., 228, 229
Friedman, U., 216
Frothingham, A., 101
Fuller, Millard, 236

G

Gaddy, Rayia, 143
Galinsky, A. D., 153
Gam, Paul, 72–73
Gandhi, Mahatma, 31, 66
Gardner, John, 172
Gardner, W. L., 77, 78
Garza, Alicia, 109
Gebhardt, M. C., 74
Gehlbach, H., 158
Generations X and Z, 49
Gerber, R., 91, 93–94, 246
Global Leadership and Organizational Behavior Effectiveness (GLOBE) research project, 73
Goals: aim for change values, 236–237; Controversy With Civility, 149–150; group aims and, 131–132; mutual attainment of, 113; SCM's, xiv
Goldman, B. M., 77
Gonnerman, Monet, 242
Goss, K., 183
Grabosky, T. K., 266
Grace, M., 49

Graf, Aurora Guillén, 209
Grant, H.M., 236, 256
Grashow, A., 144, 203
Greenberg, E., 178
Greenleaf, R. G., 9–10
Greenpeace, 215, 216
Groce, N. W., 255
Group values: about, 24, 106; Collaboration, 25, 106–111; Common Purpose, 26; Controversy With Civility, 21, 26–27; illustrated, 11, 25; power of group commitments, 94–95; *See also* Groups; *and specific values*
Groups: adaptive change by, 221–222; broad-based involvement in diverse, 118–120; building coalitions, 34–35, 187–189; celebrating success, 117; change for, 203–204; clarifying values, vision, and aims of, 129–132; Common Purpose for, 120, 127–132, 134–135, 138–139, 140–141; creating strategic plan, 265–266; decision making methods by, 142–144; defining, 128–129; development stages of, 134–135; dissonance in, 161–162; dynamics in, 269–272; encouraging involvement in, 125; exploring beliefs of, 184–187; facilitating inner work of, 226; informal exploring within, 116–117; maximizing growth of, 271; practicing Controversy With Civility, 155–157; process used in, 121–122; reaching consensus in, 143; rights and responsibilities of, 172–173, 177–178; shared vision of, 131; sharing ownership, 117; speaking truth in, 270–271; SPT's support of, 153; technology for collaborating in, 271–272; transmitting culture of, 135–137; trust building in, 116, 117–118, 125; *See also* Citizenship; Social responsibility
Groupthink syndrome, 153–154
Growth: cultivating mind-set for, 256; maximizing individual and group, 271; required with Consciousness of Self, 23; *See also* Change
Gunewardena, N., 266
Gurin, P., 164, 165

H

Habitat for Humanity, 236
Haller, Anna, 147
Halligan, Colby, 216
Halverson, C. B., 121
Hannah, S. T., 45, 53
Happiness, 66

Hashtag activism, 90
Heifetz, R. A., 9, 144, 203, 217, 221, 223, 224, 226–227
Heifetz, Ronald, 5
Heraclitus, 2
Heroes, 245–248, 275
Hickman, G. R., 17
Higher Education Research Institute (HERI), xiii, xiv, xvi, 5, 6, 10, 17, 18, 19, 20, 22, 23, 24, 25, 26, 27, 28, 30, 38, 42, 44, 57, 61, 67, 80, 88, 106, 114, 115, 116, 118, 122, 134, 144, 150, 151, 158, 173, 176, 191, 203, 234, 261
History: ignoring context of politics and, 250–251; providing awareness of, 183–184; of U.S. citizenship, 177–178
Holmes, Oliver Wendell, 94–95
Horth, D. M., 210–211
How Good People Make Tough Choices (Kidder), 74–75
Howell, J. M., 146
Hudnall, Erin, 112
Hulme, E., 50
Hurston, Zora Neale, 35

I

IDASE ("I Design as a Social Entrepreneur"), 51
Identity: impact on sense of congruence, 73–74; peer influence and, 49; values shaping, 47–48
II, S. H., 210–211
Impact America, 233, 244
Individual values: about, 22–24; Commitment, 21, 24; Congruence, 21, 23–24; Consciousness of Self, 21, 22–23; illustrated, 11; overview, 42; *See also* Individuals; *and specific values*
Individuals: adaptive change by, 219–221; aspirations and dreams of, 50–51; awareness of worldview, 157–158; change for, 203–204; civic engagement by, 182; courage required for change, 275; deficit-based perspectives of, 251–252; exploring constraining and empowering beliefs, 184–187; facilitating inner work of, 226; heroes vs. regular, 245–248; maximizing growth of, 271; mental models for change, 217–219; personal style of, 49–50; providing direct services to, 243; *See also* Consciousness of Self
Ingham, Harry, 51
Inquiry, 158–159
Institute for Global Ethics, 74

Integration, 113, 114
Interdependence, 254–255
Intergroup dialogue, 164
Irony of Service, The (Morton), 243
Isaacs, David, 141

J

Jacoby, B., 182
Jaffe, D. T., 89, 101
Janis, Irving, 153–154
Jensen, M. C., 106, 134, 153
Johari Window, 51–52
Johnson, D. W., 113, 118, 119, 129, 142
Johnson, F. P., 118, 119, 129, 142
Jones, S. R., 23, 119
Jost, J. T., 262
Jung, Carl, 43, 48

K

Kabat-Zinn, J., 58, 61
Katzenbach, J.R., 120, 129
Kay, A. C., 262
Kazepides, T., 163
Keeley, S. M., 159
Keen, J. P., 92
Kegan, R., xviii, 42, 71, 203, 204, 219, 220, 223, 224, 225, 226
Keller, Helen, 24
Kellerman, B., 7
Kenn, C.H., 92
Kerkoff, Ashlee M., 87–104
Kernis, M. H., 77
Kettering, Charles F., 31
Kezar, A. J., 5, 18, 35
Kidder, R. M., 74–76
Kielburger, C., 178
Kielburger, M., 178
King, Martin Luther, Jr., 17, 31, 213, 214, 227–228, 245, 261, 270
King, S., 23
Knowing-being-doing framework, 31, 32–33
Knowledge. *See* Self-awareness
Kodama, C., 36, 74
Kohn, A., 112, 113
Kolb, D. A., xvii
Kolb, D. G., 271
Komives, S. R., xiii, xvi–xvii, 2, 7, 8, 10, 31, 36, 38, 42, 45, 46, 55, 64, 90, 112, 122, 129, 133, 142, 157, 192, 214, 275–276
Kotter, J. P., 131, 203
Kouzes, J. M., 80, 89, 94, 118, 120, 160, 270, 271
Kramer, K. P., 82
Ku, G., 153
Kwasnieski, A., 249

L

Lahey, L. L., 203, 204, 219, 220, 223, 224, 225, 226
Language, 139
Larson, C. E., 114, 116–117, 118, 120, 121
Laurie, D. L., 224, 226
Leaders: accepting challenges, 53–54; acknowledging dissonance, 161–162; actualizing destiny of, 91; assumptions about change, 206; authenticity of, 77–79; awareness of worldview, 157–158; balancing stability and disequilibrium, 226–227; becoming conscious of aspirations, 50–51; burnout, 96; commitment of, 88–89, 99; contributing to problems, 208–209; credibility of, 94; dealing with group decision making, 142–144; defined, xvii; developing consciousness of self, 52–57; embracing power, 227–229; examining personal process, 269–270; facilitating inner work of groups, 226; finding one's passion, 91–92, 93–94; fostering dialogue, 163–165; influencing change, 215–216; learning to succeed as, 245–248; motivation and ability to learn, 45; permanent whitewater conditions for, 210–211; personal style of, 49–50; recognizing other worldviews, 158–160; resilience of, 98–99; SCM as tool for assessment, 37; self-reflection of, 51–52; truthfulness of, 270–271
Leadership: authenticity in, 77–79; challenges achieving social change, 242–248; change and roles for, 225–229; competency of, xiv; courage required for, 275; credibility and commitment in, 94; cultures with collaborative, 177–178; defined, 2, 198; evolving views of, 7–9, 13; fostering dialogue, 163–165; leveraging power, 227–229; mindfulness in, 57–60; NCLP materials on, xxiii–xxiv; resilience in, 98–99; SCM on, xiii–xiv, 2–3, 6, 9–12, 19; self-efficacy of, 36, 53, 54, 55; shared vision and transformational, 131; socially responsible, 172–173, 248–249, 256–257; within Black Lives Matter, 109–110; *See also* Leaders
Leadership (Burns), 7

Index

Leadership Reconsidered (Astin & Astin), 2, 198
Leadership self-efficacy: defined, 53; factors contributing to, 54, 55; scoring of men and women in, 36
Leadership the Eleanor Roosevelt Way (Gerber), 91
Learning: facilitating technical changes, 225–226; leadership success, 245–248; mind-set for, 256
Learning organizations, 211
Lee, R., 23
Leiter, M. P., 97
Leland, C., 10
Leveraging technology, 271–272
Lewin, K., 210
Liang, Bernard, 120
Lichtman, Karina, 223
Lindholm, J. A., 92
Linsky, D. L., 9, 144
Linsky, M., 203, 217, 223, 226–227
Lipman-Blumen, J., 8, 10
Listening, 139–140
Littlejohn, A., 267
Loeb, Paul, 214, 239, 245, 246
Lopez, G. E., 164
Louden, Jennifer, 198
Lubic, B. J., 123, 138
Lucas, N., xvii, 7, 8, 10, 31, 112, 214
Lucas, S. E., 40, 139
Luft, J., 51, 52

M

Making Our Society an Inclusive Community (MOSAIC), 251
Malcolm X, 253
Mallett, Kerry, 96
Mannix, E., 265
Marcello, Jenna, 90
Margaryan, A., 267
Marion, R., 17, 205
Marketing Charts, 190
Martin, Trayvon, 109
Maslach, C., 97
Mason, Chelsea, 175
Mason DREAMers, 47
Mather, P. C., 50
Matusak, L. R., 17, 198
Matz, D. C., 161
McAuliff, K. E., 263
McEwen, M. K., 23, 119

McKelvey, B., 17, 205
McKnight, John, 252, 255
McMahon, K. N., 7, 18, 40
McMahon, T. R., xvii, 7, 8, 10, 31, 112, 214
Mead, Margaret, 101
Measuring change and success, 266–268
Meier, A., 213
Mental models of change, 217–219
Meta-cognitive abilities, 45
MIA (Montgomery Improvement Association), 213
Millennials, 49, 162–163
Milligan, C., 267
Mindfulness: Consciousness of Self as, 23, 57; leadership and, 57–60
Ministry of Social Development of the State, 51
Mission statements, 120, 136–137
Mister Splashy Pants, 215–216
Mitchell, T. D., 236
Mizrahi, T., 188
Mobile Light and Railroad Company, 213
Monet, Claude, 29, 30
Montgomery, Alabama, bus boycott, 212–214
Montgomery Improvement Association (MIA), 213
Moore, A. J., 236, 237
Morozov, Evgeny, 190
Morse, S. W., 107
Morton, K., 242–243
MOSAIC (Making Our Society an Inclusive Community), 251
Motivation of leaders, 45
MSL. *See* Multi-Institutional Study of Leadership
Multi-Institutional Study of Leadership (MSL): about, xxiii–xxiv; findings on leadership self-efficacy, 54; predicting leadership development, 89; purpose of, 12; SCM research by, 35–36; Socially Responsible Leadership Scale, 12, 35, 57
Munro, K., 163

N

Nagda, B. A., 164
National Association of Student Personnel Administrators (NASPA), xvi, 31
National Clearinghouse for Leadership Programs (NCLP), xvi, xxiii–xxiv, 20, 22, 25, 27, 30
National Leadership Symposium, 172
Neale, M. A., 265
New York League of Voters, 246

Nielsen, 190
Nimbleness, 211
Nixon, E. D., 213, 214
Nobel Peace Prize, 91
Norming stage, 135
Nussbaum, Martha, 242

O

Ohanian, A., 215, 216
On Becoming a Leader (Bennis), xviii
On Becoming a Person (Rogers), xvii
Online civility practices, 163
Organic change. *See* Change
Orphanage tourism, 233
Ospina, S., 8
Ostick, D. T., xvi, 48, 87–104
Osuna, Rachel, 187
Outcault, C. L., 7, 18
"Overview of the Social Change Model of Leadership Development, An" (Skendall), 17–40
Owen, J. E., 182, 257
Oxfam America Club, 127

P

Palmer, S., 190
Palus, C. J., 210–211
Parker, G. M., 112, 117–118, 119, 121
Parks, Rosa, 31, 213, 214
Parks, S. D., 93
Passion, 91–92, 93–94
Paternalism, 250
Peace Corps, 91
Peer influence, 49
Peer Support Network (PSN), 160
Performing stage, 135
Permanent whitewater conditions, 210–211
Personal style, 49–50
Pew Research Center, 189, 271
Piedmont/Tidewater Rain Garden, 234
Pond, Eleanor Dorcas, 136
Porras, J., 69
Posner, B. Z., 80, 89, 94, 118, 120, 160, 270, 271
Power: bases of, 220, 228; extending with empowerment, 184–187; reconsidering, 227–229
PR Newswire, 190
Prayer of St. Francis, 139
Problem solving, 207–208

Process: becoming leader as, xviii, 6; Consciousness of Self as developmental, 52–57; examining personal, 269–270; listening in communication, 139–140; speaking truth in group, 270–271; traditional vs. organic change, 205–206; trust and group, 121; used in groups, 121–122
Prussia, G., 271
PSN (Peer Support Network), 160
Public Affairs, 178
Public relations vs. social change, 253–254
Purvis, A. J., 162
Putnam, R. D., 181, 183

R

Rank, Mark, 238
Rath, T., 50
Raven, B. H., 228, 229
Rayner, S. R., 143
Reddit, 215, 216
Reflection: efforts reflecting Commitment, 95–96; Johari Window for, 51–52; self-awareness and, 54–56
Reflective dialogue, 141
Reichard, R., 45
Reinforcing feedback loop, 209
Relationships: cultivating meaningful, 125; systems thinking reliance on, 208
Resilient leadership, 98–99
Respect, 168
Return to Love, A (Williamson), 80
Right-versus-right decisions, 74–77
Roberts, D. C., xiii, xvi, 5–16, 42, 198, 263, 270
Roberts, D. R., xix
Robertson, D. C., 123, 138
Rogers, Carl, xvii–xviii, xix, 52, 61, 275
Ronson, J., 162
Roosevelt, Eleanor, 90, 91, 246
Rosch, D. M., 268
Rosenberg, M. B., 141
Rosenthal, B. S., 188
Ross, F., 246
Rost, J. C., 7–8, 10, 17, 19
Roth, George, 217–218
Royer, Meg, 78
Rubrics: Citizenship, 192, 193; Collaboration, 124, 125; Common Purpose, 146, 147; Controversy With Civility, 167, 168

Index

Rudwick, E., 213
Rule-based thinking, 76
Rumi, 149

S

Sacco, Justine, 162
Sanford, N., 226
Sava, Melanie, 127
Schaufeli, W. B., 97
Scherrei, R. A., 10
Schwartz, L. M., 268
SCM. *See* Social Change Model of Leadership Development
Scott, C. D., 89
Seemiller, C., 49
Segregation laws, 212–214
Self-authorship, 70–72
Self-awareness: interdependence and "us and them", 254–255; leadership development and, 43, 45–47; mind-set for, 256; reflection developing, 54–56; SCM focus on, xiv
Self-knowledge. *See* Self-awareness
Seligman, M., 98, 99
Senge, P. M., 203, 207, 208, 209, 210, 211, 217, 221, 226
Sergiovanni, T. J., 152
Servant Leadership (Greenleaf), R.G., 7
Service, 243
Seven Cs: about, xiv–xv, 19; adding courage to list, 275; Change, 21; Citizenship, 21, 176, 191–192; Collaboration, 21, 122; Commitment, 21, 24, 87–88, 99–100; Common Purpose, 21, 144; Congruence, 21, 23–24, 81–82; Consciousness of Self, 21, 22–23, 60; Controversy With Civility, 21, 26–27, 166; defined, 11–12, 20, 21; illustrated, 11, 20; social perspective taking and, 153. *See also* specific change values
Shalka, Tricia R., 66–86
Sharing ownership, 117
Sharp, Marybeth Drechsler, 127–148
Shaw, Sarah Ida, 136
Skendall, Kristan Cilente, xvi, 17–40
Slack, Craig, xxiii–xxiv
Slacktivism, 190
Smith, D.K., 120, 129
Smith, Lillian, 22
Smith, Mary Louis, 213

Social capital, 181–183
Social change, 233–260; addressing root causes with, 237–239; aimed at change value of, 236–237; attributes of, 235–236; collaborative nature of, 239–240; complexity in, 240–242; Controversy With Civility in, 154–155; developing leaders for, 256–257; facilitating, xiv; leadership challenges with, 242–248; overview, 235, 258; public relations vs., 253–254; students making, 233–234; volunteerism and, 243–245
Social Change Model of Leadership Development (SCM): about Seven Cs of, xiv–xv; change at hub of, 28–29, 202–203; impact of, 12; implementing, 31, 33–35; importance of, 8–9; individual values of, 22–24, 42; interactions in, 29–31; knowing-being-doing framework of, 31, 32–33; on leaders and leadership, xiii–xiv, 6; premises of, 9–12; primary goals, xiv; publications of, xvi; questions generating action in, 263–268; relevancy and concerns of, 5; research on, 35–37; tool for self-assessment, 37; values of, 2–3, 17, 19–21. *See also* Applying SCM; Ensemble; *and specific values*
Social justice, 262–263, 270
Social media: enacting change via, 34; expanding citizenship via, 189–190; influencing organic change via, 215–216
Social perspective taking (SPT): community development of, 187; contributing to Citizenship, 181; defined, 56, 152; recognizing other perspectives, 158–159; supporting Seven Cs with, 153
Social responsibility: avoiding pitfalls, 254–256; examples of, 177–178; leading, 172–173, 248–249, 256–257; pitfalls in, 249–254; SCM's assumption of, 18
Socially Responsible Leadership Scale (SRLS), 12, 35, 57
Society/Community values: about, 27–28; Citizenship, 28, 179–181; illustrated, 11, 27; *See also* Communities
Sorenson, G.J., 17
Soul of a Citizen (Loeb), 214
Spirituality, 91
SPT. *See* Social perspective taking
Staley School of Leadership Studies (Kansas State University), 233
Stengel, Casey, 109
Stetzer, A., 190

Stop Hunger Now, 131
Storming stage, 135
Storytelling, 136
Strain, Charles, 241–242
Straus, D., 118, 121
Stroh, D. P., 203, 205, 207, 208, 209, 212, 215, 224
Students: acknowledging dissonance, 161–162; activism by, 95; constraining and empowering beliefs of, 184–187; developmental readiness of, 45; effect of deepening self-awareness on, 45–47; fostering dialogue, 163–165; learning to succeed as leaders, 245–248; making social change, 233–234; recognizing commitment in, 89–90; worldview of own and others, 157–160; *See also* Leaders
Students for Fair Trade group, 189
Subject/object shift, 219
Success: celebrating, 117; measuring change and, 266–268
Sunergos, 114
Supportive environments, 93
Sustainable Living Learning Community (George Mason University), 234
Sustainable Student Action (SSA) club, 120
Sustaining: commitment, 96–99; Common Purpose, 137–138
Syed, Nadia, 247–248
Synergy, 114
Systems thinking, 206–209, 238

T

Takaki, Ronald, 177, 178
Talents, 50
Taplin, D. H., 274
Tatum, B. D., 246–247
Technical change: adaptive vs., 217–219, 223–224; facilitating solutions, 225–226
Teh, Alex, 127–148
Theoharis, J., 213
Thompson, M., 69
Thompson, S., 45
Thoreau, Henry David, 235
Tobe, G. R., 89
Toffler, Alvin, 2
Tometi, O., 109
Tonn, J. C., 228
Tool: assessment, 57; SCM as, 37
Torres-Harding, S.R., 265

"Transitions and Tranformations in Leadership" (Roberts), 5–16
Transmitting group culture, 135–137
Tri Delta Fraternity, 136
Trust: building, 116, 117–118, 125; group processes and, 121; required in Controversy With Civility, 160–161, 168
Truth: congruence with own and others', 72–73; speaking to leadership groups, 270–271
Tuckman, B. W., 106, 134, 153
Turner, B. S., 17
Twitter, 189
Tyree, T., 35

U

Uhl-Bien, M., 17, 19, 205
Uhl-Bien, S., 8
U.N. Human Development Index, 242
United Nations, 264
University of Kansas, 184
University of Missouri Students Association Social Justice Committee, 189
U.S. Climate Action Network, 34–35
U.S. Office of Education, xv
U.S. Supreme Court, 213–214

V

Vaill, P. B., 203, 205, 210, 211
Valadez, Yanniz, 51
Values: aim for change, 236–237; authenticity in personal, 90, 91; Change, 28–29; finding groups' shared, 129–130; group, 24–27; individual, 22–24; interacting within SCM, 29–31; leading others with conflicting, 72–77; questions clarifying SCM, 265; SCM's core, 2–3, 17, 19–21; shaping leader's life, 47–48; Society/Community, 27–28; *See also specific values*
Van Velsor, E., 112, 118
Velasquez, Rodrigo, 46–47
"Virtues of Leadership, The" (Sergiovanni), 152
Vision: collaboration and shared, 114–115; personal vs. socialized, 132–134; questions to establish SCM, 263–265; transforming leadership with shared, 131
VOLS 2 VOLS peer educators, 133
Volunteerism, 243–245
Vonnegut, Kurt, 13

Index

W

Wagner, W., xiii, 55, 53–59, 182, 201–232, 233–260, 275–276
Wall, V. A., 48
Wallace, David Foster, 48
Walumbwa, F. O., 43
Wang, C. S., 153
Watson, Summer, 133
WE LEAD, 112
Weber, K., 178
Weber Shandwick, Powell Tate, & KRC Research, 162–163
Wenger, Etienne, 179
Westerheide, Monica, 53
Whale hunting, 215–216
Wheatley, M. J., 172, 203, 205
Whitmire, K. J., 17
Williams, Melissa, 180
Williams, S., 187
Williamson, Marianne, 80
Winkelman, Eli, 247
Woelker, L. R., 20, 187
Wolff, Thomas, 188
Wood, W., 161
Work avoidance, 226
Working ensemble. *See* Ensemble
World Café Community, 141
Worldview: awareness of, 157–158; recognizing others', 158–160, 168
Wright, J., 112, 118

Y

Yousafzai, Malala, 91, 92

Z

Zimmerman, George, 109
Zinn, Howard, 246
Zúñiga, X., 164